Clean Dirt

Clean Dirt

Chronicles *of a*
Farmer's Daughter

AUTHOR

JOAN M. WELLANDER-KLEPPE

iUniverse

CLEAN DIRT
CHRONICLES OF A FARMER'S DAUGHTER

iUniverse books may be ordered through booksellers or by contacting:

iUniverse
1663 Liberty Drive
Bloomington, IN 47403
www.iuniverse.com
1-800-Authors (1-800-288-4677)

ISBN: 978-1-4917-5470-2 (sc)
ISBN: 978-1-4917-5478-8 (e)

Print information available on the last page.

iUniverse rev. date: 04/23/2015

1750 – 2013

Unearthed by the Author:

Joan Steiner Wellander-Kleppe
with valuable research on the 'Swiss movement'
by Cousin Roger J. Steiner, PhD. retired professor,
language department head, University of Delaware

Michael W Stuhldreher retired architect, legendary
diving champion of Yale University, son of
Harry Stuhldreher of Notre Dame Football

Bethany Lindley, assistant editor

Barbara Rivera, assistant editor

CONTENTS

DEDICATION

To my parents: Susan E. Welsch and George J. Steiner
                   whose nurturing and pioneer spirit
                   inspired and encouraged me to treat
                   every adversity as a challenge to excel.

To my sisters: Tess, Lillian, Maybelle
                   who paved the roads that lay ahead of me
                   with stepping stones of good examples
                   for me to learn from.

To my children: Tom, Alan, Barbara
                   the whetstones of my daily grind, keeping
                   me sharp, and inspiring me to survive and
                   heal the cuts and bruises of life's jagged
                   edges.

To my grandchildren: Josh, Jake, Zach Rivera, and
                       Hayley and Morgan Wellander
                       who have made me a proud and
                       happy grandmother.

IN MEMORIAM

Mother	Ma – born July 4, 1884	deceased February 24, 1967
Father	Pa - born March 12, 1885	deceased October 5, 1983
Sister	Tess – born January 12, 1910	deceased December 4, 1995
Sister	Lil – born June 24, 1913	deceased May 9, 1988
Siste	Maybelle - born April 2, 1918	deceased August 23, 2012
Husband	Albert W. Wellander born July 3, 1921	deceased March 1, 1975
Husband	Willard Earl Kleppe born May 30,1926	deceased March 18, 1988

INTRODUCTION

"I could write a book. . ." How many times has one heard that? Many people may have lived a novel-worthy life, but putting it in the printed word is a daunting exercise.

My motivation to write a family biography emanates from the family history book that I found in our Wisconsin farm home many years ago when I was a child. It is a hard-cover book, printed in 1925, documenting our family roots as far back as the 1700's with my birth date of August 22, 1925 appearing as the last entry on the last page.

It is exciting to be part of a story that began with my father's grandfather living in the Napoleon Bonaparte era as a Corporal in the Swiss Royal Bodyguard Unit for King Louis XVIII of France. It is awesome to know that my paternal grandfather, a direct descendant, came to America from Switzerland at age eight and, a few years later, fought with the Union Army in the Civil War. It gives me a perspective of the source of my father's manly yet mischievous nature—in view of tales revealed by his father.

Since then, more genealogy research has been done by relatives on the Steiner family tree. It is a challenging undertaking to cover six generations that touch four centuries, from the 1700's to 2014—the year of this publication. I feel blessed that, along the way, there have been people dedicated to continue recording this history.

It is interesting to note the changes that have evolved over more than two hundred years. I admire the ingenuity and fortitude of my ancestors and how their ethics and accomplishments have affected each succeeding generation. Of course, my siblings and I believe we were most fortunate to have had parents who set a high bar in the areas of morality, tolerance, fairness, compassion, a noble work ethic, humility, selflessness, and love.

Because of our parents' indelible, positive influence during their nearly one hundred years on earth, this biographic history concentrates heavily on them. I believe this book will provide insight to my children and future generations of what made me the person that I am and to never underestimate the ability to attain goals they may set for themselves.

FOREWORD

My parents were true pioneers who endured incredulous hardships as they began married life in 1908 on virgin farmland in central Wisconsin. This 138-acre parcel of land, a wedding gift from my dad's father, had never been 'worked', and was accessible only via a muddy path—referred to as a 'lane' where even a horse-and-buggy could become mired.

The pristine land had to be cleared of boulders and trees, and stumps dynamited to make the rich soil tillable. Fences had to be built to define parcels for planting and/or grazing. Livestock, both cows and horses, had to be bought; a barn erected to house them; and machine sheds built to store the horse-drawn equipment. Other buildings, such as a silo, corn crib, granary, smokehouse, blacksmithing shop, and chicken barns, also were priorities in construction—second only to a house, of course.

The barn was always first on the list because farmers considered that structure to be most important. It was the hub of dairy farm income, a facility that housed the cows whose milk represented the farmers' livelihood. (The volume of milk was what showed up in the bank account.) It also was used to store the hay and grain to feed the cows and horses (the latter which served as transportation in those days, as well as moving machinery in the field for plowing, planting, fertilizing, cultivating, and harvesting.)

Two other factors were vital in establishing a residence for both man and beast: a source of clean drinking water which meant digging a well, and a road to travel to and from the farm, which meant digging deep into the money sock, usually in the hands of a lending institution.

In those days, a "water witch" (dowser) was sometimes called upon to 'divine' a source of water with the use of a tree branch wielded between the diviner's two hands. If it forcefully bent downward, it meant an underground water source was detected. (Hearing this mysterious story as a tot, I tried it with a willow branch—with disappointing results. I found nothing, not even a mud puddle!)

As to the construction of a road, Pa was always proud that he was responsible for striking a deal with the County to build a road leading from the Federal highway (Route 41) to the farm property. The legalities of the deal elude my memory, but I know it was actuated with a handshake that validated my father's 'word as his bond'. That was one of the moral ethics I have lived by: what you promise, good or bad, big or small, you keep your word—or, as my mother interjected, 'unless you've broken a leg, or DIED!"

Everything I needed to meet life's challenges, I learned from my parents—a list of traits to live up to: morality, honesty, tenacity, patience, tolerance, humility, pride, a zest for life, a thirst for knowledge, common sense, and a sense of humor.

It was a 'package deal'. And, in that package, I found an innate love of music. Although I never came close to being a serious musician performance-wise, I have enjoyed its therapeutic effect, whether I am performing or just listening. It is a God-given gift.

As to the paradoxical title "Clean Dirt", it applies to Mother Nature's packaging of many foods found on the farm, from the apples, purple plums, and cherries on the trees, to the chaff alighting on your hair or clothes (especially when loading hay), to the mud on your hands from planting a garden, to the elderberries, raspberries, currants, and chokecherries on bushes. Closer to the ground are strawberries, peppers, and tomatoes; in the ground are carrots, scallions, and celery—all of which I have plucked for a tasty treat with just a cleansing swipe across my apron. I have even picked red clover blossoms to suck the sweet nectar out of the tiny tubes, becoming a kind of human hummingbird.

My parents were years ahead of the times with organic produce. They used no pesticides on any of the crops in the fields or in our garden. No growth hormones were given to any of the animals shipped to market, or those for our personal use, including: geese, Mallard and Muscovy ducks, Guinea hens, and varieties of chickens. Believe me, one's olfactory organs affirmed the use of n-a-t-u-r-a-l fertilizer. That reminds me of the old joke repeated by Walter, Lil's husband.

He'd ask my mother, "What do you use on your strawberries?" She'd respond, "Sugar and cream"; he'd say, "I use manure."

The soil is a sacred possession when, whether big or small, you can claim it as your own. When you see people photographed as they return to a land that they love, kneel down and kiss the ground, that is how farmers feel about the soil in which their livelihoods lie.

Every day unfolded like a television 'reality' show. I'd wake up in the morning, wondering what the day might hold: maybe the birth of a wobbly-legged foal, a bloated bovine in need of a life-saving enema, the arrival of hundreds of baby chicks from the local hatchery, or something live that Pa would bring in from the field he was plowing or cultivating. If he came up to the house, with a smile on his face and his hat in his hand, I could guess it held a tiny rabbit, some Native

American artifacts like arrowheads or skinning flints, or a covey of baby pheasants.

Ma's surprises were usually of a culinary nature, always validating her cooking and baking prowess. I cannot recall anything that she could not prepare, whether it was ordinary or gourmet fare. Exquisite desserts were something that the family could expect on a daily basis: it could be a schaum torte, six inches high, twelve inches in diameter, covered with strawberries and topped with real whipped cream. I don't know of anyone outside of our family who has tasted, or even *seen,* such a unique creation. Another original concoction of hers, an "angel sunshine" cake, was moist, delicate, and too tall to fit into a cake carrier. Her secret was to prepare two batters: angel food from egg whites, and basic sponge cake using the egg yolks.

I have tried for more than sixty years but still haven't mastered her skill of creating pie crusts as delectable and short-grained as hers, to perfectly complement the fillings: fruit, cream, or custard. They were blue ribbon winners at the county fair, the most unusual being 'rhubarb custard' with all of the rhubarb flavor but none of the puckering tartness.

She served interesting substitutes for potatoes, one of which I'm not sure of the spelling, "geschnittenen pfannenkuchen", but I know how to prepare it: pancake batter cut into random small pieces as the mix hits the frying pan. She would serve a large bowl of these morsels which we would cover with her homemade rhubarb-pineapple sauce.

Then there was a traditional German side dish: spaetzle, made with a simple batter of egg, flour, salt and enough water stirred into the mix to make a smooth batter to scoop up in one spoon, then cut with another to drop into boiling water. Cook these 'noodles' until they rise to the top of the water (about five minutes); drain; fry in hot butter on both sides until lightly browned; then serve. We loved the taste and texture, but the bonus feature was that it is simple and thrifty to prepare: a cup of flour with a pinch of salt, one egg, and just enough water to make a batter.

There were no shortcuts 'back in the day'. There were no cake mixes or frozen meals, no microwaves, no supermarkets, no sales taxes. Everything was *real* and fresh. We had a cold room in our cellar where we kept all kinds of produce that Ma had canned: sweet and dill pickles, tomatoes, pickled yellow and green beans. Cherries, plums, peaches, apples, and pears.

There was a second cold area in our cellar where a cache of potatoes and carrots, harvested in fall, were kept for use during the year that followed. Five- and ten-gallon crocks filled with shredded and salted cabbage huddled in a dark corner. A heavy earthen plate, weighted down with a large rock, was placed on top of the kraut to 'cure' for a few weeks. That served as our source of sauerkraut for the whole year. Every time I was sent down to the cellar to bring up a bowl of kraut to be cooked with spareribs or our homemade smoked bratwurst, I couldn't resist indulging in a forkful as an appetizer right from the crock.

Nothing went to waste—not just because the whole family experienced the Great Depression with the rest of the country, but because of the sense of values that farmers live with as they deal with life and death issues every day. Unlike any urban setting, where people work with people and things, a farmer's spouse is his co-worker and God is his boss.

Farmers work with living things: their livestock and their crops. The disease, Garget, can wipe out a whole herd of cows with lethal inflammation that can affect their heads, throats, and dry up their udders. That devastating malady struck my parents' livestock twice. It took thirty years to recoup resulting financial losses.

Weather, too, like persistent rain, or drought, can ruin entire crops. Rainy weather can make it impossible to get out in the fields to plow and plant, or, at harvest time can rot the crops in the field. Drought, not enough moisture, also deals a lethal blow.

There were no credit cards to bail one out of debt or increase your debt. You couldn't spend money that you didn't have. Household and food items were bought in bulk to always have necessities on hand as well as benefit with the best price. A flour bin in the pantry was commonplace. Eggs and produce were used as barter at the local dry goods store toward purchases or for a "due bill" to be used at a later date.

Even though my adult life has been spent in urban environments, I still bake and cook from scratch—sometimes out of financial necessity, but most times because I prefer the homemade taste. No aroma beats that of bread baking in the oven. Although fruits and vegetables are available now year 'round in the cities where I have lived, I still buy only what is in season to reap the best flavor.

PREFACE

According to official records, beginning with the birth of my father's grandfather, Johann Steiner, the Steiner lineage is documented to have touched four centuries—from the birth of Johann Steiner in Switzerland in 1798; my father's father, Jakob Joos Steiner born in Switzerland in 1843; my father, George Jacob Steiner, born on March 12, 1885 in Dodge County, Wisconsin; and I, Joan Marie Steiner, born on August 22, 1925 also in Dodge County.

On May 12, 1908, George married Susan Welsch, born on July 4, 1884, daughter of Leonard Welsch, a neighbor and friend of George's father whose farm was less than a mile away. George's father, an Evangelical Methodist, and Susan's father, a Roman Catholic, were best friends and confidantes who regularly visited each other for serious discussions on controversial subjects over a glass of homemade wine and a fine cigar. Their friendship was tested when George converted to Catholicism in order to marry Susan. Jakob's later whole-hearted approval of the union erased any inkling of the previous disapproval.

Photos of the two fathers mirrored the likenesses of Winston Churchill (Steiner) and Franklin D. Roosevelt (Welsch). Grandfather Steiner was a balding hulk of a man, stubborn, and wise like Churchill, always having a pipe hanging out the side of his mouth—asleep or awake. Grandpa Welsch was tall and stately, and smoked an occasional cigar.

Both George and Susan had attended the little red schoolhouse, midway between those farms and within walking distance for each of them. Of course, "walking distance" had a different connotation during that period in history. People walked great distances as a matter of everyday life. Even in the 1930's, I walked at least a mile from that same little red schoolhouse to my home during first through fourth grades, weather permitting. In spring, I would stop to pick a bouquet of wild flowers alongside the road: trilliums, bachelor buttons, and yellow buttercups.

Back in those days, there weren't school buses to transport rural children to and from school and home. Parents didn't have to worry about their children being abducted on those rural roads, or from their homes, schools, stores, or playgrounds. It was a different time with a different mindset. There were neither tabloids nor news media for crackpots to feed on.

During summer vacations, I'd walk a mile to our rural route mailbox every day to pick up our mail until I finally got a bicycle. But the bicycle didn't make the trip a breeze. It was only a pair of wheels, a seat, and handle-bars to traverse the hilly, gravel road. Ah, yes, that bike! I recall the day Pa brought it home. I simulated a joyous response, as Pa rejoiced for snaring such a bargain. Only $6.00—a steal, considering it was missing only *one* wheel. He assured me that he would find a replacement in the junkyard, the only source for parts during that World War II shortage of rubber and steel. He did find one, and only too soon did I find myself astride that contraption, ready for a trial run.

I learned to ride it in one 'fell swoop' as my father gave me a push atop the barn hill, saying, "the trick of learning to ride is to focus forward"; "don't look down"; and "it's easier to balance if you go *fast*!" He was right. I went flying down that hill and didn't come to a stop until I reached bottom, headfirst into a bramble bush. The theorem was proven in less than thirty seconds.

The 'home tutoring' sessions to learn to drive a team of horses or a tractor were just as brief and terrifying. When it came time for me to learn how to drive an auto, I "hired" my mother as instructor, a woman of saintly patience.

NOTES FROM THE AUTHOR

I have tried to remain faithful to the truth regarding the content of this book, relying on my memory of events and what has been confirmed by relatives who may have been present at the time. Generous credit is given to Cousin Roger J. Steiner, PhD. who had gathered information from various sources, including research made on trips to Switzerland regarding the genealogy of the Steiner family. Roger has since passed, and I owe a debt of gratitude for his meticulous research.

The Steiner ancestors were as intelligent as they were handsome. They were inventive, ambitious, artistic, refined, and, thankfully, mischievous. It has been a badge of honor to bear the name and a challenge to meet established expectations.

Within our immediate family, the competitive spirit was always present. None of us ever waited for opportunity to knock. We have been innovators who 'made' progress happen.

The spirit of ingenuity has been passed down to each generation.

THE LITTLE RED SCHOOLHOUSE

My first recollection of life starts at the age of four when I visited the little country schoolhouse as a guest of my sister, Maybelle, who was probably in sixth or seventh grade at the time. What transpired on that auspicious occasion could be labeled 'my first public appearance as a stand-up comedienne'.

The teacher, Bernice Steiner, called upon all the visiting children to tell the one-room-school student body what they had seen on the way to school that morning. All of those present were farm children like me. I thought, *"What could they have seen that would be as interesting as my experience?"* When called upon, I proudly stood up to share the exciting scene I had witnessed: "I saw one cow riding another cow!" This was followed by my audience's complete silence, then a collective tittering which was shot down by the teacher's instruction to "please open your books."

My sister was thoroughly embarrassed. When we got home at the end of the day, our parents good-naturedly assured her that there had been no harm in my telling the truth of what I had seen, a perfectly natural phenomenon in the animal world.

I was sure I detected a little tittering from them, too. In the years that followed, I admit to being dirty; that is, I loved to play in mud. I recall

1

my mother chiding me, "How can you get so dirty in just a couple of minutes?" when I came in from outdoors.

The little red schoolhouse was a common starting point for the Steiner family. I started first grade there in 1931, right after turning six years old on August 22. The school was located at the country crossroads called Elwood Corners—about 1-1/2 miles from home, as gravel roads go. It was located across from a non-operating cheese factory, turned residential for a family that had moved from the big mysterious city of Chicago—a metropolis larger and further away than Milwaukee!

The newcomers—grandparents, and an adult daughter with her three children—occupied the second floor, accessed by an outdoor, tall wooden stairway, by-passing abandoned cheese-making equipment on the first floor.

Across the road, on the southwest corner, was the Evangelical Methodist church and cemetery where some members of the Steiner family were buried, including my paternal grandfather, Jacob Joos Steiner. I remember his interment in 1934 when I was only nine years old. World War I veterans were in attendance and provided a 21-gun salute. I had never witnessed anything like that before. I thought, *"He must have been very important!"*

The teacher, daughter of my father's brother, Fred, lived in one-half of the Steiner homestead with her parents, two brothers, and two sisters. "Miss Steiner", as she was called, was both pleasant and pretty. She was perfect. It could not have been an easy task to teach all eight grades assembled in just one room. She was "encyclopedic" (if there is such a word), meaning she knew a lot about everything.

I remember the metronomic routine as she addressed each class, going and coming from the front of the room: "stand, pass, and be seated." I always stopped to listen what was being discussed or what she was teaching to each gathering.

There were inkwells on the desks and 'stick' pens to dip and write. That was one thing that had not changed since my parents' days in school.

I never received any special attention just because the teacher and I were related. Quite the opposite. She made a point of challenging me to do the best that I was capable of, and more. I do remember being very bored when it came to coping with the three R's because of the pre-school tutoring I had received from my sister, Maybelle, who had relentless patience. She was born with the vocational calling to be a teacher, practicing on me from the time I could walk and talk. In today's vernacular, I was her "lab rat".

The first day I came home from school, I showed my parents my first-grade primer which had been handed out for us students to just look at. I explained to them that I had already read the whole dull book of "See Dick run, see Jane run, see Spot run."

At age 6, I could already read and write at third grade level and work arithmetic problems.

Every day in summer, and every weekend when Maybelle came home from the city high school, just when I was having the most fun outside playing with our dogs, petting the calves, chasing chickens, climbing trees, or just digging for worms to go fishing, Maybelle would summon me to come in the house. Reluctantly, I would amble in, wash up, and sit myself down on a little worn-off painted green child-size chair at the blackboard which hung below our wall-mounted crank-type telephone, to spend a torturous hour of spelling and working arithmetic problems, followed by a reading session.

Quiet time was not for me. I was a free-spirited youngster, a tomboy of sorts, loving the outdoors, romping with our dogs, playing in dirt, and climbing in the barn's haylofts. I liked to curry our purebred Percheron horses (a breed of draft horse that originated in the La Perche region of France), feed the cows, gather the chicken eggs, stealthily follow our old

3

'Mama' cat to find her newest hidden litter of kittens, hold baby chicks (that Ma bought by the hundreds), nuzzle little ducklings hatched by our Mallard and Muscovy ducks (native to Mexico and southern Brazil) which were sometimes referred to as "turkey" ducks, a cross between a turkey and a duck because of their size and their uniform dark-only moist meat.

After enduring the boring first grade, the school board permitted Miss Steiner to promote me to the third grade. To me, it was no surprise that the third grade also held no challenge for me. I had already conquered that level of curriculum, both from Maybelle's tutoring, and from being in a one-room schoolhouse where you get to hear everything that was being taught to all eight grades, every day, over and over and over again. You especially could not ignore the geography lessons when the big wall map was pulled down from atop the blackboard. The teacher would point to various countries, cities, rivers, and mountain ranges— whatever she was teaching. The way the map snapped back, when she was finished, amused me, too.

Maybelle's tutoring made learning all the subjects easier, but there was also a disadvantage: it gave me an unrealistic perspective that school was easy and, accordingly, it didn't foster the discipline of good study habits. Although it put me ahead of the pack academically, I was two years behind my peers chronologically. It delayed parental permission to wear make-up, go on a date, or hang out with the 'in' crowd to smoke and drink. On the up side, it kept this naïve child out of harm's way during the impressionable teen years. I never regretted spending my free time productively on the farm where, contrary to popular belief, there were no dull moments.

In the three years spent at the little red schoolhouse, I don't recall having much fun. It was often scary and unpleasant. Even though I was never a victim in the frequent shutdowns because of a head lice epidemic, there were two hazards, however:

1. Walking home from school. During the first half of the walk, I was part of a group of girls, allied against the boys who used to whip little black snakes that they found among the rocks and bushes. I soon learned that, by not screaming, I was not a target; but it may account for my lifelong fear-of-snakes phobia.
2. On the school playground, a few crude bullies were mean and nasty while we played outside when the teacher left the premises to go home at lunch time. They broke off branches from trees, dipped them in the fecal matter in the outhouses, and then whipped them as they chased us girls around the school. We never told the teacher for fear of even nastier retaliation from the bullies.

The same ruffians also used to try to peak at us girls through the knotholes of the outhouses when we were in them. One day, as I was sitting in one, something that looked like a tomato worm came through a knothole next to me. I heard some yelling and crying going on outside. I later learned that the bullies had pressed a young boy (actually, a cousin of mine) against the outside wall and forced his penis through the knothole.

During the years I attended that school, Miss Steiner took us on only one field trip: wading in a creek on a farm where one of the students lived. It was a shallow creek, only knee deep. I was unaware of what those 'blobs of mud' were, all over my bare legs. I couldn't rub or push them off. They were really stuck to my skin. That was my introduction to nature's strange creatures called *leeches*. Later, I learned that old-time pharmacists used to sell them to clear up black-and-blue bruises on people's faces resulting from fisticuffs. More recently, I again made their acquaintance by using them for bait when fishing for walleyes.

MY ROOTS:
THE FAMILY TREE

I was probably age four when I began to wonder: "How do I fit in the family tree?"

Atop our upright piano, set on a crocheted-edge runner, stood a tintype photo of the immediate family members: my father, my mother, and my three sisters. The youngest one shown, Maybelle, looked to be about seven years old. *But where was I?*

My question was answered with the explanation that the appointment with the photographer had been made before my mother knew she was pregnant with me.

Proof of my connection was found in the 'putting' of my name and birth date as the last entry in a hardcover biography, published in 1925 (the year of my birth).

According to the family history book, written and documented by my father's ancestors, my roots can be traced back to the early 18th century to a well-to-do upper-class family by the name of Steiner who lived in western Switzerland. They were highly respected and of the Roman Catholic faith.

Johann Steiner married a Protestant girl, embraced her faith and was therefore disinherited, left home, and went to Zizers—a town not too far away from Andeer, in the direction of Lichtenstein and Austria. (In fact, when the Austrian royalty was deposed after WWI, the crown princess made her home in Zizers.)

His son, Johann Batista Steiner, married a girl from Zizers whose family members were involved in saddlery. They had one son, Johann, born in 1798. When he was 4 years old, Napoleon's army crossed the Alps. The soldiers took everything they could lay their hands on. Johann's mother hid her silver spoons in her lap and held Johann on top of them, to no avail. The soldiers found and took them.

<u>My Grandfather's Father</u>

At the age of 15, young Johann decided to become a mercenary soldier in order to earn money for his family and himself. He enlisted in France at a time when Napoleon was under attack because of his defeat in Russia in 1812 and was preparing to prove himself in a decisive battle. He was deposed by the French Parliament in April 1814, signed an unconditional abdication, and was exiled to the tiny island of Elba. (If Johann was in Napoleon's bodyguard as family legend would have it, the service would have lasted only four months until Napoleon's defeat in the Battle of Leipzig and his exile to Elba.)

We do know that Johann became a corporal in the Royal Bodyguard in the army of King Louis XVIII of France where he served until his honorable discharge as evidenced in the record of his official resignation dated May 17, 1825. Johann was family here as evidenced by this discharge certificate:

ROYAL GUARD
Swiss Regiment of Besenval N.S.

1ˢᵗ Battalion   **6ᵗʰ Company of Salis**

We, the undersigned, chief officers of the Regiment and Commander of said Company, certify that Corporal John Steiner, born in Zizers, Canton of Graubunden, Switzerland, served bravely and faithfully in said Regiment up to May 17, 1825; that he has received his formal release, and that during his time of service he earned the good will of his superiors and the love of his comrades by his good conduct.

For these reasons, we give him this paper as testimony of our appreciation of his efficient service.

Rueil, May 17, 1825

The Battalion Chief,	*The Commandant of*
Rosule Oltehde	*the Company, von*
The First Lieutenant, Gaehter	*Salis Soglio*
Sergeant Clavadetscher	*The Marechal de Camp*
Corporal Raymond	*Colonel of the Regiment,*
Stephan Fluber	*C. von Besenval*
Senti Antoin	*J. Clavadetscher, Fifer*
	and Rifleman
	Andrel Pruffner, Drummer

The paper is headed by a coat-of-arms with the French fleur-de-lis, a crown, and eight flags, and signed by his comrades-in-arms as well as his commanding officers.

On January 27, 1826, he married a Romansch-speaking young lady, Anna Barbara Joos (my paternal grandfather's mother.)

Background of Anna Barbara Joos`

JAKOB JOOS (1750-1828), the son of Conradin Joos and Christine Zisli, and URSULA PEDRETT (1765-1818), daughter of George Pedrett, also of Andeer, married June 30, 1786, and had eight children, one of whom was ANNA BARBARA JOOS.

Anna Barbara Joos had traveled from Andeer to Zizers to find work during the threshing season and stayed to run a bakery. She met and married Johann (John) who set up a harness shop next door to the bakery. They lived on the upper floor where their youngest child, my grandfather Jakob Joos ("J. J.") was born on February 17, 1843. (Relatives may still operate a bakery in that area.)

Occupations of ancestors included harness makers, bakers, teachers, artists, inventors, and adventurers—all of whom were great story tellers. Because of the mountainous terrain of the Alps, Swiss people seldom left their canton (state). When they did make a trek to another community, they brought back entertaining folk lore to tell their families. I remember one in particular that my father loved to repeat:

A father, preparing to take a trip on foot some distance to the valley below, wanted to make sure that his young son would not follow him on this trip that required the stamina of an adult. He placed a large pumpkin in front of his house set high on a hill. He told his son to sit on this big orange 'rabbit egg', to hatch it, until he returned. He assured the boy that from that vantage point, he would be able to see his father traveling down to the valley.

The boy obeyed his father, and sat for many hours. Still no rabbit had hatched. He finally stood up to investigate why there was no movement in the 'egg'. With that, the pumpkin started to roll down the hill, splashed open as it hit a big rock when, simultaneously, it startled a rabbit sleeping next to the rock.

The rabbit leaped away as the boy shook his fist and yelled, "Hey, come back here. Don't you know I'm your father?!"

That was typical of the Old World storytelling—very long, and very dry humor. They had hours to while away because of their slow pace with no electricity or modern conveniences of any kind. This was still true as I was growing up on the farm where entertainment as well as the crops were 'home grown'...or groan!

The people of Andeer were descended from Rhaetians, inhabitants of an important province of the Roman Empire. They originally spoke the Celtic language of the Helvetians, but it became mixed with Roman for what today we call the Romansch language—a sister language of Italian, Spanish, Portugese, and French. Today, there are still 50,000 Swiss residents who are speakers of the Engadine dialect of Romansch. Even all of our Swiss cousins speak it. They must also be fluent in German to get a high school and college education, and to find a job.

My Father's Father

My grandfather, Jakob Joos Steiner, widely known as "J. J.", was born in 1843 of a Romansch-speaking young lady, Anna Barbara, from Andeer who had come to find work in Zizers during the threshing season. She met Johann Joos, a saddler (a leather worker who makes saddles and harnesses), whom she married in 1826.

Johann set up his harness shop in the building where Anna Barbara ran a bakery. The harness shop was at the front entrance with the bakery at the side. The upper floor was their home. Jakob Joos, their youngest child, was born on February 17, 1843 in one of the bedrooms in that apartment.

In his home town, the houses were made of wood with old-fashioned fixtures such as draw-string latches on the doors. Wood was used to heat the homes in stoves and fireplaces. There was no plumbing. They had no wells, but the water from the mountains ran clear and cool, winter and summer, through pipes to a trough cut out of a stone block. People brought their buckets to fill them, then carry the water home for drinking and cooking. This pipe also led to other large troughs where the women did their washing.

Andeer is about ten miles from Italy which can be reached through the Splugen Pass. It is surrounded on three sides by snow-capped mountains. It now has about 800 inhabitants—probably as many as when the Steiner family lived there. It is set in a valley three miles long and one mile wide, about 3,000 feet above sea level, beside a source of the Rhine River, the Hinterrhein, which flows through the town but is too wild for any boat to travel on it.

On one side of town, there was a silver mine; on the other an iron mine—both of which were in operation in the 1850's. The Italians in the community did the harder labor, such as paving and running a big blast furnace. The Steiners were business people. The younger members went to night school and learned languages, tailoring, sewing, carpentry, and many other occupations.

Dairy farmers in Andeer kept some cattle and poultry within the town limits. One could see a load of hay driven through the streets. One could hear the tinkling of the bells around the necks of goats early in the morning when they were driven over the cobblestone streets to pasture.

The valley was beautiful with snowy hills in the direction of Italy beneath which cherry trees would be in bloom in their season. These attractions were enough to make tourists from Italy and military men trade become all the more lucrative when a curative mineral water was found. A large hotel was built, and hundreds of people even in the twentieth century went there for their health.

Tourists traveling through the area, or taking cures, found Jakob so cute with his beautiful brown curls that they would give him money and gifts. One military man gave him a watch which, when he and his mother settled in America, was used to buy a cow. Johann and Anna Barbara heard of better chances in America, the land of opportunity, to support their family the way they wanted. They convinced their oldest child, Ursula (later changed her name to Julia) to try life in the New World. She and a cousin left Le Havre on May 19, 1849. The only communication received from Pittsburgh where she settled was the admonition 'not to come to the United States.

In 1850 Johann died, from sunstroke it was suspected. But the widow, Anna Barbara, left with six children to take care of, was a strong resilient person—convinced that life in America would be better than the little valley in which Andeer was set. They set sail to New York in June of 1851. Jakob's passport read "nine years old", but he was really eight.

The passage took forty-two days and nights. The Fourth of July was celebrated on the boat, an unheard of festivity for the Swiss.

The boat was heated in cool weather by a flat brick stove about 5' x 6' placed near the center of the boat. Bundles of gnarly twigs of birch and hazel brush were used for fuel. Jakob would like to sit on top of the stove where it was plastered over.

Each day, Jakob would be looking for something to do to pass the time. He was all alone on part of the deck and saw a rope hanging down near a mast. He climbed up, took hold of the rope, and wondered what would happen if he swung out on it a little bit. He swung, all right—right over the side of the boat above the water. If he had let go, no one would have known that he was overboard, and his descendants would not exist (and neither would this book!)

When they docked in New York, there was no Ellis Island. While Anna Barbara was deciding where to go next, Jakob walked off somewhere and lost the family. Looking for him and calling his name went on for more than an hour. Finally, he came into sight. His mischievous nature, and his being a live-wire and go-getter, boded well for his future in America.

They went by rail and boat and, upon arriving in Milwaukee, they went to find a widow they knew who lived north of city hall. After a short time, they moved to Third Street near the Wisconsin River, secured work, and were encouraged about life in this new country. (Nearly 100 years later, I worked as a secretary about one block from the location for the company that owned the Schroeder Hotel at Fourth Street and the River.)

In 1852, Anna Barbara married a Christopher Steinert and moved from Milwaukee to Dodge County where they bought a farm near where the village of Lomira is now. The marriage did not last.

Three of Anna Barbara's daughters married clergymen, one of whom was Charles Otto Rall. The Rall family has published three volumes of family history. A third generation Rall, Dr. Harris Franklin Rall, wrote 19 books during his career—a distinguished professor of theology at the Garrett Theological Seminary in Evanston, Illinois, becoming one of the leading theologians of the Methodist Church.

In 1857, her son Johann Batista moved from Milwaukee to Fond du Lac where he continued his trade of saddler. He also bought eighty acres of land near Elwood Corners for five dollars an acre. (Ten years later, it was worth twice that amount.)

In 1858, Jakob helped his brother Johann, clear a piece of that eighty acres and built a log house on it. Once, when he was herding cows home, he came to a small clearing on a knoll near his brother's land. He liked the place so much that he promised himself that some day he

13

would buy that land, build his house, and farm the land. After serving hitches in the Civil War, that is just what he did. His white Victorian-style gabled house became the homestead where my father grew up.

J. J.'s Service in the Civil War

The Civil War began with the surrender of Fort Sumter, April 14, 1861. There was an enthusiastic response to President Lincoln's proclamation and call for volunteers to put down the rebellion. The first blood was shed on April 19 as Massachusetts' troops rode streetcars through Baltimore on their way to Washington, D.C. and were assaulted by enraged Baltimorians supporting the Confederate cause.

Congress was called into session on July 4, 1861, and on July 13 gave President Lincoln powers in case of insurrection. Congress was still in session during the first battle of Bull Run, July 21, 1861 when the Federal troops were soundly defeated. Confederate troops under General Jackson came within a mile or two of the outskirts of Washington where they could easily have captured President Lincoln.

By autumn of 1862, Jakob Joos decided he wanted to be part of the Union forces, following in the footsteps of his father who, at age 15, volunteered to serve as a mercenary in France in 1813.

His First Enlistment

Grandpa ("J. J.") enlisted in the Union Army in December 1862 at the beginning of the Civil War and served the required term of nine months, for which he received $300 from a local lad named Geier to serve in his stead. This was an allowable practice at the time.

(I remember visiting Grandpa when I was about eight years old and listened to the stories he told as he sat in a rocking chair next to a potbellied stove in the parlor of the homestead house. I sat on the floor while he would talk out of one side of his mouth, with his pipe always clenched between his teeth on the other side. Occasionally, he'd fall asleep, but he would wake up when a spark fell and burned a hole in his clothes.)

He was never graphic about the hardships that he and the other soldiers suffered. He recounted the lighter side of the war. During the frequent lack of food, he would parch some of the mules' shelled corn to make it palatable. He was agile enough to snare a rabbit or a wild turkey for a real feast. Occasionally, a farmer would voluntarily donate a chicken.

During this first hitch in Service, time did not pass as swiftly as one can tell it. He did guard duty, holding forts where there was little action. To relieve boredom, he would sometimes find some soapstone and whittle a knickknack. One object he created was a little Bible, two inches wide by three inches high, with the word "Bible" and a cross whittled on the front. Another object was a pipe. These were surprisingly smooth and 'cool' to the touch.

Some of the time, he and three others took turns on picket duty. He was the first on duty, a dull time which caused him to look for a little excitement. He saw a squirrel scampering across the path and shot at it before he thought of what he was doing. There was to be absolutely no shooting unless it was necessary, and then it was done only as a signal. When an officer came to inquire, Jakob said that the trigger was stiff, and he must have hit the gun on the ground too hard. Later, he saw a rabbit's tracks and started pursuing them. When he saw officers coming, he got back to his post and said he was looking for water. (He had been in the enemy's lines—UNARMED!

The Second Enlistment

It really wasn't an enlistment. He went back to the Army in 1864, not as a soldier but as a hired teamster. The Army was in dire need of good teamsters and asked him to show them what he could do with horses hitched to a wagon. He did such an excellent job that he was hired for pay to drive Army wagons. Proof of this is in his 1891 pension application, alluding to his serve from May 1864 to February 1866. Jakob was 48 years of age when he put his signature to the official document, confirming his station as a teamster which was not a military rank as was his first enlistment.

He could return home for visits when permission to do so would be convenient. On one of those visits, enlistment enticed him again in the form of $300 or more to take the place of Ferdinand Fenner.

In the latter part of April 1865, Jakob went to Oshkosh (WI) to enlist. The fact that Robert E. Lee had surrendered his Confederate army to Ulysses S. Grant on April 9, 1865 did not mean that the war was over.

On April 14, John Wilkes Booth shot President Lincoln in Ford's Theatre. Many wondered if there would be a resurgence of the insurrection. The Confederate General Johnson did not surrender until April 26. No one seemed to know when the war was over. There was no armistice or treaty of peace, and Jefferson Davis was put in prison.

As soon as organized resistance ceased, the disbanding of our soldiers began. Therefore, there was no more draft into the Union Army when Jakob arrived in Oshkosh, and Ferdinand Fenner would not have had to pay money to someone to take his place. It was awhile before that information, whether or not drafting was necessary, received general circulation. Jakob went to Oshkosh in good faith that Fenner was still required to enlist.

J.J. did not simply turn around and go home. He went on with his teamster job and was sent right to Chattanooga with other teamsters, such as "Split Lip", "Missouri", and "Frenchy". Walens Ridge was part of their travels, and it took from morning until night to cross it. He had a six-mule team there and at Lookout Mountain. Later, for some monhs, he drove an ambulance. On Chattanooga's main street, the church was used as a hospital with bunks placed side by side in rows.

Jakob spent four days in the hospital where there was much death and suffering. When he was released, he reported back for duty.

Since he was a strict Methodist who didn't drink or play cards, he was unpopular at payday parties. As a result, he was once sent with a pair of white mules to obtain camp supplies while the remaining soldiers played cards. When he returned to the camp, he found only bodies and ashes.

Although organized Rebel resistance had been mastered, it was not until May that the last detached parties of the Confederates gave up the contest. Some of those Rebels attacked and burned Jakob's and the other teamsters' wagons, captured and took most of their mules, ammunition, and food, and took some of the men prisoners. Enough damage was done so they all had to stay here for over a month.

One day, while there, they went about 20 miles to cut green corn stalks for food. They stopped to sleep one night and heard some chickens. Being hungry, the temptation was too great not to follow the noise, but the chicken coop door was locked. Then they noticed a pig stable and decided that one would go inside and chase a pig out. The other two would be ready to club it.

One went in but found no pigs, so he proceeded to crawl out again. The others were ready with a club and saw him just in time. Jakob grabbed the club and said, "It made our scalps grizzly."

This should have taught them a lesson, but they still didn't have a chicken, so they went back to where the chickens were. Jakob crawled up on the roof and tore part of the corner away and jumped down inside. An old woman living there heard them and came running after them with a club just as he was coming out again. He jumped down, and they all ran to safety; but she saw Jakob enough to know he was small and wore a cap.

When she attended the hearing, the wagon master asked her to describe the man. A quartermaster's friend was also small and wore a cap, so, when she was asked to identify the man, she couldn't see him anywhere. Just then, the friend came in and she said, "That's him. Ain't that sumpin'!"

(Author's note: Jakob might have wanted to leave these little incidents unwritten, but there were so few really interesting moments in the life of a soldier, surrounded by death and destruction, that I couldn't resist relating them.)

Back to Mr. Fenner who asked for his money back caused enmity among friends. There are two ways to look at the situation: Martin received a benefit because he was relieved from the necessity of going into the Army and, therefore, could make plans concerning his family and jobs. Jakob was inconvenienced also in having to make various plans concerning family and jobs. A contract is a contract. If it had benefited Fenner financially, would he have given the money back? This dispute was the subject of conversation in the Lomira area for years.

When his stint was over, he returned home after an Honorable Discharge at his mustering out on September 8, 1963. When he got home, he was employed in threshing and harvesting. When cold weather set it, he went in the "pinery" where he stayed all winter. On New York's Day, January 1, 1864, they had the coldest day ever recorded in Wisconsin. They chopped wood all day but had to move fast and do a lot of running and jumping to keep warm.

When his mother and sister learned that he was using all of his "Army money" to buy that piece of land he saw and admired as a boy, they cried and cried because they were afraid he would lose all of his savings in a farm that might fail.

J.J.'s Marriage to Sophia K. Rehling (pronounced 'railing')

"J.J." married Sophia who was born in 1849 in a part of Germany at that time called Prussia. At age six, she arrived in America with her parents and older sister. On March 30, 1868, Grandpa "J.J." and Sophia settled on the homestead and brought seven children into the world— the youngest of whom was my father, George, born March 12, 1885.

Sophia was a devout Christian and, near her death, called each of the children to her, one by one, to spend an hour privately—counseling them about their future and urging them to continue living a moral and godly life. She died December 18, 1896.

With J.J.'s hard work, initiative, and expertise, the farm prospered and lived up to a statement that appeared in the "Cousins Congress Souvenir 1890": "His well-tilled acres, roomy and convenient barns, fine stock, and pleasant home, tell plainly of his industry, *modern* methods, and business ability." Modern? The Steiners were so modern that they had strung private telephone lines between the farms and other Steiner residences before the neighborhood had telephones!

Jakob ran his household by the adage: "If you spare the rod, you spoil child." There was work to be done, and his boys labored hard at farm work. On Sundays he might give them a quarter for afternoon recreation. (My curiosity asks: What kind of recreation was available in those days?) A quarter then would probably be equivalent to a ten-dollar bill now.

Back in Switzerland, there were limited resources, and the Swiss had to nourish themselves even while lacking refrigeration. This habit of prudence was carried over to Jakob's household. When spoiled meat was served at the family table, the children had to make at least a pretense of eating it. Fred, in later life, told how he was 'saved' by his baggy lumberjack jacket worn to the table. When his father wasn't looking, he would sneak a piece of the spoiled meat into his jacket, and so his plate was clear.

Whatever one might think of Jakob's tactics with his children, every single child grew up to be a creative asset to society. At family reunions, his descendants talked of the talents J.J. developed, despite his lack of formal education. He was often referred to as a genius because it seemed that there was never a puzzle or a problem that he could not solve.

His interest in reading, music, and the arts were passed on to his descendants as were his blue eyes and dark curly hair. He listed to Caruso and opera, made a delicious grape wine which he served sparingly, insisted that tools be cleaned and stored after each use, and that newspapers be folded just as they were when delivered. His inventive talents were evident in his sons' penchants for successfully developing and patenting agricultural implements that were ultimately manufactured and distributed.

His credit rating at the bank was one of the highest. He was able to retire in his forties after amassing as much land as amounted to a substantial portion of the little valley in Switzerland where he was born. In the 1870 census, after only four years on the farm, Jakob's worth was estimated at $6,700—equivalent in today's dollars to at least $100,000 or more.

On April 18, 1898, Jakob married Mathilda Louise Diesterhaupt, a 37-year-old eligible lady he probably met on his visits to Boltonville where he had business at a mill operated by an older sister of his first wife. Mathilda was buried in Boltonville in 1943.

Jakob's application for a disability pension at age 48 stated his difficulties as hernia, rheumatism, and neuralgia. At age 84 he requested a pension with the following comments on the application: dizzy spells, attacks of lumbago and rheumatism, eyesight is very poor (especially the left eye with which he could not distinguish objects clearly, three feet away), and seriously troubled with catarrh.

Jakob died September 7, 1934, and was laid to rest with full military honors in Ebenezer Cemetery next to the little Evangelical Methodist church at Elwood Corners. In the living-room of his home, he had hung a large sketch showing treatment of prisoners by their Confederate guards at the infamous Andersonville Prison camp. Jakob escaped the experience of torture. He had a military service that he and his family could be proud of.

I am proud to be of Swiss ancestry as a daughter of George Jacob Steiner and the woman he married, Susan Elizabeth Welsch. It is regretful that records, comparable to the ones of the Steiner family, were not maintained for ensuing generations.

The Welsch Legacy

I know very little about my mother's ancestors. By the time I was born, most of them were deceased, and no one had committed any genealogy to print as did the Steiner family. All photographs, mementos, and printed records were lost in the fire that devoured my parents' house early in their marriage.

I vaguely remember my maternal grandmother who lived on a farm with my mother's only sister. My maternal grandfather had passed away many years before I was born. I knew her two brothers, Joe and Oscar, and her sister, Rose. Each one of them was hardworking, honest, and morally upright.

Uncle Joe Welsch lived in Mayville, Wisconsin with his wife, Mary, my godmother. Their son, Ray, became a doctor; daughter Alice lived in Milwaukee; daughter Gertrude was married to a commissioned lieutenant and dentist in the Navy (residing in Hawaii with their two little daughters when it was attacked on December 7, 1941.) Uncle Joe and Aunt Mary raised their grandson, David, who was my age growing up and generously shared his toys when we visited them.

Uncle Joe was a great tease and a diabolical laugh. Aunt Mary was a great cook. She and my mother got along very well as both of them had a streak of mischief and loved laughter. She was still a jolly, astute person even though she became blind when she reached the 90's.

Uncle Oscar lived in Fond du Lac, Wisconsin with his wife, Alexia, and their six children: Leonard, Ralph, Andy, Delores, Dorothy, and Jeanette. Jeanette was the closest to my age and the one I knew best. I think Oscar was Ma's favorite in the family because he was so pleasant, generous, and down to earth as she was.

Ma's sister, Rose, was married to Jake Beck with whom she had five children: Alex, Alex, Roland, Leo, Donna, and Dorothy all grew up on farms—first, near Lomira, and later near Kewaskum, Wisconsin. Aunt Rose had a hard life, compounded by Uncle Jake's horrific accident when his arm was caught in a corn shredder. He had to free himself by cutting off his own arm above the elbow with a pocket knife given him as a Christmas present from Maybelle.

Aunt Rose had to take over her husband's chores of milking cows, plowing, planting, and harvesting crops, in addition to the household demands of cooking, cleaning, and caring for their children's needs as well as his. She lived well into her 90's, spending the last few years in a nursing home in a comatose state. She went in peace at last. My mother lived to the age of 82 which, I believe, surprised her when she compared it to the longevity of her ancestors—most of them living to the 40's, which included the Marx relatives who lived some distance away. Ma told stories about observing their over-eating habits when she visited them. Each one of the men could easily eat a whole roasted chicken is one sitting. All of them were acutely obese which was an example that kept my mother preparing healthful meals and eating in moderation.

That word, "moderation", was a sign post in her life, and she tried to have those around her to live by that rule.

<u>Every Day a Holiday</u>

I was a lucky kid growing up, and I knew it. Can you imagine waking up every morning, excited about the new day and what it would hold? During the school year, each day unfolded according to a pattern, but, even in that pattern there was enough variation to interest me... maybe a special treat in my school lunch, a place to go somewhere after school, a calf had been born overnight, someone special was coming over to visit, to measure me for alterations to a hand-me-down dress, Pa promised to play solitaire with me after evening chores, perhaps we were going to have my favorite meal that night...wait a minute, according to my mother, *every* meal was my favorite (a standing joke in our house!)

If you judged a holiday by the meal you had for dinner, every day was a holiday when my mother was still alive. Our 'main' meal was observed at noon, but the one we called 'supper' (the evening meal at 6:00 P. M.) was of equal stature, food-wise.

It included an entrée, some kind of potato, a salad or vegetable side, and—without fail—a dessert. According to Ma, no meal was complete without a dessert, even if it were only a lowly graham cracker.

Folks could drop in unannounced, any day, any time, and they were always asked, "Have you eaten?" Ma made it look so easy to whip up something that always pleased the palate. Nothing expensive but, without a doubt, better than any five-star dining experience. How did she do it? What she called "pot luck" was a meal "fit for a king", according to Pa. Before we finished one meal, she'd be planning for the next day. I have trouble planning for *today!*

Example: for Easter, we had baked ham, escalloped potatoes, an interesting fruit salad, fresh asparagus or cauliflower covered with crushed Rice Krispies sautéed in butter (which adds a tasty dimension to noodles as well). Our Easter baskets were filled with homemade fudge, popcorn balls, and eggs boiled in onion skins which gives them a rich ombre hue—an organic twist rather than commercial artificial dyes.

Our Bunny cakes came in two's (to multiply?!): one for our house, and one to give away. They were made from two cake layers, cut in half across the diameter, then each of the two halves were stuck together with vanilla or lemon pudding, and the cut edges stood on a plate. Cut a notch out of one end to create the shape of a head, stick pink ears cut from pink paper into the notch. Stick one large marshmallow in the other end for the bunny's little tail. Cover the whole creation with a boiled white icing and finish the face with jelly beans for eyes, nose and mouth, with whiskers made from colored toothpicks inserted in an angle toward the nose.

For Thanksgiving, we feasted on one of our Muscovy ducks, bread stuffing moistened with giblet broth, seasoned with a little sage, finely chopped giblets, celery, onions, and held together with a raw egg. Then the entire mixture sautéed in butter before stuffing the 'bird'. It was delicious enough to make stuffing sandwiches. There was always a choice of sweet potatoes/yams or real mashed Idaho potatoes, plus two vegetables of choice, and any one of three varieties of cranberry dishes (jellied, whole berries, fresh berries ground up with oranges.)

By comparison, the preparations for Christmas were insane—begun immediately after Thanksgiving: butchering a pig, hanging it in a shed where Pa 'shaved' and scraped its skin aided with boiling water. Using all the pig's parts, they started with making head cheese ("sulze") using its tongue and the natural aspic of the head to form it into a loaf.

My parents had various sizes of grinders and sausage stuffers, plus big sharp knives and a variety of bowls, to make summer sausage, bratwurst, krautwurst, hams, and bacon to hang patiently in our smokehouse. At least one-half of these precious, tasty gems was shared with friends and relatives as gifts.

Ma prepared fruitcakes with the finest ingredients including our home-grown hickory nuts, candied fruit, and butter—held together with a bit of buttery cake batter to lead a happy life soaking up brandy as it aged. It deserved the adjective 'gourmet'. When my folks made a present of any of these items to anyone, I *knew* that they must be really good friends.

They sold as well as gave dressed turkey ducks to people. The darker the feathers, the more pin feathers they had for Pa and me (the designated 'tweezer team') to detail. Ma would not allow us to miss one pin feather. They had to be perfectly plucked. After a few birds, our fingertips would be numb from the repetitive squeezing of the tweezers.

You never ate the kind of candy Ma made: a velvety confection she called 'marble' candy. It had to be boiled, then poured onto a marble slab where it cooled and mellowed into a smooth, melt-in-your-mouth, heavenly treat.

She baked hundreds of cookies: date/nut icebox cookies, Spritz, meringue kisses, and cut-out sugar cookies that were individually decorated for friends and family. I 'primed' them, but it was my father who showed his artistic side by adding details like saddles and bridles to the horse-shaped ones, antlers on the reindeer, buckles and britches on the Santas, brooms and buttons on the snowmen, and golden wings on the angels.

He arranged his palette of little bowls of various colored frostings like a Toulouse-Lautrec, and a container of melted chocolate set in warm water to apply with a toothpick, for eyebrows and people's names. It was fascinating to watch his fingers, made large by the many years of hard manual work of milking cows and blacksmithing custom horseshoes, yet amazingly dexterous. (His rings for his fingers were a size to fit a baby's wrist!)

Christmas Eve was the big event in my pre-teen years. I had to take a nap after super so that I could stay awake at Midnight Mass in town. I'd wake up about 8:00 P. M. to the sound of sleigh bells. Santa had arrived! Excited, but too shy to meet him. I ducked under the kitchen table, usually bumping my head quite hard. I froze in a shivering crouch as I heard a knock on the door. As the door slowly opened, I saw a pair of black boots enter.

I could hardly breathe when a low voice said "Ho-ho-ho" and asked if I had been a good girl. He asked me to say a prayer for poor boys and girls, and made me promise to be good to my parents. I was glad he didn't ask me to sing. I had trouble even mumbling an Our Father. I kept wishing Ma would show up. She'd know what to do. (I never suspected that *she* was the Santa!) As tired as she must have been, she had gone down to the barn while I napped and hitched one of our Percheron horses to a rig and attached a strap of jingle bells to its harness.)

After Santa left with a hearty "Merry Christmas" farewell, my sister, Maybelle, would excitedly call me to come "look at the beautiful tree and presents he left" in our enclosed, unheated front porch. There was a natural Christmas tree, with its fragile antique ornaments, tinsel, and candles in holders that were clamped to the branches.

Maybelle was the only one allowed to light the candles. I was permitted to douse them with my spittened thumb and forefinger. It was too cold to stay out there very long. I found the presents with my name on them and took them inside to the kitchen to open. It was exciting to get a beautiful doll each Christmas that opened and closed its eyes (with real eyelashes) and said "Ma-Ma" when she was tipped downward and back up again. It took me a few years before I realized it was the same doll. Ma touched up her 'make-up' and sewed new clothes for her. I caught on to this charade when I found buttons in Ma's sewing machine drawer that matched the ones on the doll's dress.

About 11:00 P. M., we climbed into our '28 Oakland sedan to make the four-mile trip to the church in town. Most of the congregants were hardworking farmers who, being in a warm crowded church, couldn't keep from yawning and falling asleep. I stayed awake by looking at all the new clothes that people were wearing. Seeing the same people all year, week after week, I had developed a mental picture of everyone's wardrobe.

I, myself, was wearing a new green woolen snowsuit. I wondered what the nuns would say if I wore that outfit to school—violating their 'no pants' policy for girls. Somehow, Ma convinced them that pants were more practical and modest than skirts. Besides, I'm sure those German nuns wouldn't want to alienate their source of beer that Pa would directly drop off at their kitchen door. (I still have the proof: holy picture cards from them noting in their handwriting 'for the case of beer.'

Christmas Day dinner was a carbon copy of our Thanksgiving meal except there were more desserts. In addition to pie, a festive frit and whipped cream bedecked schaum torte and brandy-laced aged fruit cake, there was an assortment of cookies and candies.

"Second Christmas Day" was a treat for Ma because we'd visit her brother, Uncle Joe; his wife, my godmother Aunt Mary; and Cousin David who was about my age. He had more sophisticated, expensive gifts like Tinker Toys and Monopoly which we'd play on the living-room floor while we surreptitiously eavesdropped on the men's (my Dad and Uncle Joe) conversations while simultaneously tuning in to our mothers' gossip coming from the kitchen—the latter more interesting, of course, about relatives, not about farming and machinery that the men discussed.

Aunt Mary was a good cook. I loved her yeast-made cloverleaf ice-box rolls. It seems everyone in the family were bread eaters in those days. I never minded being sick enough to stay home and enjoy 'bread soup'— made with homemade bread toasted over hot coals in our wood-burning range, then cut into cubes, sautéed in butter, then adding hot milk, salt, pepper and a chunk of butter on top. It cured nearly everything/

The thing that made New Year's Eve memorable for me was having maraschino cherries in my glass of pop—sneaking more out of the jar when no one was looking.

Funny, how little things like that made an occasion so special. I vowed that, if I got rich when I grew up, I would buy a jar and eat all of the cherries myself. The only guests we ha to celebrate with were my married sisters and their husbands who would stop in for a smorgasbord of homemade goodies—sausages, breads, olives, and a sugarholic spread of sweets.

Snow storms were fun back in the 30's as I recall Pa making delicious vanilla ice cream churning it in the ice cream-making bucket set in a snow bank. Sometimes, I would hitch up our husky Belgian Shepherd to a little sled that he loved to pull. If I could find even the tiniest frozen pond in a field, I would feel like 'Joan of the Yukon.'

When our 'city' friends from Milwaukee visited, they would bring their rambunctious teen sons. Pa knew how to cool them off: he'd hitch up one of our Percheron horses to a stone boat (a long flat wooden sled with no runners, ordinarily used to haul large stones from the fields) and take us for a spin—and I do mean *spin!* I sat up in front with Pa who would make the ride interesting by giving a tug on the reins for the horse to make a sharp turn, spilling the boys into a snow bank. No one got hurt, but it did put everyone on guard.

Twenty-five years later, as a single parent, living in Chicago in December 1957 with sons 3-year-old Tom, almost 2-year-old Alan, and six months pregnant with daughter Barbara. I wanted a Christmas tree, the symbol of Christmas, badly enough that, on Christmas Eve, I packed up the boys in a second-hand baby buggy. I pushed it more than a mile to the nearest tree lot where I heard that trees were being given away...FREE!

Without child support, I couldn't afford the luxury of buying a tree, not even for $2. I needed to support the children on the few dollars I made by singing at weddings and selling home-baked goods to neighbors on our block. When I arrived at the lot, it was after nine o'clock; it was closed. I couldn't see over the tall fence, but I heard men's voices. I interjected, "If there is still a tree left, just throw it over the fence. My little boys and I would appreciate it."

They did, and I happily clasped my hand around the center of the tree to balance it and walked home, smiling—the other hand pushing the buggy as snowflakes gently landed on my face. A Norman Rockwell gravure, to be sure, an unforgettable moment in time. I thanked God for being filled with a beautiful Christmas spirit and love for children like few people may ever experience—feeling closer to God than ever before. My heart and hands were too occupied to wipe the tears rolling down my cheeks.

If "memories make us what we are", I gained strength that night that helped me cope with the years that lay ahead. I realized that, every time I was tested, I got stronger. I understood that night, how the hardships my parents dealt with throughout their lives are what made them the models and pillars of strength for us children to appreciate and emulate.

COMMON SCENTS
By Joan Wellander-Kleppe

Only on a farm is there such a variety of enticing scents,
seasonally or year-round:

The smell of new-mown hay, takes your breath away.
Fuzzy little ducklings, baby pig sucklings,
    Tons of shucked peas at an outdoor vinery;
    The first Fall fire in the woodburning furnace.

Loaves of homemade bread baking in the log-fired oven,
Jams and jellies cooking on the stove, sweet heaven.
    Frozen laundry brought in off the clothesline
    Wafting a perfume of freshness throughout the house.

Candy boiling, cookies baking, beef roasting,
Sausages, ham and bacon curing in the smokehouse.
    Fields of clover and buckwheat in blossom,
    The beekeeper had hives filling with honey.

Cucumbers succumbing to pickling
Entices the use of alum and spices.
    Canning peaches, pears, and fat purple plums
    With simple sweet syrup for multiple yum-yums.

The smell of logs sawn into firewood,
Envying the aroma from the fire pit embers,
    Announcing the arrival of Fall
    And early bed times for all.

THE SEEDS THEY PLANTED

Farmers plant seeds of all kinds that yield annual crops of peas, corn, sugar beets, hay, and straw. My parents also planted and nurtured seeds of the body-and-soul variety to last a lifetime: integrity, honesty, tolerance, charity, patience, compassion, positive attitude, fortitude, unconditional love, and a charitable sense of humor underlying all.

They engrained a work ethic in all four of us girls to always do our best and give more than what is expected of us in any job we tackled. They inspired by example the kind of behavior that would uphold their good name. Their genuineness was respected by those who knew them as well as those who met them for the first time.

The one trait that most impressed me was their honesty. They never sugar-coated anything, and I knew they never lied to me. That is important to a child.

Neither one smoked or imbibed a traceable amount of liquor. Although they knew how to make excellent wine, it was a rare, celebratory occasion when they broke open a bottle of aged elderberry, dandelion, or rhubarb wine made in the early years of their marriage. By the time I was old enough to indulge, each vintage had morphed into an incredibly smooth nectar, fit for the gods.

They passed on many interests and talents to us girls not usually associated with a rural upbringing: playing musical instruments; a love of the performing arts, free-lance writing, glass etching, horse training, wine-making, meat processing, and tolerance of all people.

Our mother was amazing. I often confirmed that opinion, especially when she expressed self-consciousness about not having much formal education. Truly, she could hold her own, in fact could rise above any degree level of any person. She had an uncanny insight of people she met. I brought home any fellow I dated, even when I was in college, for a kind of 'litmus test'. I couldn't always detect a phony, but she was always 'right on the money'.

Her couturier talents were professional. It was often remarked that she could 'make something out of nothing'. She could design and make a stylish dress out of an outdated hand-me-down from merely a description given her, never using a pattern. She made beautiful fur stoles and jackets from fur coats she'd buy at a rummage sale. From the leftover fur scraps, she built stuffed animals over metal frames she and my Dad constructed. They were the size and image of a small Airedale.

Getting the Job Done: His Way, Her Way

More than one way to skin a cat? My mother subliminally suggested the old adage might be true, that there might not always be a single, absolute way to approach a situation or solve a problem...unlike my father's firm resolve that his was the only way, whereas she encouraged creativity and originality in finding a solution.

My father was succinct and direct in giving instructions which made one listen very carefully as he would explain a procedure only ONCE.

Both methods got results: the iron hand versus the velvet glove.

They were proud but humble people, believing that no job was beneath anyone's station: no matter how lowly it might be looked upon, any task was noble as long as it was honest. Their opinion about integrity: it was like virginity, you could lose it only once.

Many people looked upon my parents as a perfect match, yet their personalities and politics were not parallel—and that's healthy. However, both agreed on the principle that one's word is one's bond. You could count on that. All four of us girls honored that principle and proudly carried it forward in our lives: we never made promises that we didn't intend to keep.

Pa was multi-talented: he did his own blacksmithing, made custom shoes for the whole stable. He trimmed the horses' hooves, filed them with a rasp, and then nailed them in place. He treated their ailments with either Absorbine horse liniment and their cuts and bruises with Carbo salve.

He also made their harnesses which were hung on a row of hooks near the front door inside the barn. I loved to watch him bring a pair of those majestic Percheron draft horses out of the barn and, in one great move, throw the harness on each of them—a complicated configuration of leather straps, reins, loops, and buckles, all connected to a bridle with bit—in a perfect fit.

Of course, being my father's biggest fan (and the curiosity gene inherited from his father), I had to try doing it by myself one day. That day occurred when I knew my father had a lot of business to take care of in town. I didn't want him to see me fail.

Now, at an age when I am presumed to have a little more common sense, I admit I would never try anything so radical again, ever.

I brought a team of horses out onto the apron of the barn. They never looked so tall and wide, but, having been well trained, they stood still throughout the whole experiment. I took the heavy harnesses off the hooks in the barn, one by one, and dragged them out. I managed to lift them up onto the horses and straightened them out, without getting all the parts tangled up. Those horses stood there so patiently while I unbuckled all the connections, carried each harness back into the barn where I hung them back onto the hooks. I led the horses back to their stalls, closed the door, told nobody, felt an inner glow of an amazing accomplishment, but never did it again.

My father had artistic talent which included writing. He kept a daily journal and wrote a weekly column in the local newspaper with the by-line: "GOT to be GOOD if you GET it from GEORGE J. Steiner". That appeared on his formal letterhead.

There was a huge capital G, and the phrases that began with G followed one after the other, radiating from the large G.

I dabbled in writing publicity, press releases and flyers, ever since—wherever I worked, to wit:

> *It occurs to me now that this may be where I inherited my writing style: corny! At the age of 20, I was secretary to the president of an awning manufacturing company and was asked to compose an ad to announce the Spring collection. I submitted the first thought that came to mind, paraphrasing a line from an old song:*

> *"Don't WAIT UNTIL THE SUN SHINES, NELLIE ...order your awnings now."* The president liked it so much that he gave me the added responsibility of taking over the company's advertising program.

My Dad used to etch names and designs on glass, tiny chip by chip, using a triangular-tipped chisel and small hammer—writing left-handed with the sharpened chisel point while tapping the hammer with the right hand. Again, always the copy-cat, I secretly borrowed his tools to practice—using a large empty vanilla extract bottle. Eventually, I mastered the art without ever breaking any glass. When I showed my

Dad what I could do, he handed me his tools without a word. I hoped it meant that he approved. It did!

There Was Music in Them Thar Genes

Not quite a teenager, Pa became seriously interested in music, displaying a great talent when he 'sat in' on drums in a semi-professional brass band. He had an innate ability to 'keep time' perfectly. He was a 'natural'. The band members wanted to keep him permanently because their regular drummer was not consistent in playing or attendance.

They played at community picnics, pubs, private parties like charivaris (shivarees), and political rallies, but Pa's stepmother negatively intervened because 'it would be improper' for such a young lad to be exposed to the environment of some of the saloons where the 'Steiner Band' played.

He displayed further musical talent by picking up the trumpet, trombone, and harmonica—playing them by ear. He continued to play the trumpet when he enrolled at the University of Wisconsin (Madison, WI) and was accepted in its band. When it was announced that John Philip Sousa was coming there to be a guest conductor, the school's music department coerced my father to learn to read music in order to play under Sousa. He complied. He was so proud, inspired to have a photo taken showing him playing the trumpet, standing erect at a music stand.

He was 18 years of age at that time, staying in a rooming house for male students. Dad was quick, strong, and agile which he demonstrated when one of his 'roomies' threatened to shave off his mustache—a facial trademark he had sported since he was 15 years old. He was not about to have the 'landscape' altered in any way. When his assailant turned it into a physical altercation, the foolhardy culprit found himself at the bottom of a staircase along with the chair he had been sitting on. End of conversation!

I was six years old when my first-grade teacher announced she was taking me to the public school district competition to sing "Santa Lucia". I think I won a prize. That was 75 years ago, for me. I don't think it has been sung since then. The other popular song at that time was "My Old Kentucky Home" which also would not have been propagated except for the Kentucky Derby—a theme song accompanied by elitists sipping Mint Juleps amongst a sea of incredibly beautiful, humongous hats on the ladies.

That short-lived competitive diversion was replaced a couple of years later when I entertained at my father's Grange meetings—jigging on stage to a harmonica or acoustic guitar accompaniment. The sound amplifier was the large piece of tin I had to perform on.

When I was age 14, Dad gave me his treasured King trombone (purchased in 1910 from a Ringling Brothers circus band musician.) It was my beginning instrument in my sophomore year as Lomira High School's first band was being started by Marvin Kaiser, a kind of Harold Hill personality. By the time I was a senior, I had won ribbons in regional competitions. At graduation ceremonies, I played the same solo that our band director had played at his graduation, "The Old Home Down on the Farm". How appropriate!

Long before the invention of LP's, 8-tracks, cassette or video tapes, television, CD's, DVD's, iPOD's and the like, music was alive in our house—thanks to our vintage Victrolas, and our eclectic collection of classical and contemporary 78-RPM records. I still have the original recording of Sousa's band playing his composition, "The Stars and Stripes Forever." No one in our family could pass the piano in our 'music room' without taking time to sit down and play a few pieces on the piano from "Piccolo Pete" to Gounod's "Funeral March for a Marionette" (theme song of Alfred Hitchcock's murder series on television.) Pa could easily be coaxed into playing one of his many harmonicas or sing a 1900's hit. As an amateur 'basso profundo', his signature selection: "Many Brave Hearts Are Asleep in the Deep".

During our mid-day meal, which my mother served precisely at 12:00 noon, my father would have us listen to the hour-long music/variety/ farm market report program emanating from Milwaukee's WTMJ radio station, which featured

"Heinie and His Grenadiers", emceed by Johnny Olson. The feature we enjoyed was the segment where they interviewed young children. A little girl said she knew a poem and proceeded to recite: *"Mrs. Nickols made some pickles, on a windy day. Mrs. Martin came a-fartin' and blew the pickles away."* The band jumped into a song immediately but not soon enough!

In the evening when the dishes and the evening chores were done, we tuned to WGN for live broadcasts of dance music by big bands from Chicago's Aragon and Trianon ballrooms.

His musical genes were apparently passed down to succeeding generations. His proficiency, specifically regarding drums, surfaced in the natural talent of my eldest son, Tom. He, too, has a perfect sense of time, is a self-taught tympanist, and holds the role of percussion section leader in an adult concert band which he and I founded in 1994.

Although I still have the desire to play trombone in the same band, I retired that instrument on my 80th birthday, to concentrate on writing two nonfiction books. The first one, a compilation of children's letters to a police officer, while I was employed as a secretary in a Chicago Police Department's district station, is entitled "Kids 'n' Cops". This, the second one, "Clean Dirt", chronicles life on a Wisconsin dairy farm from the late 19th century to the present time.

My other son, Alan, and daughter, Barbara, played in their elementary school band from the fifth through eighth grades, as did Tom, but never pursued it in later years. Alan's first instrument was my antique trombone but switched to euphonium when I joined the trombone section of Chicago's Ukrainian Cathedral Concert Band. Barbara played a Czech-made wooden clarinet I had purchased from a friend.

Her sons, Josh and Jake, in turn, have displayed natural-born talent on trumpet and clarinet, respectively.

Pa still enjoyed live music until his last days. At 90, he played one of his harmonicas at the wedding reception following my eldest sister Tess's marriage to long-time friend, Francis...at age 65!. They lived with Dad up to his final breath, often arranging for a talented, senior-age violinist to visit and entertain Pa. Even when my children and I made a trip to visit him, I brought the trombone and played some of his sentimental favorites, something between "The Old Gray Mare" and "What a Friend We Have in Jesus". Go figure!

Both of my parents had pleasant singing voices—my mother, a soprano, and my father, a basso profundo, who loved to sing "Asleep in the Deep" as he pecked the piano keys, moving downward one at a time to reach the 'deep' end following the lines "Many brave hearts are asleep in the deep, so beware, beware—bee-ee-ee-ee-ware. It was dramatic to hear that last note which was two octaves below middle B-flat. That was more than seventy years ago, but it obviously made an impression on me. I can recall his sitting at the upright piano, carving out each note as he progressed to the end.

It was a real coup to get my mother to take time out to sit down at the piano. She played from memory because her music sheets were lost in the 1912 house fire. I remember a few that she recalled: "Jerusalem", "Lincoln's Funeral March", and "In the Shade of the Old Apple Tree". She loved violin music. When it was beautifully played, it always brought tears to her eyes. She said, "It's the only instrument that can cry or talk to you."

She was a self-taught pianist on this very piano given to her as a wedding gift from her father. It was one of two treasured items she personally saved from the devastating house fire. She pushed the giant upright out the door on the first floor after a courageous save of the treadle-sewing machine out of a second-floor window, knocking a chunk out of its wooden back side when it hit the ground.

Both parents loved to dance. Whenever they attended a dance, Pa was always asked to be the 'caller'. He could make up calls with rhythm and rhyme, free style—an original 'rapper', ahead of his time, nearly 100 years before it became a recognized genre.

Another first: he was the only farmer I know who had a radio in the cow barn which he played during milking hours. He theorized that it calmed the cows, and contented cows give more milk...or so the Carnation Milk Company claims.

He tried to show me how to play a tune on a comb wrapped with a tissue, the original kazoo! I could never do it because the vibration tickled my lips. He could also play a tune on a piece of wide grass held vertically between his thumbs, the forerunner of the Jews' harp. Not original but maybe worth mentioning while on the subject of musical performance: he could play music on a large saw, rhythm on two spoons, and melody by holding a wide crabgrass leaf held between two thumbs and blowing on it.

With a background like that, it is no wonder that my path in life was paved with blocks of music and the desire to entertain. The desire to please my parents makes me believe that somehow they're looking down on me and feeling proud that I was inspired by them—that my average talents have been put to good use in helping others with music and laughter to make them feel good.

CENTURY OF PROGRESS

World's Fair – Chicago – 1933/1934

It was the summer of 1933. I was nearly eight years old, had just completed third grade, and was excited about the possibility that my parents would take my 15-year-old sister and me to the World's Fair in Chicago.

The trip was made in our 1928 Oakland sedan. It was the first time we had ever traveled outside of the state of Wisconsin. We were going to Chicago. I was sure *that* was even further away than Illinois.

My father's brother and family had already been to the Fair so they had suggestions as to the hotel where we should stay: Mrs. Campbell's at 16th and State Streets. They said it was convenient to the fairgrounds, just a short streetcar ride away. We had no idea of what a questionable neighborhood it was until the next day when we boarded the streetcar to go to the Fair. The conductor asked my father, "What's a nice-looking family doing in a neighborhood like this?" Fortunately, we never had a problem, and we never told Pa's relatives about that comment.

My parents didn't appear to be threatened and were satisfied with the no-frills lodging. Mrs. Campbell was a plain-looking, older White woman (in what later appeared to be a Black neighborhood). Pa and

Ma weren't prejudiced. Of course, telling that to an assailant would probably not prevent our getting shot or stabbed.

I guess they thought, since Mrs. Campbell looked to be honest, friendly, and accommodating, that was good enough for them.

We arrived at that hotel about ten o'clock at night, very tired, and glad to have a bed to lie on. Mrs. Campbell showed us two available rooms. They were bare, clean, and cheap. Ma said she needed to have as soft a bed as possible in order to cope with her insomnia problems. She asked me to join her in trying the bed in the room assigned to my 16-year-old sister, Maybelle, and me. Both of us sat down hard and the whole bed collapsed.

With bare wooden floors and thin walls separating the rooms, the crash of the metal frame and metal bedspring made a resounding racket which brought Mrs. Campbell to our door. Ma explained that we had 'tried' the bed for softness. Both Ma and I obviously looked silly as we sat on the floor with the headboard and footboard forming an arch over our heads. We hoped she hadn't heard us laugh hysterically before she came up to investigate the noise. Very politely, she directed us to another room.

My sister and I moved to the 'new' room which had no drapes or blinds on the large window that overlooked the hotel's back stairs. We put on our pajamas in the dark and fought our way across the lumpy mattress and said our prayers, hoping we would wake up in the morning! During the night, we got a little nervous about all the footsteps and male silhouettes going past our window, and the gruff voices.

Fair Thee Well

Even though I was only eight years old, I remember a few things about the Fair—especially the one that I was not allowed to see! I could never have imagined that some day I would marry and live in the big strange city of Chicago.

Whenever our family traveled to an unfamiliar place, we always chose a landmark where we would meet in case we became separated. At the Fair, we chose the huge dinosaur, an animated figure at the Sinclair Oil exhibit. It could be seen from nearly every spot on the grounds.

I recall going to the Swiss Village because of my father's heritage where we enjoyed the yodeling and dancing.

At the Midget Village, some of the people put on a variety show. I thought they were so cute, and I was thrilled to meet a couple of them.

Along the way, there was a barker challenging passers-by to pound a ten-penny nail straight into a 4"x4" wood block, all the way, in just five tries. Ma was too honest to suspect that it could be a scam—that the block was probably hard wood, and that the nails of soft metal would easily succumb to bending.

I looked at Ma and know what she was thinking: *"He'll be surprised that a 50-year-old woman can do it. He doesn't know how many nails I've pounded, building chicken roosts and fences on the farm."* Yes, his jaw dropped as he handed her the prize, a $5 bill. He then challenged, *"$10, if you can do it in three."* She walked away $15 richer than he expected. Not a bad haul, in Depression times!

One colorful vivid memory is of my father and me standing outside of a sideshow tent that my mother and sister entered. I kept asking, "Pa, why can't I go in there?" He kept giving me the same reply, "because you're not 16." It wasn't until we returned home that I overheard my mother relating details to someone about our trip to the Fair—recognizing the part about me not being old enough to go in. She was talking about 'Sally Rand and her fan dance.' She elaborated, "Miss Rand danced nude behind a thin translucent sheet to reveal her silhouette which drew generous applause from the mostly male audience.

A couple of years later, maybe I was ten years old, I was really scarred—yes, scarred. Actually, it was a little scary, too. My parents and I made a motor trip to visit my mother's cousin, a woman about Ma's age, who lived in St. Paul, Minnesota. When it was time to go to bed, my parents went to the guest bedroom, but I drew the short straw. I got to sleep with the cousin, a woman too unattractive to act as uppity as she did.

I was a little upset with her already because I was aware she was flirting with my father. She appeared to be conceited and uptight, but she had no reason to be.

When she undressed and removed her uplifting corset, she was anything but "up or tight". I couldn't wait to tell my mother the next day about the proof of gravity, how her chest fell down to her waist. My mother really cracked up when I told her in private.

A Brief Overview of the Year 1934

In 1934, we again visited the World's Fair, but the second time didn't leave any outstanding memories for me. What I remember most about that year was the death of my paternal grandfather, Jakob Joos Steiner in September at age 91-1/2.

I felt sad that with him went all the stories that I would never hear.

THE RENAISSANCE MAN AND
HIS BLUSHING BRIDE

Married to Each Other and to the Land

A love that subliminally began as youngsters, in that little red schoolhouse, survived and thrived an incredible sum of setbacks and successes for nearly 60 years.

My mother and father were destined to be life partners. Despite their personality differences, they epitomized a mutually strong work ethic. They demanded more of themselves than even expected by their parents. Their talents, virtues and morals complemented each other.

It was probably about 1906 when they started dating each other. Although each of them had admirers, they never seriously dated anyone else. They realized they had loved each other all along.

When my mother's parents allowed her, as a young lady, to spend farm down-time during winter months with an aunt in Milwaukee, my father was a student at the University of Wisconsin. After completing his course of study there, he enrolled in a Milwaukee business college where he learned accounting and the Pitman method of shorthand. (It was interesting to compare it with the Gregg method I later learned.)

He financed his education as a singing waiter at Kalt's, a Milwaukee pub/restaurant frequented by affluent businessmen. I pictured it might have been an environment like Berghoff's or Matt Igler's in Chicago.

Upon graduation, he worked as a secretary/accountant at the Soo Line Railroad headquarters in Milwaukee. He wrote to my mother every day so that, when he proposed marriage, she imagined they would live in Milwaukee. That dream never materialized as Pa's father gave them a wedding present of 138 acres of virgin farm land near the area where they grew up.

Their parents were happy to learn the couple planned to marry in 1908. Imagine the overwhelming project looming ahead for them, as daunting as the future faced by the pioneers of the Old West. There were no roads, no electricity, no indoor plumbing, no refrigeration, no running water. Lighting was by kerosene lamps, heating and cooking by a wood-burning stove. Wood had to be cut on your own land and then hauled to the woodshed to 'season'—a shed also housing the privy.

Rainwater was caught and stored in a basement cistern. This was soft water, used for washing one's body as well as one's clothes. Water for drinking and cooking was pumped by hand from a well about 100 feet from the house, then carried inside in a pail. A dipper was used to dispense the water. In some houses, the whole family drank right from the dipper. Pa told a story of the time he visited someone and, as he was drinking from the 'far' side of the dipper, a small child informed him, "That's where my Grandma drinks, too!"

The couple's fathers, Welsch and Steiner, had been lifelong friends, intelligent men who met regularly to discuss deep subjects—Ma's father with a good cigar, Pa's dad with a pipe dangling from his mouth—sometimes drifting off until an errant hot ash would fall and jolt him awake.

Now, the difference between each family's religion became an issue for my Dad's father. My mother came from a practicing Roman Catholic family; my father's family professed to be Evangelical Methodist. Although the senior Steiner admired my mother, and acknowledged she would be a wonderful wife to my father, he decided to not attend their wedding—a gesture for which he profusely apologized to her for many years thereafter. He complimented her for encouraging my father to convert to her faith.

They married on May 12, 1908, in Saint Mary Catholic Church in Lomira, Wisconsin. When George proposed to Susan, she said, "Yes, I'll go anywhere with you." She was teased about that promise many times during her life, adding that he did not lead her down the proverbial garden path. To her chagrin, he led her down a muddy path to a bleak 138-acre landscape of virgin land where was no road, no buildings, no dreaming, no kidding. While work was in progress preparing their 'homestead', they lived in a little two-room log house about a mile yonder.

Pa's Pen Mightier Than the S-word

Pa's many talents were not what were generally thought of as sprouting from the soil of a humble Wisconsin dairy farm. He was a man of his word, whether it was spoken or written. He was a convincing orator and a prolific writer. While a university student, he wrote an award-winning thesis on the merits of water vs. milk, purporting that without water there would be no production of milk. In fact, no living being could survive without water.

He wrote a powerful proposal to the governmental body in charge of rural roads that successfully brought construction of a road from the nearby federal highway right to our barn door. That meant no more traveling down a muddy path to deliver the cans of milk to the dairy factory, to church, to take wheat to the grain mill in town, and eggs to the country store in exchange for groceries and dry goods

He kept a daily journal and wrote a weekly column for the local newspaper with the by-line of "Got to be Good if you Get it from George J. Steiner—each capitalized phrase beginning with a capital "G" lined up in a column in front of a single, huge "G".

Haulin' Oats

When it was time to thresh the grain, Pa would tie a bandana around his face, covering his nose and mouth, and protective glasses for his eyes, so that the chaff would neither be breathed in nor his eyes scratched, while he spent hours in the barn loft spreading the blown-in straw which would later be used for bedding the animals.

Hay There!

The other lofts in the barn were yearly restocked with alfalfa, used as the bulk of the winter diet for the horses and cows in lieu of pastures to graze on. Wagonloads of hay were brought from the fields, pulled up the barn hill into the upper floor of the barn, between the lofts, where a huge pair of 'tongs' was lowered into the hay wagon by rope with a 'trip' mechanism. The rope was attached to team of horses who had been unhitched from the wagon and positioned at the opposite end. The horses were directed to slowly walk down the barn hill.

As they were descending, the 'tongs' were triggered to clamp onto a big hunk of hay. The hay was picked up, moved sideways on a track to the middle of the intended loft. It then tripped, opening its 'jaws', and depositing the hay onto the loft. (On a miniature scale, it mocked the claw machine found in some restaurant lobbies.) This operation was repeated until the wagon became empty.

It is imperative that hay is absolutely dry before bringing it into the barn. This prevents a spontaneous combustion fire. It was common to hear of a barn fire so caused, often taking livestock with it. Whenever farmers observed smoke in the distance, they immediately dropped whatever they were doing, to help a neighbor. There also was an unwritten code by farmers to help each other in any crisis, including rebuilding a burned-out barn or house.

Crowd Pleasers

There was a presence about my parents that endeared them to all who met them: teachers, preachers, store owners to itinerant workers, or the hoboes and gandy dancers who traversed the Soo Line railroad tracks that bordered our farm.

My parents were a 'hit' wherever they went, mixing with young and old, because of their refreshing sense of humor, diverse interests, intelligent contributions on subjects, and their naturally charismatic charm. Despite the disparity in educational backgrounds—my father having attended college versus my mother's formal education cut short at third grade level, they fared equally well with persons of any ethnic, social, or economical status.

They were neither pretentious nor judgmental. Their sense of humor was not about telling jokes. Although they were captivating story tellers, it was their ability to laugh at themselves. They always saw the humorous side of life, no matter what the situation. My mother was especially vulnerable to having a comical reaction in times of seriousness. As hard as she tried to maintain a sober countenance, the abdominal jiggling under her apron invariably betrayed her.

Animal Whisperers

Pa had a natural rapport with animals. His basic advice was, "Don't let them sense any fear; keep a firm but gentle upper hand, letting them know you're in control."

He patted them while speaking in assuring low tones that made animals trust him, whether he was working with horses, cows, or dogs. Oh, yes, and pigs—the most intelligent of the bunch, he said, and it's been proven.

Ma had a 'way' with animals, too. In the early years on the farm, she raised geese until the day when one gander fell in love with her. The geese were allowed to roam freely around the grounds, and my sweet mother would talk nicely to them as she sprinkled some grain as treats for them, and filled their water troughs. I wouldn't doubt that she may have sung or read poetry to them.

Evidently, one gander construed her attention to be a romantic gesture. He began to hang around in front of the house like a nervous suitor—waiting for Ma to come out. He would run toward her, grab her skirt with his beak, then flap his wings so hard against her legs that they would turn black and blue. Finally, she had to give him away—for someone else's dinner. She knew she couldn't bear to see him on her dinner table.

Geese are known to be aggressive. I recall reading about a penal institution that kept geese around the prison yard instead of dogs, to keep the prisoners at bay. My experience with swans shows that they're even more confrontational than geese. In fact, some municipalities use them to keep the Canadian geese in line.

Ma admitted she was a tease, even to chickens. When the young roosters got big enough to sport a little red comb, and squeak out a cock-a-doodle-doo, they displayed a little spunk. They would show off their masculinity by hopping up and down when she'd raise her foot toward them in a little kicking motion. They soon began responding when she entered the chicken barn. Her little teasing backfired—she couldn't turn her back on them when she went to collect the eggs out of the hens' nests. There would always be some feisty roosters looking for a little action.

Of course, after hearing these stories as a youngster, I thought it would be funny to try the same thing, teasing the roosters with a little kicking motion. It was not so humorous when they started to look for a fight, even flying up into one's face. I stopped before it got serious.

Home on the Grange

Pa and Ma had many interests in common but also pursued separate activities. Ma had her quilting bees with the neighbor women. Pa attended Grange meetings where farmers met to discuss legislation affecting agriculture, followed by socialization, potluck suppers, and family entertainment.

On a few occasions, I was the entertainment. I was probably seven years old when Ma fashioned my 'celebrity' wardrobe: two taffeta-ruffled dresses with short puffed sleeves, one with green gussets, one with red gussets—so I could alternate between the two.

The Grange officers put a large metal sheet on stage in the little country hall where the meetings were held. I would dance a jig to *"Turkey in the Straw"* which my father played on his harmonica. (Every time I hear that tune, usually played by ice cream vending trucks, I remember my jigging days.) One time, a young Grange member volunteered to accompany me with his guitar, playing chorus after chorus of *Red River Valley,* until my legs could no longer move.

All the Stage Was Her World

Ma's creativity showed itself in the way she could create a fashionable ensemble without a pattern. She could work from a sketch or just an idea explained to her. She could create a fur stole, utilizing the best sections of a rummage sale coat, cutting out the necessary pieces from the underside with a razor blade, sewing them together by hand.

Her secret greatest love was the theatre. On Friday afternoons, when she finished delivery of eggs and dressed poultry to her clients in Fond du Lac, she would step inside the Garrick Theatre where live actors were going through a dress rehearsal for a weekend performance. She sat in the back of the theatre to relax and laugh herself silly.

She described one comedy where the main male character insisted that his servant hold an umbrella over his head, no matter where he moved—over a couch, table, chair, whatever was in his path. She said it was hilarious, waiting for the servant to miss a cue, which he never did (in spite of the fact that he was obviously drunk.)

At home, she loved to play characters to entertain me, enjoying it most when I could join in some improvisational bit. She also enjoyed going into department stores in the city, using an assumed name, trying on dresses and furs, to see what it would be like to be rich. Store owners always 'bought' her act and insisted she take home the items with no money down. She was that convincing, but honest enough to decline.

Partners in Grime

A wife to a farmer is a lifelong partner, twenty-four hours a day. To be successful, they must learn to defer to each other's wishes and needs. As stubborn and dynamic as Pa was, Ma was tolerant and soft-spoken. When Pa issued a one-way edict of doing things, Ma would counter with an alternative solution to serve the purpose from a different angle. I never heard her raise her voice in anger or use foul language. She was patient; he was impulsive. He was a Republican; she was a Democrat.

I was always proud to introduce them to my friends, teachers, and employers because they could fit in with any strata of people. They were able to converse on an amazing amount of subjects: animal husbandry; crop rotation; breeding of cows, horses, chickens; writing and story telling; musicianship; love and support of the performing arts; tailoring; beer and wine-making; cooking and baking; building fences and houses; crime, criminals, and law enforcement; Native Americans;

Jews; administering to sick humans and animals; child birth; discipline for a healthy mind and body.

Yet, in spite of their many talents and accomplishments, they were a humble pair, devoted and loyal to each other. Every day, after Ma's passing at age 82, Pa felt a debilitating pain in the loss of his life's partner of nearly 60 years. For the next sixteen years, until his death at age 98-1/2, he got tears in his eyes whenever anyone spoke of her. Looking at him, I could see in his eyes that, while he was talking to me about other things, he was thinking "I miss your mother".

It has been nearly forty years since the loss of my mother, and I still get a lump in my throat when I think about her. I wish I could make just one more telephone call to hear her voice and to tell her what's going on in my life.

A few years after my father's death in 1983, I lost my husband—a Chicago police sergeant with whom I shared less than ten years of marriage. I cannot hear a police car siren without thinking of him and shedding a tear. Now, after twenty-five plus years of being a widow, I think of him and the love we shared—every time I see a police car. More than anything, we were great partners. I can understand more than ever what a bond there can be between husband and wife. Like my parents, we worked alongside each other and 'got' each other. Losing your best friend is what my dad and I have in common.

MY FATHER'S FOOTSTEPS

The size of his shoes, probably a size 10, belied the size of his steps which were Bunyan-like in the amount of territory he covered in his 98-1/2 years on this earth.

He began life as a fragile boy, the youngest of seven children, who lost his mother when he was eleven years old. Some of his three brothers and three sisters had already married and were gone from home while he was still a youngster. He was expected to work like a man and was left to fend for himself for the next six years without the nurturing of a mother figure to look after him.

His brothers had their own agendas, leaving him to take on chores too taxing for a boy of his age and frailty. His father, who was not in robust health himself, let the boys run the farm—not realizing that George needed more nourishment and guidance.

As Pa recounted those years, he remembered that he often got the leftovers of bread gone stale, and milk that soured, for supper. No wonder, when he married Ma, he made a point of thanking her every day for the meals she prepared: "Thank you, Susie, for the good food." Even as a child, that impressed me as being the mark of a loving husband, grateful for something that most people take for granted—something commonplace: a meal.

When his brothers would be gone for a day, teenage George went into a body-building mode. The regimen included wrestling with calves, using them as sparring partners, until he could take down a calf in one hold. He practiced one-handed fence jumping until he could easily scale a fence, with inches to spare. Determined to take on his brothers in a fisticuffs challenge, having literally 'taken the bull by the horns', he had the confidence needed to prove that he could subdue them. Eventually, when they egged him on, anticipating a one-sided fight, he whipped each one in succession and quickly earned a respected rung in the sibling ladder.

Pa was not a stranger to hard physical work, once taking on the job offered him by a neighbor to bury a dead horse in the winter's frozen ground, for which he was paid fifty cents! I can attest to the enormity of a 50-cent piece when that is your only income. I experienced that joy at age 16 when waitress's tips averaged a dime or a quarter at the restaurant where I worked to earn room-and-board money. At age 18, it covered a week's bus fare to and from the university campus when I worked for room and board at an off-campus private home.

My Dad was thirteen when his widowed father remarried. Her name was Mathilda, and she became a loving grandmother to all of Grandpa J.J.'s grandchildren. These grandparents lived in one-half of the Victorian farmhouse known as the 'homestead.'

I remember Grandpa as being stern but affable patriarch, puffing on a pipe that was hanging from a corner of his mouth as he sat in a rocking chair beside the potbellied stove in the parlor. My Dad's brother, Fred, lived with his family in the other half. Memorable family 'congresses' (reunions) were held there and photographs taken that chronicled the gathering of the large extended family.

ADVENTURES SHARED WITH MY FATHER

My chores on the farm were divided between helping both parents. My father often was the butt of teasing by friends that he could not sire a son; he had to hire farm hands. Since I was the youngest of his four daughters, born in my parents' forties, it wasn't likely that the future held any hope for a boy. I was happy to become "Pa's little helper"—spending one-half of the free time after school or vacation time with him, and the other half with my mother.

I loved the outdoors and wasn't averse to work or dirt. Any job with Ma or Pa was fun. They always had stories to tell and made me feel that, whatever I was doing, was really important and a big help to them. I learned about flora and fauna from Pa, and about flour and fabric from Ma. By age six, I was qualified to help with many chores:

- Turn the emery wheel as he sharpened the triangular-shaped mower blades, one by one; the scythes and sickles that were used to cut tall weeds and grass by hand;
- Feed hay to the calves in their pens, to the cows in their stanchion troughs, to the horses in their stalls, and cleaning out their water dispensers;
- After doing the dishes from our evening meal, I went down to the barn to help at the milking by carrying buckets of freshly

squeezed milk to the milk house where I poured them into the milk cans cooling in the water tanks;

- Every morning, I was needed in the milk house to stir the morning's milk to cool it while my father was up at the house eating breakfast. The milk factory in town required that the milk be brought down to a specific temperature. While my father was up at the house eating breakfast, I aerated the milk, can by can, with a long-handled tool that had a flat, perforated disk at the bottom end (similar to a potato masher), with an up-and-down motion, over and over.

- After a monotonous half hour, I could expect my father to come to the milk house, check the temperature with a floating thermometer, thank me for the good job, load the heavy cans holding about 100 pounds of milk onto the pick-up truck, and head for town.

The Fish Out of Water

On the way to the milk factory, he dropped me off at the parochial school. The routine never varied. But one morning, in the midst of the innocuous routine of cooling the milk, MY EYES POPPED OPEN when I saw movement in the water next to the can. Did I really see what I saw? Curious, I rinsed off the stirrer under a faucet, then stuck it into the water tank to check out my suspicion. It was no apparition. Quicker than I could say it, I had landed a big slippery catfish on the disk which slid right into the can of milk.

EXTREME PANIC set in as I heard my father approaching. Words came to mind that I had never used before! I feverishly tried to find the fish in the can, up-down, up-down, but no luck. Now, what can I do? I was petrified. I quickly took my seat in the truck's cab as usual. Pa closed up the cans, loaded them on the back of the truck, and away we went.

Dumbstruck, absolutely mute, I could not muster the nerve to confess to my father. All I could think of was, "What would they do to my father? Would there be a serious consequence?" Telling my father that it was an accident would sound too...fishy. I sweated with guilt all the way to town. Before I knew it, I was being dropped off at school.

As the day progressed, I felt sicker and sicker, not able to concentrate on any of the schoolwork. I promised myself that I'd tell my father when I'd come home from school. But that didn't happen. The longer I procrastinated, the heavier my guilt became. I couldn't think of a way to bring up the subject to kind of *ease* into it. I couldn't even tell Ma. It wouldn't be fair to ask her to intercede for me.

Days, then weeks, went by before the incident lost some of its sting on my conscience. Time does have a way of diluting one's memories and guilt feelings. Then, one evening, at the supper table as the family was finishing the meal, everyone seemed to be in a jovial mood, and I was enjoying my favorite dessert of cherry pie a la mode. My appetite seemed to be normal again.

My Dad, who sat directly across the table from me, began a story: "A funny thing happened at the milk factory a couple of weeks ago." (*Dear Lord, I thought, is this going where I think it's going?*)

Pa continued: "After I unloaded the milk cans one morning, and just about to pull away, the supervisor called to me: 'Hey, George, you been stopping along the way to water down the milk?' I didn't know what the heck he was talking about until I was invited to go inside and saw the long whiskers of a catfish swimming around in the huge vat of . . .'"

As soon as I hear the word 'swimming', my mouthful of cherry pie and ice cream became airborne, flying across the table. There was laughter, then silence. I had 'blown my cover'. There could be no doubt about that being a confession of guilt.

I tried to apologize, but my father said I had suffered enough punishment in the guilt and worry I had carried around for weeks. He added that the supervisor and he had a good laugh as Pa was jokingly accused of stopping at a creek to 'water down' the milk for more volume. What a relief when that was over!

Actually, one day, on the way to school, my father stopped the truck on a dime next to a creek. He jumped out of the truck and, in one lightning-like swoop, caught a muskrat behind its head and put it in a cage on the truck. He later delivered it to a muskrat farmer to earn a small bounty. It happened so fast that I didn't have time to ask myself, "How did he do that?!" Pa wasn't a small, thin, or young man, yet he accomplished the feat as if it were an ordinary daily regimen—out, down, grab, up, and back, in about ten seconds.

When I told that to my mother after school that day, she didn't act surprised. She said that, in the early years of his marriage, as they traveled a country road in a horse-and-buggy rig, my father went through the same motions to snare a wild goose on the side of the road...for a Sunday dinner.

Any time I had to ask my school-age children to help me with a messy task, I always had a messier experience I could recall from my childhood. The following is one of them:

Public Enema No. 1

One morning, while waiting down at the milk house, ready to leave for school, my father showed up with something that looked like a tire pump. He asked if I would give him a little help. He knew me well. I was always the girl who 'cain't say no.'

As the two of us stood behind a bloated, star 'milker', he handed me that 'pump', explaining THAT would force warm water through the suppository tube he was holding. If this enema worked, it would save the cow's life. Believe me, it worked! This was not a 'cutesy' story like the one I told when I visited school at age four, and not one I ever repeated to amuse my friends.

Frogging

I didn't know it at the time, but our family enjoyed what were later revealed to be gourmet delicacies. Besides having squabs for a special dinner, we also dined on turtle stew and fried frog legs.

Turtle stew, admittedly, was a rare treat, but I could never consider eating it if it were not prepared by my mother, where the base was of a rich, mahogany hue, with a delectable taste beyond description. I remember the last time my father brought home a turtle—probably well over 70 years ago! I was about ten years old, and I believe that was the last turtle that ended up in a gourmet stew in our home. The turtle was full of eggs that looked like ping-pong balls to me. I was disappointed when they didn't bounce.

Frogging was not a common happening either. I only remember two such occasions which were exciting and, apparently, unique, as I never heard of any other kid tell of dining on frog legs.

It took three of us—my father, my sister Tess, and me—to capture those elusive jumpers. In the far parcel of wooded land on our farm, there were a couple of freshwater springs. They were not only a source of fresh drinking water for the young Percheron colts who grazed there, but, for the frogs, the continuing flow of fresh cold spring water was a perfect habitat.

My father reached down into the spring to get the frogs, then handed them to my sister who, in turn, dropped them in the gunny sack I was holding. An average 'harvest' would net us about twenty frogs which, of course, translated into forty frog legs.

Ma prepared them for the frying pan by lightly dredging them in flour and then sautéing them in butter. The only way I can describe the enjoyment of their tender, white, non-fishy-tasting meat is to say it 'didn't taste like chicken.' It was better. This gourmet delicacy was strictly for our own family's consumption. Let me validate a myth here: those frog legs *did* appear to be jumping in the frying pan!

The 'Eyes' Had It

My father was proud of the premium-grade potatoes he grew, with much of the annual crop sold to a first-class five-star hotel dining-room and some very fine restaurants.

The following is a series of experiences involving potatoes: 1 potato, 2 potatoes, 3 potatoes, 4; but if the potato bugs get them, there'll be potatoes no more! But that's ahead of the story. Here's the cycle from beginning to the harvest;

a) The Planting.

This is preceded by preparing the 'seeds'—potatoes cut into uniform pieces (larger than a walnut, smaller than a golf ball) that will not jam the planting machine; then dipping them into an antiseptic solution to prevent disease. Each piece must have at least two 'eyes' so that at least one of them sprouts to produce a potato vine.

b) The Purging of Potato Bugs.

These black-and-yellow striped beetles, a little larger than kidney beans, feed on the leaves of potato plants. Purging them involves going up and down each row, examining the plant, plucking the bugs by hand and putting them in a receptacle where they're carried away and destroyed by fire later.

c) Harvesting the Ripe Potatoes.

Potatoes are ripe when they have reached a pre-determined growing-period length, when they have reached the normal size for its particular variety or your preference, and has no green under the skin. For me, this always occurred shortly after the start of school in the fall.

A horse-drawn digger uprooted the spuds. Then a crew of human pickers, including me, separated the potatoes from the vines and put them in bushel baskets—continuing to move forward until the baskets were filled and left in the aisles (between the rows). A wagon or truck would then be used to haul the filled baskets out of the field.

A few days of this backbreaking labor required rubdowns with horse liniment in order to be able to walk upright again. It was like a vacation to get back to school.

Attract Her With a Tractor?

I learned to drive a tractor before I learned to drive a car, or even a bicycle. It was no cushy rubber-tired John Deere. (Many years later, 'gentlemen farmers' had tractors with radios, lights, and air-conditioned cabs.) Ours was an iron monster: a Case tractor with cleated wheels and a hard metal seat for a rough, bumpy ride.

It still amazes me how I accomplished the challenging and dangerous feat of bringing in loads of hay, especially at night when we tried to beat an impending thunderstorm, with only lightning to guide me as I, on the tractor, pulled a wagon with a dinosaur-looking hay loader behind that. The loader had a conveyor-type action that picked up the hay, row after row, continually dumping it into the wagon where my father wielded a pitchfork to evenly distribute it.

This three-vehicle caravan made it tricky to negotiate the wide turns at the beginning and end of each row, but I strongly felt the duty to not miss a strand of hay. I was scared to death but determined to be brave in helping my father.

There were fun times, too, like competing with my father in whipping crab apples off the end of a sharpened, limber tree branch to see whose flight would go the furthest. He could be coaxed into entertaining me with a few simple magic tricks. My favorite was the way he would use his fist to pound a chalk mark through a wooden table.

It was no trick per se, but it was *tricky* the way he could braid a strip of leather that had no severed ends. I figured out how to do that, and I also could wiggle my ears—to the surprise of my small audiences at home and at work.

Pa, the inveterate story teller, liked to recall a tale about a fellow who approached a farmer, expressing an interest in purchasing the mule he saw in the farmer's field:

> *The farmer hesitated in giving an answer. The fellow pleaded, insisting he really wanted to buy the animal. Again, the farmer hesitated, saying that he was attached to the old mule who 'no looka so good.' Finally, the farmer gave in and gave a good price to the fellow who loaded the mule onto his truck.*
>
> *A few days later, the fellow came back to the farmer, spitting out his anger that the mule couldn't even walk a straight line, and kept running into things as if he were blind. The farmer, not the least bit apologetic, reminded the fellow, "I told you, he no looka so good."*

Thanks for Pranks

Capitalizing on my folks' history of being pranksters, I usually avoided a scolding by coating my misbehavior with humor. (I use the term 'scolding' because by the time I came along, my parents didn't have the strength to spank.) Besides, whenever parents tell stories of things they did when they were young, it subliminally gives a child permission to do the same—they learn by example. I know I did!

Pa spoke of his mischievous pranks at the little Evangelical Methodist country church across the road from the farm where he grew up. As a young lad, he just didn't view religion seriously, knowing many of the congregants were not *that* holy.

One night, knowing the Ladies Aid Society was meeting at the church, he and some accomplices dressed in white sheets and making ghostly noises, scared the b'jeezus out of the women when they threw open the entrance door. As the women screamed hysterically, the pranksters made a quick exit so no one ever knew who they were.

Occasionally, when Pa was coerced to attend a service, he sat up in the abandoned choir loft where he could always find pigeon eggs. He admitted to quietly leaning over the rail and dropping an egg onto a bald man's head and then disappearing just as quietly.

Ma insisted that his mischievous streak began as early as first grade in the little red schoolhouse that both attended, probably about 1890, when they both had bench seats with two pupils to a bench. When Ma tells her version of the story, Pa was a real pain-in-the-neck kind of guy because he sat behind her and her classmate. He surreptitiously tied their pigtails together. When either one of them got up to answer the teacher, it annoyingly tweaked their necks...to which Pa countered: "she must have liked it a little because she always chose a seat in front of me."

Pa was not a hunter though he could shoot straight. One summer, when I was about fourteen years old, my parents and I attended a county fair. Walking around the midway, Pa noticed a shooting gallery equipped with rifles. I had never held a rifle before, actually not any kind of gun, not even a BB gun, but I accepted Pa's challenge to try to hit a bull's eye.

The targets were two circular gongs about 12" in diameter, mounted close to each other on the back wall of the concession stand—about 15 feet from where I stood. On my first shot, I hit the center of the gong—a hole about 4" in diameter. It made a loud ringing sound and surprised me more than it did my father. He calmly said, "Now, try the other one," as he handed me a dollar reward.

I was reluctant to try it when the carnie interjected in a condescending tone, "That one's got a center hole only about the size of a quarter." Even at my young age, I was up for a challenge if there was the slightest chance of success. My father coached, "Don't try to hold a position. As soon as you have the target in sight, shoot!"

I did just that. It seemed like the whole fairgrounds stood still. I was dead on target. The noise of success was deafening. I could feel the staring of eyes behind me. Pa shook my hand, placing two dollar bills in it. When I turned around, there was a small crowd of people behind me, giving me a wink and a smile!

PRANKS A LOT !

Ma and Pa were inveterate practical jokers. Our family, like others of that era, "made their own fun", a common expression describing home entertainment before the advent of television. Our home entertainment centers consisted of AM radios and record players—hand-cranked ones that played rubber, not vinyl, 78-RPM platters. Our albums came in hard-cover binders with paper sleeves that held the records, with a hole on one side to display the song title, recording company, and artist(s).

<u>Wooden You Know</u>

Sometimes, in the early evenings of summer, after dishes and outside chores were done, I would sit at the piano in the first-floor den. Suddenly, I would sense that I was being watched. When I turned toward the room's only window, there would be a huge animal head staring at me from the outside—one of Pa's taxidermy specimens, a 12-point buck, that he would hold up to the window. I eventually stopped screaming. Incidentally, the deer head was a gift, not from an animal that my Dad shot. He never hunted; he hated guns. But he kept a shotgun in the pantry above the door in case he had to shoot a rat or weasel in the chicken barn.

It must have been fun for him to scare me because, other times, he would come into the house with his hands behind his back and ask me to guess what he was holding. It could be candy, an Indian arrowhead found in our fields, or a live critter—perhaps a bird whose wing or leg he had mended, but, more often, it would be a tickley soft baby rabbit. Whatever it was, it always got a squeal out of me. Of course, I HAD to guess, in case it was candy!

In the winter, when the 'tough' city sons of my parents' friends visited from Milwaukee and wanted some action, Pa would hitch up one of our beautiful Percheron horses to a stone boat (a kind of wooden sled without runners) and take us all for a ride in the snow—making fast, sharp turns to spill them into a snow bank (the 'softer' side of Pa's humor).

In the early days of farming, my parents sometimes hired a transient to help with immediate chores. One such fellow had the need to visit the outhouse before getting started, and thereafter about every fifteen minutes, therefore not being of much help. On checking the facility between his time-outs, my parents discovered it was a bottle of booze he was actually visiting.

Ma related a story of her over-the-top prank that she concocted which could have had a disastrous ending. After giving a hobo a nice supper meal and a warm place to sleep, he got up the next morning and, after being treated to a sumptuous farmer breakfast, he went down to the barn. My parents found him stretched out on a bed of hay, making it clear that he did not want to work. Having revealed in conversation the night before that he was afraid of ghosts and was sure the devil was after him, my mother decided to validate the phobia.

Ma put a white sheet over herself and, with a pitchfork in hand, went down to the barn—eerily calling his name to 'get to wor-r-r-rk." Seriously frightened, he leaped up, ran to the house, where he threatened to jump from a second-floor window. Realizing that he had taken the sham seriously and, not wanting to be responsible for a broken neck, she threw off the shroud to reveal her real self—shouting to identify herself but to no avail. He did come out of the house and scurried off in the direction of the railroad tracks, mumbling something about the 'devil'.

The next scenario was the result of a collaboration of both parents:

Strange Bedfellow

My sister, Maybelle, and I shared a double bed on the second floor. One evening, as she and I prepared to go upstairs to bed, my parents were acting quite suspiciously--Ma was sitting on Pa's lap, giggling and instructing us to 'go upstairs, but don't turn on the light *so moths don't come in.*

Strange...they never said that before. We were puzzled; we had screens on the windows. We never heard that warning before. Our curiosity won over obedience.

We went upstairs to the bedroom and turned on the light. Aha, at the foot of the bed, hanging down from under the bedspread, was a black satin ribbon. Where did that come from?

We hadn't noticed any ribbon when we made the bed in the morning. My sister threw back the spread and covers, and there, far down between the sheets, was a big live bullfrog with a black ribbon around one leg. We saw his bulging eyes looking at us.

We faked a couple of screams to make our parents believe their prank-planning was successful. They were disappointed that we had not encountered the 'plant' with our bare feet.

The pranks perpetrated by Maybelle and me seem pale by comparison, like putting small screw-top lids from baking powder cans, for instance, fill them with water, and put them atop the kitchen door so that when Ma came in from outside, they would spill that little bit of water on her. It never worked.

I had a scientific trick I learned in high school science class: fill a glass with water, put a piece of cardboard across the top, tip the glass upside-down very quickly, and then hold it over my mother while she was resting on a chaise lounge in our den. I knew it wouldn't spill, but it always got a rise out of her.

With that history of pranks in my background, I couldn't reprimand my children when they thought of devious ways to '*get*' me. They were teenagers when I got my first car, my one-and-only new car, a four-door 1970 Chevy sedan—a gift from my father and sister, Tess. It was 'born' with carburetor trouble so that I thought nothing of it as I drove to the local shopping mall when it started to sputter and make popping noises, followed by smoke spewing from under the hood. Then I became concerned. When I pulled over to the curb and checked under the hood, I found that two sparkplugs had been disconnected to accommodate a smoke bomb. I could not become angry because I knew my sons thought I'd take it in good humor, which I did. In fact, I took it as a sort of compliment that they could feel comfortable in playing a joke on me.

How My Garden Doth Grow

When I sold our single-family house and moved my children and me to a brick two-

flat, there wasn't any room in the backyard to plant a garden, so I cleared a strip next to a fence and planted a few seeds: green beans and carrots. I didn't pay much attention to that area until about six weeks later. I saw that, not only had my seeds sprouted, there was a single row of some kind of flower or weed—plants about 10" high with beautiful lacey leaves. I didn't recognize what they were but were interesting enough to let them grow.

That decision met a humorous reaction from my children that they couldn't contain.

They said an acquaintance of theirs planted seeds that were not expected to germinate, but, feeling rather foolish, I realized they were cannabis plants. They were so pretty that I hated to destroy them. However, I pulled out all of them—except one in the corner, between the fence and the garage, that grew to be 6' tall. No one ever noticed, not even the police officers that came to the house to have reports typed. One day, it turned up missing, and I didn't want to know where it went.

Diesel Surprise You

Although my 1970 4-door Chevy sedan was the only new car I ever had, its style and color definitely projected an uncool ownership, so that my idea of installing a diesel horn (like that of a semi-truck) would be fun. My son, Tom, with an auto mechanic background, bought one and installed it. Now for the right moment. The moment arrived, and it couldn't have been better if it had been scripted.

The deep tunnel project was underway in Chicago, and one of the selected locations was the intersection next to our house. I had to negotiate the tight squeeze in order to get through the intersection. I pulled up to it and waited for traffic to stop. While I waited, one of the engineers came off the curb toward me while reading a map. He never looked up. In fact, he put one elbow on my car's fender as he was perusing it. At that moment I blew the diesel horn which was right under his map. Omigosh, that poor fellow was shaken into an awakening.

I had the good fortune to help employees of two offices where I worked as a secretary. I champion the under-dog when management takes advantage of their loyal, hardworking employees. I got benefits at one such place for employees who were victims of the bosses' flagrant nonviolent abuse. I became privy to their tactics as I took notes at the board meetings chaired by the president who instructed the department heads to increase the demands of the workers' output until they could not keep up with the quota increases. These unsuspecting unappreciated employees were then fired and replaced by new victims, always keeping the pay rate at its lowest level.

Another job that I held, briefly,was working the call center phones on the first floor where lights on a console lit when a circuit was being used, but therefore I couldn't tell if the call was incoming or outgoing. It occurred one time that an executive made a call which I couldn't tell the source of course. So, when I asked, "May I ask who is calling?" He blared, "Mr. Abernathy, goddamn it!" I could hardly keep from bursting into laughter and tell my buddy, Bruno, who sat across from me.

We were the only clerical people working in that first-floor area. We had plenty of visitors to keep us amused, except they were of the rodent kind. An obnoxious female vice president had a sumptuous office behind us. She ignored our information that we had a rodent infiltration; in fact, she did not believe us. I confided in Bruno that I had a plan, but he had to swear that he would be able to keep a straight face as part of the plan.

The plan: I would buy the most realistic-looking mouse at a novelty shop when I'd go home for lunch. Bruno would have to put it under her telephone with just part of the tail protruding out. He did as he was told and didn't even crack a smile when she came back from lunch. Good! We didn't look at each other; just became engrossed in looking at our desk tops, waiting to hear her door close. We looked up at each other, right at the moment we heard her blood-curdling scream. Bruno and I calmly, seriously went back to the job we were working on. No one ever knew.

The office manager approached us, thankfully on another issue: let's all dress in costume for Halloween, herself included. Bruno said he would wear his cap and gown from his recent college graduation. I decided to wear my red-and-white striped flapper dress with beads, a white feather in my hair, a long cigarette holder, and period make-up.

I drove to work, made my entrance and, to my chagrin, no one was in costume. The plans had changed in the interim. I went home and never went back. It reinforced my plan to quit anyway.

At the next place, I discovered that all forty employees, office and factory combined, were not being paid for their hours of overtime. The National Labor Relations Board came in, interviewed a few employees at random, to verify the allegation. Two weeks before Christmas, each employee received a sizeable check for a very merry holiday season. My underhanded bosses never knew it was their hardworking secretary who took matters into her own hands and got those folks the pay they so rightly deserved. I really felt proud of myself when I heard employee after employee exclaim, "I got a check! Did you get a check?" Merry Christmas, indeed.

IF YOU KNEW SUSIE

Pa often sang the beginning of this famous old tune: *"If you knew Susie, like I know Susie"* It seemed fitting to teach that song to my 3-year-old daughter, Barbara Sue. She performed it with expression in a musical vignette at my parents' 53rd wedding anniversary. She repeated her flawless performance on stage with a professional dance band in Fond du Lac's (WI) concert-in-the-park series. Equal time was given to her brothers: Tom, 6 years of age, and Alan, 5 years of age who sang and danced to *Ballin' the Jack*.

To meet Susie, my mother, was a sweetly memorable experience. She had an earthy, charismatic charm that put a person immediately at ease and eager to share a friendship with her. There always was a loving glow about her that endeared her to young and old.

She had an innate ability to analyze and understand the psyche of anyone she met—a great judge of people. I always sought her verdict about any girlfriend of mine or about any fellow I contemplated dating. Somehow, she could discern whether the person would become jealous or possessive, ambitious or slovenly, truthful or deceitful, caring or unkind.

True Love Knows No Bounds

Ma worked harder than any woman, or any two women, I have ever known. I've never gotten the picture out of my mind of how she started married life on the farm.

After living a hard life on her parents' farm, until she reached womanhood, she secretly hoped to live a city life in marriage. She loved my father unconditionally and always thought that, since he had completed a business course and worked as a bookkeeper for the Soo Line Railroad Company, they would leave arduous farm life behind.

From the time she could walk, she had to keep up doing chores with her two brothers and could only attend elementary school during the winter months when there was little outdoor work to do. During the rest of the year, she had to help with everything—the worst job of all was sheep shearing. It was a disgusting job because, as she quipped, the sheep's wool was 'lousy with lice', and she was the one who had to hold the sheep while someone else sheared them.

None of the field work was mechanized. The rows of hay had to be lifted with pitchforks onto horse-drawn wagons. Manure had to be shoveled from the gutters in the barn, behind the cow stalls, onto a horse-drawn spreader, then out to the fields for fertilization.

Harassment Even in the 'Good Old Days'

There were no neighbor girls to play with. An innocent pastime was to take a hoop from a barrel and see how long you could roll it with a stick. A couple of crude farm boys in the area decided to check out this lone farm girl. Farm life was not the innocent environment as one may suppose. She was at these boys' mercy as one of them held her down while the other one exposed himself. When she refused to participate in their sick game, they put her in a big wooden barrel and rolled her down a hill on the bumpy gravel road. It was a horrible experience. Besides the severe headache, bruises, and nausea she suffered, she was afraid to tell her parents for fear of reprisal that the culprits promised her.

What's in a Name?

Her father occasionally had a refined, wealthy but overbearing businessman visit him. When he saw the man's horse and buggy coming down the road toward their farm, he'd jokingly say in a low-German dialect, "Hier kommt der gruesen apf." (Translated: "Here comes the big ape.")

Ma didn't know the low-German dialect; she only knew high-German which was spoken in the home—so she thought "Gruesen Apf" was the man's name.

The visitor sat down in their parlor with her father to share expensive cigars he always brought to share and enjoy while discussing world events. He saw a look of curiosity on Ma's face as she peeked around the corner at them. He said, "I know your name, but I bet you don't know mine."

Ma very knowingly replied, "Yes, I do. It's GRUESEN APF." I can't imagine how embarrassed her father must have been. He probably coughed or choked a little on those mighty fine cigars. The man was understanding about the little girl's faux pas. When he visited again, she heard her father thank him profusely for leaving him a whole box of these 'especially smooth, great tasting' cigars.

Close, But No Cigar – Please!

She and her brothers decided to sneak one each for themselves to smoke out in the field where they were working. After a few puffs, they turned green with nausea and got so weak from vomiting that they lay in the field until the usual time to go back to the house.

They managed to cover any telltale signs of their deed, until their father lit up a cigar after the evening meal—causing them to run outside to puke their guts out. Their father had suspected their guilt and deliberately lit up, knowing the smoke would effect more punishment than he could inflict. (This incident reminded me of a scene from the WWII movie, *"The Sullivans"*, who tried the same experiment—all of them seeking relief over the old-fashioned bathtub.)

In those turn-of-the-century days, children had to miss a lot of school days to help on the farm, during plowing and planting times in the spring, and harvest time in the fall. Also, it was thought that girls didn't need an education because they would just get married anyway. All they needed to know were just wifely duties: cooking, cleaning, washing clothes, satisfying a husband's needs, and having babies. That kind of thinking is what kept my mother from going beyond third or fourth grade.

A Taste of City Life

In 1900, when my mother was 16 years old, her parents allowed her to go by train from Lomira to Milwaukee to spend time with an aunt. This hiatus from farm life was possible because there was little outside work to do in the winter months.

While on those brief vacations, she found various jobs to earn a little spending money while enjoying the conveniences and the magic of city life. In those days, there was a disparity between what you could buy with what you could earn. For example, a blouse cost $5.00 which translated into a week's pay—about a dollar a day. On each of these vacations, she had experiences that a little country girl could never have imagined or anticipated.

She once found work as a chamber maid in a nursing home where she discovered she had an aversion to 'old people'. Ordered to clean under the bed of one elderly resident, she tied a dust cloth to the end of a broom handle to do the job—much to the ire of the elderly lady who spittingly chastised her for not coming closer so she could see her better. (Reminiscent of Little Red Riding Hood and the Wolf?!) Ma always feared that God would punish her uncharitable attitude when she would get old herself.

My mother then volunteered for kitchen duty, but her stay was very short because of the shabby treatment of patients and the unpleasant living/working conditions for the employees. It was an eye-opening experience when she saw the poor, distasteful food given to the residents and the workers as compared with the sumptuous high-quality meals reserved for the nurses and doctors.

As she was preparing meals for the favored staff, she cleverly pilfered some of the fine edibles for herself. She felt badly that she could not alter the policy as regards the mistreated patients. One of the other female employees always looked for something she could sneak to take home. When she couldn't find anything to pinch, she told my mother, "All I can find is a drink of water, so I'll take THAT!" She HAD to take SOMETHING!

Although Ma found a way to eat better by 'sampling' the good food she prepared for the staff, the sleeping quarters (where all the hired help were assigned) were dank, dark, and disgusting. Mostly below ground level, its small, dirty windows faced onto an alley frequented by derelicts and dogs, both of which urinated on the windows, day and night. She was happy to leave that job.

Another time, Ma got a job in an upscale grocery store where she had unlimited access to the imported fine fruits, vegetables, and chocolate confections—none of which was ever available back home on the farm. She had never seen such big, beautiful apples and oranges nor tasted such fine chocolate candy. The first week, she ate more chocolates than Lucy and Ethel in that famous sitcom episode. Soon, even the smell of chocolate nauseated her.

She turned her affection to the big delicious apples and huge sweet oranges and decided to take a few oranges back to her aunt's house by stuffing them inside her voluminous bloomers. As she walked, the oranges gradually shifted concentrically, becoming encumbering as they gathered and bounced against her thighs—causing her to walk like a penguin, stiffly, with her legs gradually being forced further apart. She could appreciate the sight she must have formed, but not the sight of her face when she looked in the mirror. It was covered with red blotches, obviously a bad case of the hives from over-indulgence of fresh orange juice.

White Slavery

Her aunt had warned her to be aware of 'madams' working the train stations, prospecting for naïve young girls—particularly innocent-looking farm girls—to recruit for white slavery houses. They would lure the girls with seemingly kind offers to help them get settled, offer them a little spending money, a place to 'rest' or 'refresh' themselves, a light libation, and a reasonable lodging in a girls-only safe haven.

Her aunt described these girl 'scouts' as being refined-looking middle-aged women, generally dressed in black with large picture hats, handbags, and perhaps a walking stick. Yet, my mother eventually let her guard down and fell for one who used the line, "Your aunt sent me to meet you."

She sounded sweet and convincing, offering to join her in a lemonade after a long and dusty train ride. She accompanied my mother to a kind of pub where, after being seated in a booth, she disappeared—leaving my mother to be accosted by a strange man and locked in the place. When he insisted on her having a drink with him, she let him pour a glass for her.

By this time she realized what kind of predicament she was in. She managed to stay calm and engage the man in some innocuous conversation while she planned a one-shot gamble to escape. She decided to do something radical to get out of there. She threw the glass over the cubicle wall toward the bartender whose sympathy was aroused enough to come over and escort her to the exit door.

Attempted Rape

The worst experience of all, on one of those mini-vacations, was at another aunt's house whose second husband, a man she had not met before, attempted to rape her. Waking up, still in bed after her first night's sleep, she was startled by the appearance of a huge, red-faced burly man coming toward her, dressed in long underwear opened all the way down to reveal his obvious intention. Not deterred by her screaming for help and begging him to go away, he assured her it would do no good because his wife was down in the basement, washing clothes, and would not hear her.

He insisted that she was faking reluctance, saying, "You've got a boyfriend, so I know you've done it before." As he climbed atop the bed, putting his hand over her mouth to still her, she bit his thumb so hard that she nearly severed it. He left, yowling in pain. The incident remained a secret; she was sure her aunt wouldn't believe her over the husband anyway.

In those days of the early 1900's, mothers generally didn't talk to their daughters about intimate things like menstruation, sex, and pregnancy. I remember, even in the 30's when I was growing up, those words were not commonly used. If someone was pregnant, it was referred to as being in the 'family way'.

Just Where Do Babies Come From?

On one of my mother's stays in Milwaukee, she accepted an offer from a young man, whose intentions seemed chivalrous, to accompany her to her lodgings. When they arrived there, he moved to give her a goodnight kiss, a la French style, followed by his comment, "Do you love your boy?" She instantly became panicky, thinking she was just made pregnant with that kiss, and somehow he knew it would be a boy.

Her last and most memorable employment as a young lady was at the elegant Avon (later named 'Pfister') Hotel in Milwaukee. She started as a dining-room waitress. One of the most critical and challenging residents was the owner's wife who demanded unreasonable attention. She rattled everyone's nerves who served her. When it was my mother's turn, she followed the regimen of setting the private table before the bossy woman entered and, while doing so, she accidentally dropped and broke the lid of the china teapot.

With only seconds to spare, she put the lid back together with a dab of honey. It seemed to work perfectly...enough to hold it for a bit. The woman lifted the lid to remove the tea caddy, when the lid fell to the floor and 'broke', and there was no one to blame but herself for the 'accident'.

The chef at the Avon Hotel saw more talent in my mother than just waitress duty. He discovered her talents when she substituted for an absent (inebriated) pastry chef, baking the most elegant pies he had ever seen—from the bottom crusts of phenomenal texture to the tasty fillings and billowing meringue toppings.

She was quickly promoted to pastry chef. She loved working in the kitchen, and her first contact with Negroes (the politically correct term at the time) who made up the kitchen staff. They were congenial, soft-spoken, and respectful of everyone—especially of Ma. The first time she brushed against the head chef's arms, he caught her looking down at her arm, and good-naturedly teased her, "Did you think it would rub off?" They became good friends, leading to her lifelong non-racist and non-judgmental attitudes toward all people.

She got a taste of city life, as a teenager and as a young woman, every winter when she still lived on her parents' farm. She dreamed of the day when she would become a sophisticated urban wife, dress in designer-type clothes, maybe even have a 'colored' maid whom she would treat like an angel, take walks through a park, and go to live theatre, regularly. She loved stage productions, and any movie starring Rudolph Valentino. She fantasized that some day, from behind a bush, a sheik-like Valentino would jump out, catch her in his arms and whisk her away to some exotic rendezvous.

Good Answer!

When my father popped the question, whether she would marry him, even if they would have to live in the country, she responded to his proposal with, "Oh, George, I'll go anywhere with you."

She had to live with those words for the next 38 years, from 1908 until they retired from the farm in 1946, when she was 62 years old. She had naturally assumed that, because of my father's business education and experience, they would settle in a big city—something she had long dreamed of, a reward for the many years of hard work growing up on a desolate farm.

A few weeks before the wedding, Pa (the 'sheik') called for her one Sunday morning in his fine horse and buggy and whisked her off to the 'kingdom' they would soon call their own—that hinterland tract of land, more accurately referred to as primeval wilderness, given them by his father.

As he proudly announced, "There it is!", she saw nothing but prairie acreage and trees. There was no palace, no buildings of any kind, no road paved with gold (or even gravel), no servants, no neighbors, no kidding. This was no fantasy; this was real life. The 138 acres of rich black soil was theirs. Dreams of becoming big-city dwellers turned into the reality of becoming pioneers instead. She didn't complain then; she didn't complain ever.

During the time it took for a house, barn, and outbuildings to be built, fences to be made to cordon off various-sized fields to accommodate planting crops and grazing cattle, to purchase dairy cows and a team of draft horses to pull basic machinery, they lived in a tiny cottage on one of Dad's brother's farms close by.

While Dad and neighbor volunteers worked to make their new home fit to be occupied, Ma spent her time experimenting on cooking meals to surprise my Dad when he'd come back at night after working on the new homestead all day.

There was not much to do to keep herself from being lonesome. Dad surprised her one day by bringing her a little terrier dog to keep her company. Ma and the newcomer, Pinky, became great pals until the day he 'betrayed' her. She had decided to bake some bread, from scratch, to surprise my Dad. The experiment was a disaster. The loaves came out of the makeshift oven as hard and heavy as bricks out of a kiln.

Ma quickly went outside, dug a hole, and buried them before Pa came home. As he was walking toward their cottage that evening, Ma saw the little turncoat terrier digging up the evidence. She felt badly that she had wasted what amounted to pennies' worth of ingredients and embarrassed at her failed surprise. But they had a good laugh, and the incident was the subject of a long-running inside joke.

Progress by 'Leaps and Bounds'

When they finally settled on the property, she pitched in as a real partner. She plowed a field next to the railroad tracks, pregnant with their first child—having to take wide leaps behind a one-horse plow, the reins tied behind her back, hanging onto the plow handles as the horse went full throttle forward. She admitted, glancing at the railroad tracks, that she was ready to turn over the reins to the first sheik (hobo) that came along.

I can't imagine how exhausted and aching she must have felt at the end of a day. No recliner to sit and relax in front of a television. There was wood to chop to feed the kitchen stove, lanterns to light, water to heat on the stove, no warm bath or shower. Warm water came from either heating a pot full on the wood burning range or dipping into the stove's built-in reservoir.

As I reflect on the array of her talents, I cannot think of anything she could not do or had not already done. Her reputation was untouchable in the arenas of cooking and baking. All of her children and grandchildren have aspired to carry on the tradition of preparing palatable offerings. She set the bar so high that we are still trying to match her offerings.

She referred to her style of cuisine as being cosmopolitan. By that, she meant her bill-of-fare included a mix of German, Italian, Polish, Hungarian, and China dishes. (China dishes. . .isn't that redundant?!) She could duplicate almost any creation.

When I worked for room and board while attending college, cooking was my most important chore. It was a real challenge because I never had to cook or bake while living at home because Ma insisted on doing it herself. She measured with her hands and eyes: it was a handful of this, a pinch of that, and it was 'ready' when it 'looked' right. But now I had to learn in a sort of crash course. This is how we tackled "Cooking 101": she took a handful of something, we'd measure it; then a pinch of something else, and we'd measure that. It worked so well that I continued this 'scientific' method the rest of my life. When someone asks me for my recipe, I can honestly say, "I don't have one."

Sew What?

My mother had an enviable reputation for her couturier talents as well as her culinary prowess which, for the most part, probably evolved because of necessity—the need to economize—particularly in the Depression years, to be able to make 'something out of nothing'. As an example, working from only a description of what I'd envision, she'd create stylish garments without a pattern from out-of-date hand-me-downs...a kind of recycling.

I believe there is much good to be said about the utility of inventions in their early days. The 1900 treadle sewing machine, a gift to my mother from her parents on her sixteenth birthday, kept us in stitches for the thousands and thousands of miles of material that traveled beneath the pressure foot. Its power and speed depended on the foot that rocked the treadle, not on electricity.

The operator, from time to time, would have to replace a bent or broken sewing needle or change it to a different size. The other moving part was the belt which moved the needle mechanism up and down. It was a simple procedure to replace a worn one or to oil the machine regularly.

I learned to sew on that treadle machine at about age six when my foot could barely reach the treadle. Learning to sew a straight seam was imperative to be a successful seamstress. Therefore, my mother had me sew hems on the fifty-pound flour sacks that she had washed to be used for dish towels.

Rug-ed

I graduated to sewing cotton strips about 1-1/2" wide (that were torn or cut from discarded shirts and dresses), joined together in a continuous length, to be rolled up into a ball about 6" in diameter. Ma would then compute how many balls were needed to make a throw rug or runner of a certain pattern and length. They were then taken to a rug weaver who used a loom and carpet warp to customize these rugs according to the color and amount of strips to fashion a pattern. These rugs withstood wear and washing better than any factory-made rug. I have kept and used one of those rugs as a sentimental reminder of those days, which may be about 70 years old but still in its original shape, when at home it rested on the floor next to my bed.

In those days, nothing was ever thrown away that could be used somehow. That applied to food as well as dry goods. It just wasn't referred to as 'recycling' back then. Ma could magically disguise a leftover to a new and tasty concoction. I'd sometimes tease at mealtime, "We'd better finish the liver now, or it'll appear in muffins tomorrow."

Her inventiveness and frugality served me well when, in later years as a single mom with three small children to provide for—living on a poverty income in Chicago but able to feed them well—I was able to make everything from scratch and stretch a dollar to ten times its size. Again, 'necessity being the mother of invention", I realized that my upbringing was a blessing, indeed. It prepared me for life's many hurdles and challenges that lay ahead.

What I Learned From My Mother

What she lacked in formal education was dwarfed by the things she did well, and by her incredible common sense, immeasurable compassion and intuitive powers.

A list of her attributes include: humor, patience, generosity, gentleness, tolerance, decency, moderation, determination, ingenuity, honesty, kindness, pride, and an unquenchable thirst for learning until the day she died.

Her physical prowess included cooking, sewing, baking, canning, crocheting, rug making, quilting, stripping feathers, fur tailoring, planting, driving, raising and dressing poultry, varnishing, building fences, plowing fields, making soap, bottling soft drinks, making dandelion/rhubarb/elderberry wines, turning out all sorts of sausages, and smoking them along with the hams and bacon in our farm smokehouse.

When the farm was sold in 1946 and my parents moved to the city, most of those accomplishments no longer appeared on her incredible resume. But she still pursued a list of new things yet to try: she started seeking out fur coats in mint condition at rummage sales to transform them into stoles and jackets. To make sure she was doing it correctly, she took a course in her 70's at a vocational school.

She hired a cleaning lady to come to our house so she could observe the kinds of duties that were expected of a domestic. Then she answered an ad in the local newspaper for cleaning upscale residences because, not only would she be tested on her work, she would see what those houses hid inside and what the upper-crust people were really like. She actually liked that venture—more fun than cleaning her own house, and getting a few dollars besides.

Her enviable reputation for her couturier talents and practical culinary style were developed and applied, in part, because of necessity. She had her own formulas for feeding a family and visitors in the Depression years. Not a scrap of material or food was ever wasted. She was a 'kitchen magician".

She could dance, sing, and play piano. She could carry on a conversation with anyone and endear them with her fresh sense of humor. She was a hard act to follow, as they say in show biz, but that hasn't kept me from trying.

Ma was ahead of her time in suspecting the harmful effects of too much sun exposure. There wasn't any sun block in the 20's and 30's, but she insisted that all of us wear bonnets to shield our faces and cover the backs of our necks. Those bonnets were styled like the one on the Dutch Cleanser can: there were panels on the front section about 2" wide and 8" long in which we slid cardboard strips (removable for laundering) to form the bonnet shape. The kind of skirt all around at the bottom protected our neck area. We wore cotton stockings on our arms with holes cut into the foot end to accommodate our fingers.

Offers I Couldn't Refuse

Ma's psychological strategy to get anyone to help her was to ask in a positive tone, like "You can do the dusting now, if you want to" or "I'll let you hang the clothes as I wash them" or "when you have the time". She never ordered me to do anything. She asked in a way that I couldn't refuse. How could I say that I didn't *want* to; the word *let* implied permission or a privilege; and no one knew better than she that I did *have the time*.

She never expected me to do anything that she wouldn't do. She always worked beside me and did the harder part of the task whether it was weeding the garden, cleaning a chicken barn, or polishing the furniture. Her philosophy was effective without being confrontational or dictatorial and demanding. It put a positive spin on the request, bringing a positive rather than a negative reaction.

Somehow, she could think of a way to make a job interesting, or she would promise some kind of reward for a job well done—a sort of rainbow after a storm. It could be a special dessert, having a friend visit, going bullhead fishing in Horicon Marsh, picnicking at Fond du Lac Lakeside Park, playing hooky to see a classic movie (such as *Gone With the Wind, Grapes of Wrath, Of Mice and Men, Snow White and the Seven Dwarfs*), or spending an afternoon at the county fair. Focusing on the future made the present much easier, sometimes hilarious or even weird.

Dining With the Freaks

The second bright idea was Ma's permission given me to accept a supper invitation from the carnie connection. Imagine how appealing it was to sit at a long, common table with all the carnies and freaks: bearded lady, rubber man, half calf/half boy creature, alligator man, the Popeye'd woman, and the goat boy. 'Nuff said!

Living Like an Only Child

There was an advantage in growing up like an only child. With the two eldest sisters married, and the third either away at school or in a teaching assignment, I had her undivided attention, her sound advice and always pleasant times. Even though I worked on her huge garden, cleaned chicken barns, gathered and washed eggs, or helped her dress the dozen fryers she butchered every weekend for her city clientele, the chores did not seem as demanding as my father's assignments.

After we delivered the dressed poultry in the city to doctors, lawyers, restaurant and hotel chefs, she would take time out to go to a movie, carnival, or a pub where they had Friday fish fry specials. Some places offered three pieces of fresh lake perch, potato salad, and a few slices of rye bread—all for only ten cents! With it, we'd have a nickel beer. I was a teenager but, back then, you could be served if you were accompanied by a parent. In fact, most of the taverns had 'family' entrances where a family could gather to enjoy home-cooked food and a glass of beer.

Ma taught me how to crochet edgings on pillow cases and handkerchiefs, and make doilies. I also crocheted miniature baskets with a handle, to hold nuts and mints that were meant to be placed ahead of the dinner plates, and a large basket to hold a water container for cut flowers. All of these baskets were dipped in a heavy sugar bath which acted as starch to hold their shapes. With cotton rug warp, I crocheted 'jackets' in variegated colors to slip on the bottom of tumblers so they wouldn't leave wet ring marks on wooden tables. We also crocheted place mats.

Together, we made hooked rugs—some using yarn, some using narrow strips of cloth; woven 'wheel' rugs; and braided rugs using strips of wool cut from salvaged coats and skirts. Occasionally, we found time to put together a patchwork quilt or a patchwork cover to slip over a fragile quilt.

Smocking. . . another lost art. It was almost a tradition to 'smock' a harlequin-shaped large pillow to use as a gift to someone, especially as a wedding gift. As I remember, you needed to first make the pillow using ticking material and feathers or other stuffing material, as the base. Then using calico material for the exterior surface, you would choose one of the three colors—calico always had three variations of a color for its squares, dark, medium, light (usually white). You could smock only one color, and keep it within the harlequin shape.

When reaching the necessary dimensions, three sides would be sewed by machine, leaving one side open in which to insert the stuffed pillow form. You would finish by hand-sewing the fourth side shut as unobtrusively as possible.

WEED IT AND REAP

Growing strong, healthy crops depends on cultivating—destroying the weeds that choke crops—allowing each seedling to stand up straight, unbending. That can also be analogous to human behavior: getting rid of bad habits, and nourishing good ones to be upright individuals who reap positive results in life's ventures.

The cultivation of rightness, embracing the straight and narrow choices in life, was exemplified by my parents. Their discipline was melded with unconditional love, trust, and encouragement. They gave my three siblings and me a solid foundation on which to build our lives.

Having been born and raised on a dairy farm gave me a set of values that comes with the inherent life-and-death experiences on a daily basis, equally relevant to the crops as well as the animals.

The day my father made a statement that he was not a gambling man, my sister, Tess, countered with the logical argument that he was, indeed, a huge gambler as a farmer: crops could be ruined in minutes by rain, wind, or hail; and a herd of cattle could be wiped out overnight with any one of several catastrophic diseases—which actually happened twice in their early years of farming, causing the loss of a whole herd to garget disease. Those tragedies caused indebtedness that took my parents nearly thirty years to eradicate.

The hard and simple work ethic learned in childhood was a natural part of life that became an unwritten reference in adulthood when applying for a job. Since I was the youngest of four daughters, much younger than my siblings, I became a 'hired hand' to my father, and a 'confidante' to my mother.

I inherited not only the chores formerly assigned to my elders, but I also earned some special privileges because of my docile, sensitive nature. I never argued with or talked back to either parent, but they made me feel free to offer an opinion or suggestion. As I reflect on my upbringing, I don't recall that my parents ever raised their voices with me. I do remember overhearing my mother remark, referring to me, "I never have to scold her...she is so sensitive."

I never audibly thanked my parents for the intangible gifts given me, such as encouragement to get the most out of academic study, support of participation in extra-curricular activities and, above all, behavior consistent with the family's good name, and pride in my own life. Complying with their argument in favor of remaining celibate until marriage was a reward in itself when I walked down the aisle at age 24, still a virgin.

All four of us girls worked for room and board at some point in our lives: when we sought higher education or gainful employment some distance from home.

We reflected a persona that we could be trusted, especially with money matters. My eldest sister, Tess, at age 35 was the first female ever selected by a bank's board of directors to be the lone Cashier/ Manager of their bank. As for myself, at age 16, the owner of a large city restaurant put me in charge of the cash register, whenever he had to be absent, excluding all the other waitresses despite their long history of employment there. He always let them know that the 'farmer' was in charge. That is when I first realized it was an asset to be a farmer's daughter.

When I chose to work for room and board while attending the University of Wisconsin (Madison), the student placement office suggested I contact the football coach/athletic director, Harry Stuhldreher, even though that family had another girl under consideration. The decision to take me was quickly made when it was learned that I, a farm girl, was available. They probably based that decision on the previous experience they had had with a farm boy from the same area that I came from—perhaps because they believed we were 'grounded'. They would never have had to worry about my integrity, honesty, or work ethic.

I was honest, eager to learn, and willing to work beyond what was asked of me. I immediately fell in love with their four sons: "Skippy" (Harry, Jr.), Michael, Johnny, and Peter, of approximate ages 13, 11, 9, 7, respectively. It was a memorable period in my life and, hopefully, in theirs also as I loved them dearly.

Both of my parents led by example. That was a good thing. I was always willing to do whatever they asked—no matter how unappealing the task was. They were patient in explaining how they wanted a job done, and what the rewards would be if I did a good job. They always worked beside me and never expected me to do anything that they themselves wouldn't do. I still get choked up just thinking about everything they did for me, the sacrifices they made, and the encouragement given to me to pursue my interests in the arts and education.

I helped my father in the barn, feeding the calves in their stalls, carrying the buckets of freshly 'squeezed' milk to the milk house and emptying them into the cans which were set in the water tanks to cool. I helped my mother by daily gathering the eggs (except having to reach under the old 'clucks' who guarded their eggs as if they were celebrity babies, inflicting pain as they pecked the back of your hands), cleaning chicken barns by scraping the roosts and floors, following by spreading limestone on the floor, and a layer of fresh straw on top of that, on a weekly basis. Every weekend, I dusted all the furniture, upstairs and downstairs in our house. It always looked as if we were expecting 'company'.

Additionally, in summer, I mowed our huge lawn by pushing a prehistoric manual rotary mower. I helped to weed the vegetable and flower gardens, and pick strawberries from our large patch in the garden. I remember the summer of 1946 when together Ma and I picked 1,000 quarts of strawberries, always at daybreak when the mosquitoes were bloodthirsty and lying in wait for us.

Summer also meant that a circus, carnival, or county fair would be on my parents' agenda. Since we loved parades, especially if they included marching bands, my father was willing to go an extra mile to enjoy it. If a classic movie came to the closest city, my drama-loving mother would take me to see it even if it meant keeping me out of school. I was secretly impressed that she could fool the nuns at school.

She and my father used to entertain at local functions in the early years of their marriage. Pa dressed up as a 'big brown bear', and Ma brought him into the performance area where she would play the piano while he performed some song-and-dance routine. I am grateful for their encouragement of a love for the performing arts which has lasted a lifetime for me and my children.

When Barbara was three years old, she performed a vintage ballad on stage with a prominent orchestra, having learned the song only hours before, to honor my mother and father with *"If You Knew Susie"*. Her five- and six-year-old brothers were given equal opportunity. I can attest to the importance of parental support.

Until their deaths, they never missed any of my children's or my performances in any show or concert, from the time I was in grade school to when I was in my forties and lived 150 miles away.

Observing the kind of cohesive partnership my parents had to have for living and working together twenty-four hours a day was a realistic example of how people have to get along with each other. A farm is a place of full-time employment with no Union stewards to arbitrate complaints about working overtime, pay raises, and paid time off. A farmer is committed to being on the job, whether in good health or not, mornings and evenings on an absolute schedule. You don't milk cows when you 'feel' like it. They are udderly programmed by nature.

I grew up with the philosophy that all labor, no matter how menial, is noble as long as it is honest. It came with the territory. I passed this dogma on to my children who, although raised in the big city of Chicago, always worked hard—beginning at an early age. Both sons, Tom and Alan, had paper routes while they were still in grade school. Their little sister, Barby, took over when they moved on to other jobs. Long before they were old enough to legally work, all three had helped contribute to the household. They knew if there were to be any "extras" they'd have to earn them.

Later, in their teens, they ran a small neighborhood restaurant while the owner was in the hospital. Tom was the short order cook; Alan was the dishwasher. When the owner returned to work, he refused to pay them for the hours they worked-- claiming he had no proof of their service since the manager refused to back them up. They were never paid and never forgot the betrayal by those adults. It was a bitter lesson learned about trusting people.

My youngest child, Barbara, also wished to be a 'breadwinner'. At age four, she went from door to door on our side of the street with her little red wagon selling homemade banana cupcakes. The little corner grocery store supplied me with overripe bananas. I learned from one of her customers, a next door neighbor, that they paid $1.00 for each cupcake. Apparently, Barbara misunderstood my instruction that the cupcakes were 'four for a dollar', not 'for a dollar'. But the customer said he couldn't resist paying whatever she asked because Barbara was so cute and serious, a really convincing salesgirl.

As a one-parent family, with no relatives, friends, or funds to help with child care, I worked out of my home until Barbara was in school full-time. I did some baking for caterers, sang at weddings, and did clothes alterations (adjusting the hems on the parochial schoolgirls' uniforms), and on coats and dresses for an elderly alcoholic lady who usually sprayed me with liquid conversation as I sat on the floor to pin up the hems. On Sunday afternoons, I answered listeners' calls at WGN-TV where I also computed survey results for a sponsor of Bob Elson's program regarding mattress sales, and other clerical tasks they found for me to do.

The children loved my affiliation with WGN-TV because I could take home prizes left over from Bozo's Circus program. They got an invitation to be special sequestered guests on the live Garfield Goose Show with Frazier Thomas, and rare tickets for the Bozo Circus show which had an eight-year waiting list.

At night, after the children were in bed, I transcribed correspondence for about a dozen department heads at Blue Cross/Blue Shield insurance company. On week nights I typed from 8:30 P.M. to 3:00 A.M., then slept until 7:00 A.M. in time to get the boys off to St. Andrew School. The completed typing was picked up at noon by a courier so I could do a little homework and then 'recharge my battery' until the boys' exuberant arrival after school.

I did all of that typing on an old Underwood manual typewriter, often having to make four or five carbon copies which required some heavy-handed pounding and very difficult method of correcting copies if I made a typo. The oral text was given me on antiquated, wax mini-records on a Dictaphone machine which had to be operated with a foot-controlled pedal. How primitive was this forerunner as compared with modern-day computers and photocopiers.

I always had the comforting company of a parakeet I was bird sitting. As soon as I sat at the table near his cage, he'd scold until I opened it and let him out so he could sit on my shoulder and 'listen' with his beak next to the Dictaphone earpiece—a tickling experience.

When Barbara was only four years old, she was articulate and mature enough to act as my secretary to answer the phone so that I didn't have to stop whatever I was doing. I wished she would stay that age forever—never complained, always entertaining. I remember the day that the piano tuner arrived—the official tuner for the Chicago Public Schools. He was refined, and blind. Barbara pulled up a stool next to the piano, keeping him company for the hours he spent at the piano, giving him a sales pitch about her mother who 'doesn't have a husband' and 'would he like to marry her', listing more attributes for me than appears in Webster's Unabridged dictionary. I was in the kitchen, thoroughly amused, but never came out of the kitchen until it was time to pay him. Meanwhile, his wife waited in the car for him.

It was unusual for her to talk to strangers. She probably felt safe being at home with her mother close by. When I took her to Wieboldt's department store to buy some yard goods, she tugged at my skirt when I was talking with a salesperson and whispered in my ear, "Do you know her?" I replied, "No." She cautioned, "You know you're not supposed to be talking to strangers."

THE TRAVELING SALESMEN

Meet the Farmer's Daughter and the Farmer's Wife

No farm story would be complete without bringing in recollections of traveling salesmen who visited us. None of them slept with the farmer's wife or any of the farmer's daughters, but they did add another dimension to farm life when they appeared at our house. And how my mother loved to stir up a little excitement with the strangers who visited us.

My sister, Maybelle, and I were up in the attic on a lovely spring day, basking in the sunlight coming through the windows overlooking the front yard. We could even see the road leading up to our property. We observed an unfamiliar car making a turn toward our home. It must be a salesman approaching.

We ran down the two flights of stairs to our kitchen to alert our mother. She preferred to not let these men in the house, so she would keep them at bay outdoors on the lawn. The salesman this day was from the McNess Company. There were others from the Raleigh or Watkins companies. He was pushing a line of personal care items, like deodorants, hand creams, toothpastes and toothbrushes.

Ma always listened intently, occasionally asking a pertinent question that would really get the salesman more animated. My sister and I were listening from behind a cracked-open door. We heard the man lay out a whole display of toothbrushes as he pitched toothpaste and mouthwash products. Finally, my mother excused herself as a cue for him to leave, which he did.

Ma came into the house, carrying the whole fold-up display of toothbrushes which he obviously had forgotten. Maybelle and I took it, ran back up to the attic vantage point and started dividing up the toothbrushes—one for you, one for me, etc.

Glancing out the windows, we saw the salesmen's car coming back up the road to our house. We put every toothbrush back in place and ran downstairs just as the salesman arrived at our door. Ma took the display case and handed it to him. He apologized for any inconvenience and left, never knowing what evil had lurked in the hearts of these innocent-looking females.

Another time, on a lovely summer day, my sister and I were in the kitchen doing our chores when we overheard voices outdoors in front of the house. It was a gruff-talking salesman trying to coerce my mother into buying whatever he was selling.

Maybelle said she'd give me a nickel if I'd go out, peak around the corner, and say to the salesman, "'zit so?" I did it and got the nickel.

Then Maybelle promised me a dime, a whole dime, a week's allowance, if I'd go out there again, stick my head around the corner and say to Ma, "Don't let him kid you, Ma." The look on my mother's face was priceless. She was awestruck as I had never said a sassy thing in my life up to then. I barely got back inside the house to collect my dime from Maybelle, when I heard my mother making excuses for my rude behavior, and the salesman assuring her that he had a really large pill to cure me. His threat went unfulfilled; Maybelle and I had already disappeared quietly to the closet downstairs.

Ma had an encounter with a salesman during the school year when neither Maybelle nor I was at home. This time it involved a vacuum cleaner. The salesman insisted on demonstrating how much dirt would be extracted out of my dad's pillow. Ma thought, *"This is going to be interesting because I just picked it up from the dry cleaner's yesterday. Now I can tell if the dry cleaner really did a good job."*

So, the salesman put a filtering cloth over the end of the hose that plugged into the cleaner, to catch all the farm dirt from my dad's head. He vacuumed and vacuumed, finally removing the filter in a dramatic gesture. There it was, clean as a whistle. Disappointed, of course, he could only say that my father did have a clean head.

Years later, when we had moved to the city, a salesman came to our door one winter night in a blustery snowstorm. Ma couldn't refuse his request to come in out of the storm to demonstrate his line of pots, pans, and strainer. He stacked his wares in the middle of our living-room and said they would withstand even his jumping on top of them. He was a middle-aged man, a little stocky, and very sincere. He jumped on top of the stainless steel pyramid that he built, smashing it out of shape. To assuage his embarrassment of a demonstration gone awry, we treated him to coffee and some of Ma's homemade coffee cake.

THE BIRDS, THE BEES, AND
THE HICKORY NUT TREES

Birdland 101

First, let me tell you about the bird, but let me preface this escapade with a little 'background music.' My mother occasionally would verbalize her fantasy—maybe founded in an old fairy tale—that a crow could be taught to speak by splitting its tongue. My father didn't subscribe to this possibility but, in his inimitable loyalty to her and commitment to never pass up a challenge, he had a plan in mind to humor my mother.

He confided in me one day that he had been keeping an eye on a crow's nest in a tree in the far corner of the farm, watching a fledgling crow and hoping to capture it before it left the nest, to present it to my mother.

I will never know how he finally captured it, but he brought the ultimate gift home to her one summer afternoon. Her long-running joke had become a reality. Calling her bluff almost put her in shock! But, trooper that she was, she decided to follow through on the experiment—short of any tongue surgery, however.

She gave her new-found 'student' a clean, comfortable home in one of the vacant, cozy little chicken barns behind our house. She called him,

"Petie", and visited him several times a day to talk to him, to give him some corn kernels, grapes, water, and speech lessons. I agreed to co-host the experiment. We took turns coaxing him to "Talk, Petie, talk", say "Susie", but his only answer was a sharp peck of his beak.

After several weeks in captivity, Petie showed no signs of any interest in becoming a linguist. Finally, admitting defeat and suffering disappointment, and injury (ours, not his), my mother decided it was best to release him back into the wild. She bade her feathered protégé farewell as I rode off into the sunset with Petie safely tucked inside a carrier box mounted on my bicycle handlebars. Down the country road I went to free probably the first crow to ever have a bicycle ride.

Making a Bee Line

As for the bees, there were a few incidents in my life involving the attack of the bees.

In some cases, they may have been wasps or hornets, but who has the courage to take a close look.

When I was ten years old, while playing with my four-year-old niece, June, in the front yard of my sister Lil's farm house, a swarm of bees got into my thick head of hair. In a flash of reaction, I started to violently shake my head to keep them unsettled while I ran at least 100 yards to the barn where I plunged my head into a tank of water in the milk house. I don't know how I thought of that response so quickly, but it worked. I didn't get stung. I got stunned! I mean, *really dizzy!*

Another incident involved my mother on the farm. I was waiting for her in the driveway next to our car, ready to go on an errand. My mother came out of the house and decided to make a 'pit stop' at the last minute—in the outhouse enclosed in our woodshed, rather than go back upstairs to the bathroom in our house.

The next moment, she came screaming out of the privy, flailing her arms while doing a wild jig with her bloomers down around her ankles. As she was in the midst of this bizarre dance to shoo a bee out of her britches, she was not aware that our gasoline supplier, Elmer Octane, had pulled his truck up next to the pump down the driveway a bit and had stopped in his tracks to observe this comedic scene. Ma reacted nonchalantly as she pulled up her bloomers and climbed in the old Chevy.

As for me, I discovered you don't necessarily have to be in an outhouse to attract these stingers. My grandsons do not want a visual reminder of the day that they and their mother were waiting for me in their van, when suddenly, as I was about to embark, I suddenly dropped my drawers as I was being stung by something that had crawled up my slacks leg.

Another time, my husband was enjoying breakfast at our kitchen table when I stepped out the back door, still in my pajamas, to briefly admire our climbing roses. Like a flash, I flew back into the kitchen and dropped my pants to the floor. As my husband dropped his jaw in witnessing this unexpected nudity, I screamed, "There it is!" as a bee flew directly to the kitchen window. I wondered, "How do they know where the windows are?"

A Nutty Tale

To relate the hickory nut trees tale, I travel once again down memory land, to a far corner of the farm. That's where the grove of nut-producing trees was located, both hickory and butternut trees. Many of my comical experiences involve my mother, and this is one of them.

It was in fall, and Ma was working in our attic, probably getting our winter clothes out of mothballs. Years ago, we had natural fabrics, like fur and wool, that served as tasty morsels to moths, and everyone used mothballs to store clothes made of those fabrics.

From the vantage point of the attic windows, she could see that distant grove of trees and what looked to be poachers moving around them. Always hell-bent for a little excitement, she said to me, "Let's drive over there and surprise the trespassers." We got in the old family car and headed for the showdown. When we pulled up at the crime scene, we saw three people filling their gunny sacks with nuts. Ma could hardly keep a straight face when she announced to the shivering trio, "These are our trees." The thwarted culprits immediately dropped the sacks of pilfered nuts and fled in their jalopy.

We took the bounty home and found the joke had backfired on us: as we started to crack open the nuts, we found all of them were wormy. It would have been a better (bitter?) lesson to the thieves if we had let them get away with the ill-gotten goods.

FOUR-FOOTED COMPANIONS

There was no shortage of pets during my lifetime: horses, donkeys, cows, calves, dogs, cats, white mice, hamsters, parakeets, and turtles.

GOOD HORSE-KEEPING

My father was a registered breeder of purebred Percheron draft (work) horses—familiar to anyone who has seen the teams used by the Joseph Schlitz Brewing Company of Milwaukee to pull their beer wagons.

At one time, we had 12 adult Percherons in our stock—some of which my father had broken and teamed up into working pairs. We usually had at least three working teams at any point in time, plus a black stallion named Jack (his father was a regal-looking example of equinity, with a typical white star on his forehead, named King.)

Four of the younger, unbroken ones—two grays and two roans— were kept in a fenced, wooded area where they could graze, exercise freely, and have access to a freshwater spring. They would sprint to the entrance gate when they heard Pa's pickup truck approaching to make his daily check on them. One of the roans would lean over the gate to give him a kiss on the cheek; the other one would take a handkerchief from his overall bib pocket and 'wipe' it off!

A pair of yearlings named Dick and Dan were tame enough for me to ride bareback. An old mare, Maude, that I could take out in the fields to pull a stone boat or other conveyance, was steady and well-behaved. If it started to rain, I could stoop under her for shelter while she stood perfectly still.

Horses, like tires, work best as a matching pair that is used to working together. Compatibility of their personalities and strengths does make a difference and has to be taken into account when pairing them. Pa was an expert at breaking the colts and fillies to be gentle, compatible work horses. It was an exciting, breathtaking sight to watch him in action, never letting them sense any fear, always maintaining his control. They loved and respected him.

Pa, a veterinary-oriented farmer, made 'horse calls', treating lame horses with liniment for muscle aches and strains, and carbo salve for cuts and sores.

Gee and Haw

These are the 'turn signals' for horses, donkeys, and most other beasts of burden. "Gee" means turn to the right; "Haw" means turn to the left. Pa used these terms most frequently with the pair of donkeys we had, "Jack" and "Jenny". Jack was as stubborn as a mule, and Jenny was as sweet as Jenny Lind. Occasionally, on a summer Sunday afternoon, Pa and I would go out for a jaunt, bareback on these creatures. I got to ride mild-mannered, obedient Jenny, while Pa chose the challenge of staying astride the cantankerous, frisky Jack who tried, but never succeeded in catapulting my father over his head. Jack would alternate between getting down on his knees and kicking up his hind legs When he finally conceded defeat, he became a well-behaved conveyance.

These donkeys were not just 'pets'—they served a functional purpose, invaluable and unbeatable when pulling power was needed to extricate a vehicle from a mud hole, for instance.

Wholly Cow

For bovine breeding purposes, Dad kept a fierce-looking bull in a fortress-like stall in the cow barn. Occasionally, my father would allow the bull to exit the barn to get some fresh air and exercise as it could roam freely in the gated barnyard. When it was time to bring him back to his stall, my father would round him up with the help of our collie, Sport.

The last time my father had to bring him in, Sport was not around to assist—he had passed away a few weeks earlier. As the bull made a move to charge my father, Dad instinctively called out the dog's name, "SPORT"! The bull stopped short and headed for the open barn door and, like clockwork, entered his stall. My father's life was saved with the 'ghost' of his faithful dog—truly a man's best friend.

I couldn't get too attached to the cows and calves except for feeding them when they were in the barn, and could massage that part of their heads just below their horns. How they loved that. My mother said when she and her brothers were kids, they'd release the calves in the barn and try to ride them. That never occurred to me to be much fun, and far too dangerous.

The Up's and Down's of Horses and Cows

I made what I think is an interesting observation about the difference equines and bovines in the way they lie down and the way they get up: opposite of each other!

A horse, for instance, will get up using its front legs first, then the hind legs. A cow rises first with its hind quarters and then its front legs. The procedure is reversed when they lie down: the horse lies down first with its hind legs, then down with its front legs. A cow lies down first with its front legs, and then down with its hind legs.

Young Tess's Dog

Besides my parents, Tess and I were the dog lovers in the family. Tess related the story of her dog "Pinky", her inseparable companion when she was a young girl. She brought this dog to a well-attended family reunion and, when it came time for the group photo, she protected its face from the camera explosion by turning its derriere toward the camera rather than its face.

Sport and Fanny

We usually had two dogs at the same time—one large and one small one. The first pair I remember was a Collie named Sport and a Fox Terrier named Fanny who were inseparable. I watched Sport chase a cat to a hayloft in the barn—the level of hay being about 10 feet high. Fanny climbed the vertically straight ladder to chase it down. They never harmed the cat. It was just a playful game.

However, out in the fields, it was not play time. They would position themselves on each end of the grain shocks and then surf for rabbits. When they came upon a gopher hole, each would start digging at opposite ends. After a bit, they'd look up at each other and then exchange positions. They would dig until one of them would latch on to one end of the gopher. As the gopher would try to exit in the other direction, it would get nabbed again—making the ensuing action a see-saw motion until one would pull the gopher out, disgustingly stretched out to twice its original length.

Teddy and Blackie

The next pair was made up of a handsome Belgian Shepherd named Teddy and a less lustrous Cocker Spaniel named Blackie. Teddy was broad, brawny and brainy. He learned many tricks very quickly: sit up, play dead, hold a pipe in his mouth, put his front paws on a chair, with his head between them as if he were in prayer, until someone would say "Amen".

When my father came home from town after making his milk deliveries, he'd park his truck by the barn and have Teddy bring the mail in his mouth to the house. He could even carry a glass milk bottle in his mouth. The only thing he couldn't do was BARK, and he never learned to raise his hind leg to urinate like other male dogs.

My mother didn't have success in teaching a crow to talk, but now she had another student, this time to teach a dog to bark. Every day, she'd coach him, "Teddy, say WOOF". This went on for months. One moonlit summer night, after everyone had gone to bed, we were awakened by a low, distinctive bark of a dog beneath our bedroom window, clearly articulating the word "WOOF". He finally got it! But it forever sounded like the word 'woof'.

He never learned to lift his leg to urinate. We made my mother promise to not teach him to do that. He did catch on to doing a chore usually attributed to Border Collies: he knew what to do when I'd say, "Go round up the cows." I would walk with him up the lane to one of our distant pastures, open the gate, and then ask Teddy to corral the herd of cows and drive them down to the barn for the evening milking. It saved me from walking all the way to the back of the field to get the cows' attention to move.

Blackie, a Cocker Spaniel, was with us for only a short time until we gave it to my Aunt Rose which she wanted for her young children.

Heidi

Heidi came from a litter of puppies, born one November, owned by a park district theatrical coach. She and I were good friends, so she let us have our pick of the litter, free. Two nights before Christmas, we were invited to visit her home and choose a puppy. The children agreed on the 'sleepy' one whom they named Heidi. They held that little blond ball of fur all the way home and slept with her on the living-room floor that night.

There wasn't a day in that dog's life of 13 years that my children didn't show their love for that dog. When they came home from school, they'd say 'hello' to Heidi before they'd acknowledge me. Their friends would come over to see if Heidi could really say "I love you". She really could, on command.

They dressed her up in underwear, and had her pose with a hat and cigarette holder to assume the look of a Hollywood director. She learned to turn doorknobs with her paws in order to let herself in and out of the house. She knew each of my children's names so that I could ask her to go upstairs and get whichever one I wanted. Her bark easily identified which of the neighbors' children were passing our house—especially the ones who teased her and whom she didn't like.

When my son, Alan, brought home baby chicks from school, he kept them in a box in his upstairs bedroom. One day, I heard a little muffled "peep" that seemed rather near. There, at the top of the landing, was Heidi gently holding the little chick in her mouth as if to say it needed help. Heidi apparently sensed the chick's listlessness was a reason to bring it to my attention. She was simply the best dog you could ever own, or rather, we were all owned by Heidi!

Fritz

A police friend of mine left a litter of five Shepherd puppies for me to dog-sit while he went on a four-week furlough. Two of them were promised to one of his colleagues, so there were three remaining in my custody. He decided I could sell or keep them. I named them"Annie", "Fanny", and "Fritz".

I gave Annie to a young couple who had a carpet installation service and wanted a watchdog to guard their materials in their truck while they were on a job. Fanny went to the home of one of my Junior Patrol choir boys where she was renamed Chloe. We decided to keep Fritz. What a handsome specimen he turned out to be.

Heidi was not at all thrilled with her roommate. It was so comical how he went about trying to win her over: he would lie down beside her, doze off, and then swing his head over to nudge her. All he got was a Marge Simpson growl.

When he was a year old, I got the brilliant idea of having Fritz audition for the Police Department's canine unit. Two officers came to the house. They agreed that he looked like a great candidate, but he 'lacked aggressiveness'. They were kind enough to not call him an out-and-out coward. . . just because he barked and jumped backward with every step they made forward.

A bar owner on Clark Street in Chicago heard about him and was thrilled to have him for security purposes. Some months later, we had an opportunity to visit him when his owners moved to the suburbs. They lined up some chairs in a row for my children, myself, and a friend. We knew it was him by his trademark habit of taking a drink from the toilet and opening his mouth when he walked out with his mouth still full of water. It was interesting to watch him, puzzled, as he sniffed each one of us. All of a sudden his memory kicked in. He came over to my chair and tried to jump in my lap and slobber me with kisses. It was amazing.

When Heidi passed away, I vowed to never get another dog. The next week I weakened. One of the salesmen at the office said he couldn't keep his black Labrador because he was moving from the suburbs to his city girlfriend's apartment where dogs were not allowed. I brought home this wild five-month-old bundle of perpetual energy. We named her 'Misty'.

Misty

She was loving and smart but so uncontrollable. We hardly completed even one session of obedience school—too many dogs, too much noise, too much pain inflicted by the trainer who cracked her across the bridge of her snout with a trank. It may have been a recognized procedure in training, but I couldn't stand it myself. We decided to have the trainer come to the house.

Misty was only about six months old and proved to be not only a quick learner, but had a great memory. As the trainer came to our house, sat at the kitchen table with my husband, she let one hand dangle under the table. Quick as a flash, Misty moved quietly under the table and bit the trainer's hand, obviously remembering who hit her across the bridge of her nose. But Misty remembered the tiny bit of training she received in that one obedience session. Although categorized as being passive aggressive, she became the perfect pet and alert watchdog also.

Sheba

Sheba was a puppy when my police sergeant husband rescued her in the middle of a gypsy street disturbance. He opened his squad car door when he saw she was in danger and coaxed her to enter. Then he turned her over to a police woman under his supervision and suggested she bring the pup to our house in the district. Sheba had some crazy hang-ups: she hated the sight of running water, and she tried to eat bees. The running water phobia may have been caused by someone turning a hose on her during the street disturbance. I can't explain her appetite for bees!

She was a companion for our Labrador, Misty, and had about a 13-year life span.

On an Easter Sunday, when I was preparing dinner for a group of people, I looked out of the kitchen window and saw Sheba having a horribly big seizure. She looked back at me as if to ask for help. One of the dinner guests volunteered to take her to an animal hospital where they decided it was best to put her down.

Both Misty and Sheba lived to be thirteen years old just like Heidi before them. When they were gone, I 'inherited' Max, a Basset Hound, from my son, Tom, whose new home had no landscaping, only bare soil—not suitable to train a puppy.

Max

I planted some cucumbers the summer I began caring for Max. One morning he brought something very strange-looking to me. It turned out to be a small cucumber with both ends chewed off. Tom's wife, Pam, solved the mystery: when she used to prepare salads for themselves, she'd cut off both ends of cucumbers to keep Max from getting underfoot. Apparently, he got to like the flavor!

This was my first experience with a Bassett Hound. I found out what a good disposition they have, even a sense of humor. At my house he had 1/3 acre to sniff and search every day. If I changed even ONE item in the yard, he would notice it immediately and bark at it. My daughter had bought a gazing globe for me which I put in the backyard, near the door, so Max saw it the moment he came out. It was hilarious how he jumped backwards and barked at it as soon as he saw it.

Mama Cat

When it reigned, it purred! She was queen of her turf, a very sweet, solid gray, big female cat. It's the only one I recall ever living on our farm. She was cagey, becoming very illusive, which I found to mean she just had a litter. I had to be very nonchalant when I tried to follow her. She had a sixth sense about what I was doing, so I took a long way around and eventually she led me to the spot.

111

I had bad luck with kittens; it bothered me for years even though it was accidental.

One incident happened in our music room as I sat on the round piano stool which could be spun to go up or down. It was one of the rare times that we had a kitten come into the house, but I forgot that as I started spinning on the stool. I lost my balance and tipped over. The seat hit the kitten in the neck and killed my sweet little buddy.

Another time, I was older—probably about 15, a cheerleader in high school, and practicing doing cartwheels on our lawn. In the middle of a cartwheel, I accidentally lost my balance and went down hard—right on the head of a kitten I adored. I was so sad; it took a long time for me to assuage my guilt about it.

White Mice

Advice alert: don't ever get white mice. I allowed my son, Alan, to have a few. It wasn't bad until they reproduced. The 'fragrance' was overwhelming. I placed an old 78-rpm record over the box, but the fumes were strong enough to come up through that little hole in the middle. The odor stayed in my mind when I went to a political meeting that night, arriving a bit late because I had my son move the creatures to an area where we wouldn't be exposed to the unpleasantness. At the meeting I mentioned the dilemma to State Representative John Merlo. He surprised me when he said, "I know what you're talking about. My son had them, too."

Hamsters

Daughter Barbara suggested we get hamsters, but we had no luck with them. I gave in and off we went to the pet shop. The owner swore that we had a male hamster on our hands. Well, did Barbara get a shock, a painful shock, when she went to clean the cage a week later and pulled out her bloody finger. The 'male' hamster had a new litter of babies and bit clear through her finger in protecting the little ones. The mama didn't protect them very well shortly thereafter. She ate them all, much to Barbara's chagrin.

Rabbits

We had no better luck with a cute black-and-white bunny that we called 'Snoopy'. I had a large crate for it to have plenty of room. I put a big screen across the top so it got air but, apparently, it may have been in a drafty place—something dangerous for any animal—and so, one morning, we found him cold, stiff, and very dead.

Turtles

We had a variety of short-lived small turtles, and one three-legged large one found one summer on a Wisconsin rural gravel road. It survived that summer, but when there were no more overripe cherries falling into our yard from our neighbor's tree, he would eat nothing else. We gave up and he gave in.

The latest additions:

Sophie

Sophie was a pedigreed American-English bulldog, built like a brickhouse, all muscle, no flab, so playful, but as solid as a 65-pound sack of bowling balls (you'd understand, the first time she ran into you), and had a unique connection with everyone in the family. But when our house was sold after I moved into Alden Poplar Creek Nursing Home, the rest of the family couldn't keep her in the places they had to rent. Luckily, a wonderful home was found for her, but she is greatly missed.

Arthur and Sully

Grandson Jake read about these unusual cats of which there are only two breeders in the state of Illinois. Arthur is silver and white, with a long chassis and short legs which makes him look like a furry slinky when he walks. He climbs, rather than jumps, to reach necessary heights—to get up on a bed or sofa. We call him a "Munchkin", but technically he is a 'Napoleon." Sully is also a male cat, orange and white blended color, and is a Standard. They were highly socialized in the breeder's environment of five children, three dogs, and twenty cats and kittens, so they're not afraid of being with strangers—humans or animals.

Stewart and Scout

My daughter (Jake's mother) was impressed enough to buy a brother and uncle of the kittens that Jake has, also both male. Scout is a silver and white brother of Arthur; Stewart is a Dreamsicle-orange/white long-haired handsome feline—a little more cautiously curious than Scout.

Scout is fearless in his quest for knowledge and food. Scout is also the more curious of the two. I doubt if there is a square inch in his house that he has not personally investigated—climbed into or over. They are both loving and entertaining.

Chloe

Granddaughters Hayley and Morgan convinced their father (my son, Tom) to get a puppy, and what an adorable creature she is: all blond, except for two brown ears. It looks like a cross between a Golden Lab and Shepherd—very smart. Tom has trained her as he did with a previous dog, the Basset Hound named 'Max', and she responded well. (She appeared with Hayley and Morgan on the family's Christmas card.)

Baby and Slinky

These were son Alan's companions who lived in his house in Chicago. Baby was a good-looking Shepherd and fearless watchdog of the premises, both inside the house and of the backyard—a formidable-looking caretaker. Slinky is a Dachshund and just cute, with no responsibilities to look after anything.

THE WARM DAZE AND NIGHTS
OF SUMMER VERSUS THE COLD
DAYS AND NIGHTS OF WINTER

For Butter or Wurst

Summertime

The years I spent in grade school and high school fell into the era known as the "Great Depression" which lasted from the stock market crash of 1929 until the onset of World War II. Yet, some of my happiest memories occurred during that period. As farmers, we were not rationed as were city dwellers. We had non-rationed food that came from our garden and fields: vegetables, and meat from the chickens and hogs that we raised.

Ma made our laundry soap bars from the hog fat that she rendered, mixed with lye, and cooked it in a large black cauldron until it was ready to pour and cut into bars. Of course, we always had plenty of milk from our dairy cows, and cream to whip for dessert topping.

Our cold cellar had a year's supply of potatoes, root vegetables, and crocks full of sauerkraut. Also occupying a small space of the cellar was a room with shelves of home-canned goods: pickles, beans, beets, tomatoes, plus sweet cherry and plum sauces that were used for instant desserts.

There were eggs, bacon, ham, and sausages—thanks to our chickens and pigs. Ma made a separate income for non-essential items such as, kitchen curtains, things for us kids, and hair coloring for herself by selling eggs and dressed chickens every week in the city. She had a loyal clientele who not only gave her some 'mad' money but a feeling of independence.

Every town held a firemen's picnic, free dances, and free movies. The picnics were fundraisers for the volunteer fire departments or for a needed civic project. There were games of chance like bingo, darts, and turtle races. Pa was the resource for supplying the little turtles, drawing a pie-shaped playing field, and painting numbers on their shells for the purpose of betting on them. Sometimes there were also a dunk tank, a nail-pounding event, sack races, and raw-egg-in-a-spoon relays.

There was always a parade through town to precede the event which included marching groups and local theme-inspired clown acts. When my pre-teen children participated in such a parade, entrants were required to have a slogan besides being dressed in costumes. I wore a white satin clown outfit with deep pockets to hold 100 small rubber balls which I dropped behind the burlap horse costume inflicted on my two youngest children. For the eldest son, I fashioned a ringmaster costume. He carried our slogan board: *"Don't play with fire, It could be your doom. You could be pushing up daisies instead of pushing a broom."*

As I walked behind the burlap 'horse', I dropped the rubber ball 'horse apples' and swept them into the crowd. We won first prize: a whole $5!

I made one big mistake, however—making my own clown shoes, not realizing I'd have to walk flat-footed through the whole parade. My thighs became so painful that I couldn't walk up stairs when I got home, but probably still not comparable to my children's discomfort.

The food at these rural picnics was a big attraction because it was homemade good: bratwurst braised over hot coals, coffee with a slice of homemade pie or cake, ice cream cones and floats, and cotton candy. There was always a stand for beverages of beer and pop, and a popcorn wagon that pulled you to it with its naturally captivating fragrance.

Each surrounding hamlet sponsored free dances, and free movies if they had a place to put up a screen and a grassy area for people to lie and watch the movies. Some people brought folding chairs; the young romantic crowd brought blankets. No one cared if someone next to him was chomping on popcorn or fish fries or having a drink. For a nickel you could get a schooner of beer; for ten cents you could get a meal of fried fresh-caught lake perch, potato salad, and two slices of rye bread and butter. The merchants made a few pennies on additional purchases by customers, enough to show these "B" movies.

One night, when my four-year-old niece was visiting us, Ma and I took her with us in our family's 1928 Oakland sedan to our home town's free movie. It was only four miles from our farm, but it turned out to be a very l-o-n-g four miles. As we were leaving town about 10:00 P.M. after the movie, there was an unexpected torrential downpour of rain. Halfway home, the car's headlights started to dim. The car slowed down, finally coming to a stop as Ma pulled off onto the highway's shoulder.

The night was pitch dark. A lightning bolt revealed our bearings: next to a cemetery which we knew was about 100 yards north of a relative's farmhouse. Using a flashlight, Ma verified that the car had cleared the edge of the highway. We had no road flares. So far, there hadn't been any traffic, but we prayed that any motorist would still have working headlights to see and avoid us.

My niece was still asleep in the back seat. Since I was ten years old, Ma thought it would be all right for her to go to the relative's farmhouse to call my father. She took the white blanket from the front seat, covered herself with it and, armed with the flashlight, she took off. I watched her light as she passed the cemetery. What a haunting image that was—ghostlike! It seemed to take forever for her to return.

When she did, she said she had awakened Pa who would be coming in a short while with the pickup truck. That news was welcome, but she wondered how Pa could have fallen asleep, knowing that we were out in the storm. Men!

No sooner had Ma got back in the car, when a man appeared out of nowhere. He said his car stalled down the road, and he didn't want to weather the storm alone. Again, men! Ma said he could sit in the back seat as long as he didn't wake up my niece. It was good to have male company, even though he didn't appear to be of any help, and we did take a chance of it being Public Enemy No. 1 (John Dillinger) who was on the loose that summer.

That was a more interesting than usual movie night. Regarding the dances, there was always a good band that drew big crowds. Usually the female patrons were admitted free; the males seldom had to pay more than a quarter. There, too, sales of beer and pop made it worthwhile for the dance hall owners.

The nights spent on the farm were pleasant times. As a youngster, after chores were done and evening drew on, I'd clean up and relax on the lawn with a blanket big enough to hold me and my dog. I'd look up at the stars to find the Big and Little Dippers and ponder what I might grow up to be, listen to the sounds of the farm animals chortling in the fields and an occasional barking dog. Sometimes, I could hear singing or laughter in the distance, the chirping of katydids, or croaking of frogs filling in the background beats. My trombone-playing high school buddy, who lived on a nearby farm, would inspire me to bring my instrument outside and answer his fanfares with a few warm-up measures.

Pa would come up from the barn after chores, go in the house to clean up, and then bring a snack for us and a cup of coffee for himself. He said the horn blowing reminded him of the way his ancestors in Switzerland may have communicated with their neighbors, using alphorns associated with the Swiss. (You might remember them from the Ri-Co-La commercial.) With a little coaxing, I could get him to tell me stories of the 'olden days'. This was one of his favorites:

THE MAN, THE WOMAN, THE PIPE, AND THE DOG

A man with a pipe in his mouth, sat across the aisle from a woman with a dog, riding a train going from Milwaukee to our little home town of Lomira. As the man sat contentedly, puffing on his pipe, the woman kept waving the smoke away from her space—complaining to the man, and finally opening her window. The man ignored her complaints and gestures, continuing to puff away, with occasional remarks about her stinky little dog.

Mile after mile, the woman continued to harass the man. Finally, as the train got closer to their destination, she could no longer tolerate the pipe smoking. She reached over, grabbed the man's pipe, and threw it out the window. In one swift move, the man grabbed her dog and threw it out the window, too. As the train pulled into the station, the sobbing woman was relieved to see her precious little dog walking the tracks, coming toward her. What do you think was hanging out of his mouth? The pipe? No, its tongue—panting all the way to the station!

The Cold Winter Days and Nights

There were few interesting things for me to do in the winter, but I did have a routine. I would go down to the barn after I did the supper dishes and finished my school homework. As my father and hired man were milking the cows, I carried the buckets of milk to the milk house to empty them into the milk cans that were set in cold water tanks.

Sometimes, I'd feed the hay to the horses in their stalls, or just lie in the hay piled in front of their stanchions. It was cozy and relaxing to listen to the cows chewing their cud and the muted strains of music coming from an old AM radio mounted on the wall next to a telephone intercom system. Pa insisted that music, especially "barn dance" style, calmed the cows and, like the Carnation Company touted, our milk came from contented cows—and contented cows give more milk. I must rephrase that: Pa said it was a misnomer that cows *give* milk...you have to *take it* away from them!

After Dad and the hired man finished the evening chores, they came up to the house, washed up, and relaxed a bit before bedtime. Pa would read the daily newspaper, eat a pint of ice cream, write checks to pay bills, or work on his weekly column for the town's chronicle. His by-line was: Got to be Good if you Get it from George J. Steiner. The whole household was generally in bed by 9:00 P. M. As they said, "six o'clock comes mighty early in the morning."

Our daily farm operations were on a strict schedule: arise at 6:00 A.M. for the morning milking (no matter what time you got in the night before), breakfast at 7:00 A.M., followed by loading the milk cans (which I aerated every morning, to cool the milk while Pa ate breakfast) on the pickup truck to deliver the milk- processing factory in the same town where I attended the parochial school.

Ma had dinner ready at precisely 12:00 noon (farmers typically had their main meal in the middle of the day); supper at 6:00 P.M. which featured lighter fare, perhaps leftovers and something new, too. One thing was sure: there were potatoes at every meal and always some kind of a dessert.

This might be the appropriate spot for me to expose Ma's ruse in finishing off any leftovers. She would cleverly disguise them in a different offering. For instance, if it didn't 'sell' at face value, it might end up as tidbits in a casserole dish or in the ever-suspicious muffins. Waste not, want not.

I don't want to imply that my mother wasn't an excellent cook. She was amazing, and thought it was sinful to waste anything worth saving, and our family grew up with that mindset. When I was the sole provider for my three young children, I could stretch a 39-cent fryer into meals over three days. The first day, I cut up the chicken and used the back, neck and wingtips for soup, adding chopped onions, celery, carrots, parsley, a little chicken concentrate that I got for free from my friends at Wyler Company, and some homemade noodles.

The second day, I dredged the rest of the chicken parts, browned them in a little butter, put them in a covered roasting pan, topped with a few onion slices and, by the time they were done, they were juicy and had made a tasty self-gravy.

The third day, I removed the tiny bits of chicken remaining on the parts I used for soup, added some little pasta shells and salad dressing, to make a very palatable chicken/pasta salad. Thankfully, I was inspired by my mother's inventive frugality. These were simple creations and now lovingly passed down to my grandchildren.

When my father shaved, even in his 90's, he used the same straight razor all of his adult life. I used to sit at the table beside him, very quietly to not jiggle his mirror because I loved to rummage through his shaving box that contained a menagerie of interesting little items: bitter, hard, black licorice sticks about the size of a cigar; a sex-detecting needle on a thin red string that swung back and forth across your palm if you were a male, and in a circular motion in detecting a female; magnets; puzzles; mints; a joke book; silver dollars and some foreign odd-shaped coins; Indianhead pennies; a pocket knife; a comb; barber shears, and, of course, the shaving mug and brush.

The leather strop, which he used to sharpen the razor, hung in the washroom off the kitchen. I liked to hear the rhythm and see the slapping movement when he used it, always wondering how the leather could sharpen the long straight razor blade. It was the same mechanical movement he made when shaving the hide of a butchered pig as it hung in a shed. I didn't hang around any longer when it came to cutting up the parts.

The next time I saw that meat was in our basement when both parents used the various parts in preparing slabs of bacon, ribs, hams, roasts, and grinding up some of the pork for making various sausages (summer sausage, bratwurst, krautwurst), and a delicacy called "headcheese" made with natural gelatin from the head and knuckles, pieces of tongue and other bits of meat, and then pressed it until it 'set' and could be sliced for sandwiches. It took me years, until adulthood, before I could bring myself to discover it made a tasty and enjoyable sandwich with a little mustard on rye bread.

My parents set up a long table in our basement, lined with meat grinder, stuffers, seasonings, and casings. Sometimes, I helped turn the handle on a stuffer which helped me realize how hard it was for them to spend hours into the night until they finished, cleaned the equipment, and hung the products in our smokehouse.

Ma and I spent some evenings in the basement, next to our wood-burning furnace, while we stripped the down off of feathers saved from the fowl that was butchered in the summer. She used the material to fill pillow ticking. Occasionally, I would sit down there by myself to crack hickory nuts and butternuts harvested from our small grove in a corner of the farm. They gave a gourmet touch to cookies, frostings, and butter layer cakes.

I remember Ma hosted a real quilting bee, inviting friends for a productive social gathering as they sat around the quilting frame which took up our whole family/music room. The visiting women brought homemade desserts, coffee cakes and such, which I enjoyed along with them and, admittedly, also enjoyed eavesdropping on their "woman talk".

Ma was a genuine, ahead-of-her-time recycler by cutting up cotton garments into 1"-wide strips, sewing them with smooth joints where each strip was added, then removed from the treadle sewing machine, snipped the thread chain at each joint, then rolled the resultant long strip into a ball about 6" in diameter. She knew the formula of how many balls would make a rug. Then she took them to a rug maker who used a loom and wove the rugs according to Ma's suggested color scheme. I have one of those rugs that was made 70 years ago, and it's as strong as new.

Ma also got 'hooked' on braided rugs. For those, she cut strips from woolen coats, skirts, and pants. This material was also used for an original 'wheel' design of braided rugs.

Pa had his own sewing projects that only a treadle machine could handle, such as: mending leather harnesses. He spent the winter months preparing machinery for the next planting and harvesting seasons: sharpening individual blades on the mowers used to cut pea vines and corn stalks. The machines also needed cleaning and oiling. He studied past crop records to plan rotation for the coming year.

If we had a snow storm, I could usually convince him to set the ice cream-making bucket in a snow bank and crank out a smooth, delectable batch of vanilla ice cream or a citrus sherbet.

Sundays were reserved for going to church in the morning after chores, and then go home to prepare a chicken dinner 'fit for a king'. always allowing for the possibility of guests dropping in. About once a month, I accompanied my parents as they visited old friends or relatives on a Sunday afternoon where I was allowed to share the tradition of having a glass of wine with a piece of cake. *Viva la tradicion!*

THE GREAT DEPRESSION

The Way Things Were

It was the economic crisis that began with the stock market crash of 1929, which continued through the 1930's, until the industrial boom triggered by the explosive effect of manufacturing wartime items for WWII began in December 1941.

As a youngster, I thought it was a great time, a time of bargains and fun. Families did things together, mostly free events like visiting friends or relatives on a Sunday afternoon. Of course, as a pre-teen, a youngster thinks that most things in life are free. I secretly enjoyed all of the attention given me as the youngest of four daughters, especially when acknowledged with "so you're the *baby!*" (I had been a surprise arrival for my 41-year-old parents.)

People they visited were of my parents' generation and happily followed the tradition of offering guests a piece of cake and a glass of homemade wine. I didn't mind sitting still on a mohair-upholstered, stiffly padded upright chair, listening to the adults' boring reminiscences of the 'olden' days, vocally recalled in a hybrid mix of German and English—as I waited for my glass of wine, a fair reward!

Our basic grocery shopping for flour, sugar, and other staples was usually done at what was known as a 'dry goods' store in the closest small town 'general' store about four miles from the farm. Sometimes, we would only take produce or eggs to this store to get a 'due bill' to be used as cash for future purchases.

Transactions that took place on the store's ground level, whether it was for a due bill or change due from a purchase, were expedited by the sales clerk by way of a small metal canister that traveled on a cable from the sales clerk to the second-floor bookkeeping department.

Purchases that could be, would be, wrapped by the sales clerk in white or brown craft paper, tied securely with white cord from a ball of string that sat on the counter, and cut with a kind of ring that had a cutting hook on it and worn on the clerk's little finger. This is quite different from modern-day packaging: plastic bags, boxes, or tagged with a store sticker—all of which must first be scanned by the sales person, to avoid a store alarm which detects unscanned, unpaid items.

For everything else, we shopped at the nearest large city about ten miles from our farm. While my parents shopped, I would wait at Woolworth's five-and-dime store, going up and down the aisles to look at the toys or costume jewelry. Occasionally, I would just sit at the food counter and ponder the difficult decision: how to spend my weekly dime allowance. Should I get a five-cent mug of root beer with a five-cent hot dog, or 'blow' it all on a triple-dip rainbow ice cream cone?

In those days, most housewives wore cotton dresses and aprons. Ma would make a trip to the city when there was a special at Penney's where ten cents would buy a cotton dress or a cobbler-style apron. She made a point of never being one of the first customers when the store opened its doors, to avoid being crushed in the rush of the eager crowd.

While jobs were at a premium, my eldest sister, Tess, was fortunate to find employment (after graduating from high school as a valedictorian, and subsequently from a business college) as a bookkeeper at the local Chevrolet dealer at the astronomical salary of $25 per week.

For entertainment, we listened to radio programs during our noon meals and after the evening chores were done. We had an Atwater-Kent console radio in the house.

I recall the weekly disagreements during summer vacations between my sister, Maybelle, and me on Thursday nights at 7:30 P.M. She insisted on listening to dance music broadcast live from the Aragon/Trianon ballrooms of Chicago. I wanted to listen to 'another exciting episode of *"The Lone Ranger"* and his ever-faithful friend, *Tonto*. If she won out, I would go down to the barn where my father had a radio playing music to keep the cows 'contented', but he would allow me the half-hour Lone Ranger 'interruption'.

Major movies were luxury entertainment but, thanks to Ma's love of the theatre, she pulled me out of school to share classic films like *Snow White and the Seven Dwarfs, Grapes of Wrath, Johnny Belinda, The Corn is Green, Of Mice and Men, and Gone With the Wind*. Without critics' review in the local newspaper, I don't know how she assessed them as 'must see' movies which did become timeless 'greats'.

My parents occasionally visited friends in Milwaukee whose children often took me to their neighborhood theatre where we saw a double feature plus a cartoon, all for only six cents!

Back home, during the summer months, all the surrounding hamlets even beat that deal: they offered weekly FREE outdoor movies— usually oaters, with a cartoon or two. These were sponsored by local merchants to bring some dollars into town. Some of the family-run taverns offered free lunches of beef sandwiches or plates of fried fish with slices of rye bread and cole slaw. (Was this practice responsible for the 'happy hour' phenomenon?) It was not such a happy memory for my aunt and my mother on their 'girls night out' for a movie in the city, and a hot beef sandwich with a beer at a nearby pub...to later find out that the 'beef' was actually muskrat—so tender and in a tasty gravy. (Ugh!)

Granted, as farmers, we didn't have much income because selling prices were comparatively low for everything we produced: milk, grain, chickens, eggs, and potatoes, considering it still took the same amount of hours and labor to produce and sell these commodities. Cows still had to be fed and milked every morning and evening; the barns had to be cleaned every day and the manure hauled away; eggs had to be collected, cleaned, sorted, and packed; all the livestock and poultry had to have food and water daily; fallen trees had to be sawed into logs and then split and stored in the woodshed for use in our wood-burning range and furnace—a valuable resource of fuel for cooking and heating.

Admittedly, on the positive side, we always had food on the table—not only for ourselves but for anyone who came to our door, whether they were relatives, friends, or strangers (even hoboes or homeless ones who traveled the Soo Line tracks bordering our farm boundary.) On Sundays, we automatically placed a couple of extra settings on the dining-room table to make unexpected guests feel welcome to share 'feasts fit for a king', as my father labeled the meals.

In later years, when I moved as a bride to Chicago and became friends with people there, I learned first-hand of the hardships experienced by city folks during the Depression years. They walked the railroad tracks with a bucket to pick up pieces of coal dropped from freight trains to burn in their pot-bellied stoves to heat their apartments. They supplemented their meals with "Depression soup" consisting of fat rendered from bacon for flavor, and flour browned in the fat for body, adding boiling water and noodles-from-scratch to make enough soup servings to feed the family.

My mother was known for miles around for her culinary results, be it pot roast, turtle stew, chicken and dumplings, or ham and escalloped potatoes. She mastered any dessert known to man: schaum tortes, cream and fruit pies, Jello and whipped cream parfaits dramatically presented in a huge leaded-glass crystal bowl. Other specialties included bread pudding served warm with an amber-colored wine sauce, angel-sunshine cake, cream puffs and chocolate éclairs, nondescripts, or melt-in-your-mouth candies.

I don't recall any meal after which my father didn't compliment my mother for the especially good and tasty food. I can't think of anything that irritated him more than someone coming late to the table and his having to announce a second time that the meal was ready and on the table.

My mother made everything from scratch, always tasty and artfully presented. Pa appreciated how hard she worked. She not only put great effort and love into cooking and baking, she kept the house and herself impeccably clean and orderly—no matter how tired or ill she might be. I never heard her complain, use foul language, or raise her voice. She always had an ear ready to hear whatever anyone wanted to say.

There were no conveniences for doing the laundry. She made the soap from lye and lard rendered from butcherings. We had one of the oldest surviving Maytag washing machines to do our laundry and additionally used a washboard to scrub the heavily-soiled articles. All the laundry was hung on a line with clothespins—winter and summer. It was a comical sight in winter when the frozen long underwear was brought into the house and stood up in a room off the kitchen.

There was no permanent press fabric in those days. We did the pressing with clip-on solid irons that were kept hot on a wood-burning stove, alternating them as they began to cool. And we did iron EVERYTHING—from bed sheets to dresses and blouses to handkerchiefs. The most challenging were the rayon accordion-pleated skirts. She sewed and mended clothes for herself and her four daughters on a treadle sewing machine. I learned to weave by darning holes in the men's work socks with 'store string', stretching the target area over a bulb-shaped wooden darner.

She raised and dressed poultry, not only for our own consumption but for her city clientele. She maintained huge flower and vegetable gardens; made homemade soap, root beer, and various kinds of sausages which were smoked in our own smokehouse. She canned fruits, jams, and jellies and, of course, baked breads and rolls weekly. We worked together to sit by the basement wood-burning furnace to strip dried chicken feathers to stuff pillows, in winter; she canned fruits, jams and jellies in season, in the summer; and, of course, all year-round she baked breads and rolls at least once a week. We harvested and cracked hickory nuts and butternuts to use in cookies and cakes.

There were no garbage disposals; they weren't needed. Few food products were packaged in metal or glass containers. Glass bottles might be returnable to the store, and glass jars could be used for canning jams and fruits. Things like fruit and potato peels were fed to the pigs. Table scraps, that were rare, might be added to meals for the cats and dogs. Sour cream or milk was used in baking desserts, such as devil's food cakes. Somehow, my mother always found a creative solution for things like table scraps or leftover material remnants from a sewing project.

The Depression was more challenging for urban dwellers than it was for farmers like us. We had food to fuel our bodies and sources of trees to cut down as fuel for our stove and furnace. After my father and hired help brought logs to the woodshed behind the house, I chopped firewood on a chopping block for household use, in a size that would fit into our kitchen range.

I was one of the fortunate kids in elementary and high school whose mother packed a good, appetizing lunch. It made me feel guilty to have a thermos bottle filled with hot chicken noodle soup and bologna sandwiches on tasty homemade bread, with always a piece of cake or a cookie or donut for dessert. The city kids had plain lard sandwiches, period. I shared my lunches with kids who had none. I couldn't bear to have a 'feast' when I gagged at what I saw they had. In those bleak days, city dwellers had to stand in long bread lines for food, and walked the railroad tracks to pick up stray bits of wood and coal to keep their pot-bellied stoves burning for cooking and heating purposes.

Every week, especially on Sundays, we could expect friends to drop in to visit and enjoy a great meal of chicken soup with homemade noodles, roast chicken with the trimmings, and homemade fruit or cream pies, or a giant Jell-o parfait presented to the table in a prism-cut crystal bowl, topped with real whipped cream.

Lessons for Life

I felt secure growing up under the watchful eyes and hands of each omnipotent parent. I always doubted my ability to fare in the grown-up world without them and their wisdom at my side. It prompted me to learn as much as I could every day from them—by doing, watching, or merely listening. Keeping the history in mind of their perseverance and intestinal fortitude held together with an undaunted faith in God gave me courage to survive the times of crisis in my life.

My ill-fated times were miniscule compared with theirs: their house burned down on Christmas morning in the early years of their marriage when their first child, Tess, was still an infant. There was my father's close brush with death during the WWI flu epidemic, and the devastating debt-building losses of two complete herds of milk-producing cattle from which they didn't emerge until retirement age.

To help bolster income, my mother survived the brink of a nervous breakdown caused by sleep deprivation in having to tend the flocks of baby chicks. She had to get up several times during the night in mid-winter weather, go out to the chicken coop in her nightgown and coat to make sure the brooder stove had not gone out to cause the chicks to freeze, or had gotten too hot causing them to be asphyxiated. Her sleep pattern, therefore, was forever distorted.

Things She Taught Me

When I was six years old, my feet hardly reaching the foot pedal, she had me hem towels made from laundered 50-pound or 100-pound flour sacks in order to learn how to sew a straight seam. When I had that mastered, I was eager to learn the zig-zag way of joining cotton strips that went into making loomed rugs.

She baked the most delicious butter-tender shortcake biscuits, then sinfully mounded them with sweet, juicy berries and topped them with our own pure whipped cream—sometimes gilding-the-lily addition of a scoop of homemade ice cream. Her original creation of rhubarb custard pie was a not-too-sweet, not-too-tart meringue-topped flaky crust, gloriously light and tasty treat. It was just one of her baking triumphs. She was known for miles around as being an exceptionally good cook and a baker without equal.

THREE SISTERS: RELATED

As a youngster, in the elementary school years, I didn't know what I wanted to be, but I knew what I HAD to be: as good or better than my preceding siblings who had set the bars really high.

As a first grader, when I was six years old, my eldest sister, Tess, was twenty-one, Lil was eighteen, and Maybelle was thirteen years old. I loved each one in a special way. They were uniquely different but always generous with their love—not always with each other, but always toward me.

One thing we unanimously agreed upon was the fact that we were blessed with especially good, caring, talented parents, head and shoulders above any others whom we knew. They were highly intelligent, capable, moral persons of integrity, respected by all who knew them. It was a badge of honor to wear their surname. They were advocates of a moderate lifestyle. We had an advantageous start in life.

<u>What I Learned From Them</u>

My eldest sister, Theresa (Tess), was born on January 12, 1910 during a blizzard. In a phone call to the delivering country doctor, Dr. Raymond, my parents were told that the snowstorm prevented him from going any further by horse-and-buggy beyond the point where the main road (U.S. 41) met the lane to our farm—more than a mile from our house.

Pa responded by quickly hitching up a team of horses to a sleigh (the typical vehicle often depicted on Christmas cards) and picked up the doctor just in time to deliver the baby who probably weighed more than 11-1/2 pounds (which was my weight as the smallest of us four girls.)

Ma told stories of how Tess who, at age two, hated to wear soiled underwear. If she had an 'accident', she would rinse out her bloomers in an outdoor water tank and then hang it up to dry on the garden fence.

I didn't get to know Tess until she was an adult who watched over me until I became an adult. Tess was of an age and attitude to be 'double cast' as a mother to me. In fact, Maybelle and I sometimes referred to her as 'Mama #2' (in a good way!) She was authoritative, serious, sensible, opinionated, unequivocally honest and moral.

She had graduated as valedictorian of her high school senior class in 1927. Being of the same heredity cloth, I knew I would be expected to bring a similar honor upon our family name. Being the first born, with sterling attributes, it seemed logical that she must be my father's favorite. In a word, she was 'perfect'. As I matured, I realized that not one of us was a favorite. Our parents made a deliberate attempt to treat all four of us equally and fairly. My mother confirmed that not one of us was perfect—each one of us had good points and not-so-good points, she commented.

Coincidentally, I did graduate as valedictorian from the same high school and under the same principal that Tess had fifteen years earlier—a wonderfully pleasant man, E. E. Packard. He was unmarried in his first stint at the high school and had a date with Tess after graduation. She said she was so nervous about going out with him that, when he picked her up at the farm in his Model A Ford, she banged her head getting in. She never told him that it cut her scalp. She bled silently.

After graduation from business college, it was the beginning of the Great Depression era. She was fortunate to get a job paying $15 per week as bookkeeper in the office of a local auto dealer. There was little left, after paying room and board in town, but she was luckier than most people who had no job at all. To me, her office job seemed like something I might like to do when I was of employable age.

More than 10 years later, my first office job after graduation from the same business college at age 17 paid $85.00 a month at the prestigious Schroeder Hotel company in Milwaukee and, out of that, I paid $8/ week for a room and bought all my meals.

Looking back, I can see that our lifes' paths were almost parallel—our jobs, our husbands, our divorces, our second marriages. In the 30's, she married a 'closet' alcoholic—the son of an affluent couple in a nearby town who, like my first in-laws, didn't reveal their son's addictions, hoping that a 'good girl' would change him.

He was a man who knew everything there was to know about major league baseball but little else. After suffering physical and mental abuse from him as well as infidelity, she sought a legal separation from him after 10 years—divorcing him in 1945.

Thirty years later, learning of his death in 1975, she married a long time friend of the family, Francis. He was a good man—good to her, to our parents, to all of us and our children. He had been a teacher and a semi-pro baseball player in his younger days until he chose the United States Postal Service as a career. He chalked up 38 years without missing a day's work—first as postmaster in his home town, and then as a rural route carrier.

Tess and Francis were 65 years old when they married on All Souls' Day in 1975 in a wedding Mass at Fond du Lac's St. Joseph Catholic Church. The priest conducted the lovely ceremony very informally, joking that their pre-marital conference was short and easy since they could skip the part about procreation. I had the privilege of singing Schubert's "Ave Maria" and Gounod's "Panis Angelicus". Their Godson, Frank

(Maybelle's eldest son) sang Cat Stevens' "Morning Has Broken" in accordance with the bride and groom's wishes. The priest invited a round of applause from everyone present after the ceremony.

At the ensuing wedding reception and dinner, our father at age 90 entertained with tunes on one of his many harmonicas. It was a beautiful occasion that Tess and Francis could finally be able to marry after a thirty-year courtship—a wait endured because of their religious convictions. They believed it was worth the wait and hoped they would have at least five years together. They deserved every happiness in the 20 years they eventually shared.

After my husband passed away and our Lake Puckaway retreat was sold, I missed those days of getting together with them there. After that, I started making the 150-mile drive to their home to visit and bring some of their favorite meals that I loved to cook: chicken and dumplings, oven-baked beef stew, and American chop suey. Between visits, I regularly telephoned them with the latest family news. It was chilling to get the news of their unlikely, simultaneous deaths on December 4, 1995.

The irony of their tragic deaths still haunts me. I miss and think of them every day.

Their absence has burrowed a deep chasm in my heart and life.

Turning back the pages of history to 1983, Tess and Francis had lived with our father and gave him loving care until our Dad's passing that year at age 98-1/2. His care didn't become intense until his last year when he could no longer bathe, shave, or feed himself. They never left him alone for a minute, always trying to make him as comfortable as possible. They responded to his requests for visits from his longtime friends and from the parish priest who brought the Holy Eucharist to him at least once weekly.

In 1986 they liquidated the house in Fond du Lac, gave away most of the furnishings and made their full-time residence in Brownsville where Francis had a lovely house built in 1955, paid for with cash. (Neither he nor Tess ever 'charged' anything; they paid for everything with cash.) They joked about living next door to a medical clinic where they were only steps away from the services of a doctor and dentist. It gave them a sense of safety.

They were extremely frugal and lived a very private life. Tess didn't ever leave the house. She said that she didn't want anyone to see how crotchety she had become. Besides, her legs were quite weak, and she didn't want to take the chance of stumbling or falling down and breaking a bone. She felt safe in the house and mostly stayed in bed. My son, Tom, installed a telephone in her bedroom within arm's length of her bed on a cedar chest. As time went by, a potty chair was placed between the cedar chest and her bed so she didn't have to make the difficult walk to the bathroom.

The only other person who had a key to the house was Francis' brother, Rich, who lived on their homestead farm about a mile away. The only regular visitor they had was our sister, Maybelle, who 'made the rounds' every Thursday: she started from her rural home to visit relatives in a nursing home, then picked up some restaurant home cooking to take to Tess and Francis, visit awhile, and then back to her home.

However, on that ominous cold week in December 1995, Maybelle had an appointment elsewhere that kept her from the routine Thursday visit. The following Monday, the Senior Center four miles away called their house. No answer. The Center was concerned that Francis had not shown up for a few days to pick up the $2 dinners. He had never failed before. To be sure that nothing was wrong, the Center called Francis' brother, Rich.

Rich went to the house. No one answered his knocking on the door. He peeked through the garage window and saw their car was in there.

He went back to the house and unlocked the back door. As soon as he opened it, the horrible odor of decomposition hit him. He saw his brother lying dead who apparently had fallen from a heart attack and slid partially under Tess's bed. Tess was lying in a position that looked like she had tried to reach the phone. She, too, was in a state of decomposition. They probably had lain there from the previous Wednesday, the last time anyone recalled seeing Francis. They were probably already deceased on that Thursday when Maybelle wasn't able to stop in.

It was a heart-stopping moment when I got the phone call from Maybelle, "Tess and Francis are dead." How could it be real? My first thoughts were, "Were they in an accident? Were they victims of a house invasion? Murder?"

There they were, in a surely safe place, living a quiet private life, and yet died in a horrific set of circumstances. It reinforces the fact that only God knows how and when that fatal day will come.

Lillian (Lil) was born in June 1913 in our farmhouse, delivered by Pa, who was alerted by the hired girl "the baby is coming" as she fled past the barn to run home.

This girl was specifically hired to help Ma with housework in her final days of pregnancy but, like Butterfly McQueen in "Gone With the Wind", she knew *nothin' 'bout birthin'* and wanted no part of it.

Lil was a climber. When she was about four years old, Ma came out of the house and called her name when she couldn't see her playing anywhere A little voice answered, "Look how high I am." There was Lil, peering down from the top of the windmill. Ma quickly thought not to panic or scream, to not cause Lil to fall. Instead, she went along with it, asking very calmly, "I bet you can see really far. Can I come up and look with you?" Lil cheerfully invited Ma who was afraid of heights but who gradually ascended the rungs until she reached Lil. She shared the breathtaking view, and gently coaxed Lil to come down for lunch and a nap—after which she removed enough rungs of the windmill ladder so no child could climb it.

Lil was the middle child between Tess and Maybelle for seven years before I came along. It has been my private, personal belief that she was the unwitting victim of the middle-child syndrome. She attended a junior high school but just couldn't buckle down. The principal said it was a shame since she was really bright and could have graduated if she could only attend two or three days a week. She wanted to live life in person, not through books. In spite of much pain suffered throughout her life, emotionally and physically, I knew her as a wonderfully warm, pleasant, loving, and generous person. For someone having to cope with an early pregnancy at age 17, she presented herself as happy, easy-going, full of life, and always ready for a hearty laugh.

She bore the baby girl, June, and married Walter, the father—a handsome, neighboring farm boy—the only man she had ever dated and loved. I thought he was so sophisticated, the only man I ever knew who wore spats (short for spatterdash, popular in the late 19th and early 20th centuries.)

Lillian was a beauty, born, I'm told, as a towhead (with light blond, almost white, hair) which turned into an auburn color and naturally curly in her adulthood. She and Walter were caught up in the habits of an older twosome with whom they double-dated. It was in the day of prohibition where drinking was done in a speak-easy, in an era of 'free love'.

Baby June was my parents' first granddaughter, and me as a five-year-old aunt. As she graduated from high school and received a full scholarship to the University of Wisconsin, she chose to work in the University's primate lab where she met and married Dr. Hiroshi Odoi. She moved to Chicago with Hiro where they lived on the south side because of his employment at the University of Chicago and became the mother of five children.

Lillian and Walter had two more children: Shirley, who married a local entrepreneur, with whom she became the mother of six daughters—all of whom received degrees in the medical field. Rita Mae married and became the mother of two precocious, professionally successful daughters.

Lil had an unenviable life. She began married life as a vulnerable teen-ager with a small baby, a jealous husband, on a small farm perched high in a remote hilly area--far from any signs of human life. Imagine the isolation, a house with no electricity, and no indoor plumbing. Yet, she was a good mother, loving wife, and an immaculate housekeeper. Her hands, once lauded by a jeweler to be beautiful enough to model, became enlarged and calloused from all the hard down-and-dirty farm work she had to do which included milking cows by hand.

She was an excellent cook and expert baker of breads, cakes, and pies. For my birthdays, she always made my favorite cake: poppy seed cake with custard filling and caramel frosting. She churned her own butter and slathered it in, and on, everything edible. She had been a hard worker since childhood, more than any woman should be. She seemed to thrive on work but shunned education beyond grade school, in spite of a junior high school principal who promised passing grades—if only she could attend school two or three days a week. He said that she was that bright!

Ours was a family of girls: my grandmother was a girl, my mother was a girl, my three sisters were girls, my sister Lillian had three girls, and two of those girls had girls. Maybelle and I 'broke the molds': each of us had three children, the first two being males.

Now, a little about Maybelle who arrived in this world on April 2, 1918, incarnated as a teacher—yet another sister whose example I tried to emulate in my life's pattern. Unlike me, she knew at an early age what she wished to be, a teacher, and I was her 'lab rat'.

My first memory of her existence comes to mind as I recall a scene occurring many times over—actually daily for the next few years— of me, at age three or four, kneeling before a low-hung blackboard mounted beneath our crank-type telephone in our farm kitchen. That is where I spent an hour every day learning to write letters, then words and numbers, until I could work simple addition and subtraction problems.

By the time I got into first grade, I read the whole primer the first day of school. I recall coming home and telling my parents how boring it was, sarcastically quoting from the book, "See Jane run, see Dick run, see Spot run."

While I was attending the little one-room country schoolhouse, Maybelle chose to attend the 'big city' high school in Fond du Lac where the diverse curriculum offered the subjects she wanted to explore: French and Latin. She was the ultimate scholar. Her senior class numbered in the hundreds, yet she graduated as second-highest in her class, a miniscule grade point below that of the valedictorian, Fahey Flynn, who later became a respected, capable, impressive newscaster on a major Chicago television news team.

She came home on weekends. I couldn't wait to see her and what she'd bring me—candy, a pencil, a ball, or a knick-knack. It was exciting to hear her stories of where she lived and things that happened in that big city school. One story, funny and easy to recall, was about the first place she lived. It was an elderly woman, extremely frugal, who would ask Maybelle to turn out the light (a 15-watt bulb in the hallway outside her bedroom) so it wouldn't get too warm in the house.

Maybelle was intelligent, well-read, industrious, and definitely independent in thought, action, and fashion. She successfully defeated the prognosis at birth of an early demise. Her strength lay in prayer and tenacity. In spite of her fragility, she channeled her stubbornness into a positive attribute to attain her high goals. In family circles, she was known as the 'talking machine.' She was articulate and could speak with authority on various levels of a myriad of subjects.

She went on to graduate from Oshkosh (WI) State Teachers College (now known as University of Wisconsin-Oshkosh) as the only student on the commencement program with three asterisks after her name—standing for HIGHEST HONORS, head and shoulders above everyone else.

She taught school for nearly sixty years, students of all ages—from youngsters to remedial tutoring for adults, even beyond her formal retirement. Her children are a testament in her ongoing participation in religious, civic, and educational interests. Her eldest son, Frank, is a high-profile realtor; Mark is a self-employed CPA and financial adviser; and daughter, Sue Marie, is a respected teacher, assistant principal, and Stephen minister.

<u>So This is the Baby!</u>

That's what I was always greeted with when visiting old-time friends of my parents. It seemed to be news to everyone that I was born nearly eight years after Maybelle, my mother being 41 at the time. It seemed a little weird to be so introduced, even after I was college age.

I remember looking at the family portrait on top of our upright piano when I was about seven years old. There was my mother, father, and three girls—the youngest about my age. It was Maybelle, not me. My mother became pregnant shortly after the tintype photo was taken. I was born the following year. My sisters liked to tease me that I really was 'adopted'.

What I Learned From Them

Then along came Joanie, or 'Joanikins', as Tess often affectionately called me. She was also the one who labeled me 'Grinny' because, every time she checked on me as a baby, I would be awake—grinning, not crying. She admitted to our parents that, instead of accompanying them on an outing, she would rather stay home to take care of me. And that is what she did, until the day she died.

By the time I was old enough to retain memories, Tess was living in our home town and working as a full-time bookkeeper at the local Chevrolet auto dealer. She then married a bar/restaurant owner and moved a few miles further away. The only time I got to see her was whenever my parents would stop in that place of business or when I got to spend short vacations there. I didn't much enjoy those vacations as Tess was always tending business while her husband was either gone or 'not feeling well' in bed.

I'm sure now that she enjoyed my company, to cheer her up and help her with food orders she prepared for the dining-room attached to the bar, and do some light ironing in the upstairs living quarters. I silently detested lunch when it included liver and onions, but I applauded her best-ever hamburgers and the treat of ice cream for me and their dog, Mitsy.

The pleasantness ended when, one evening, her husband got into an instant drug-driven rage, threatened us with a gun, and chased us up to the third floor where she and I locked ourselves in a storage room until he left. I understood then (in the eyes of a ten-year-old) why Tess always seemed so serious, never joking or laughing. She lived an unhappy life, often in terror—incarcerated by marriage vows she observed as a strict Catholic.

Memorable Events We Shared

When Lil and her husband moved to a bigger and more modern farm than that first primitive location, I enjoyed vacationing there. I didn't have to do any work. All I had to do was play with my four-year-old niece, June. Lil was always pleasant with fun things to do, places to go, and wonderful home cooking just like Ma's: country-fried potatoes, fresh-made applesauce, bratwurst, homemade bread, and pies—all of which were picture perfect. She had learned well from our mother.

When I was on vacation there, I got to ride an old, retired race horse named 'George' that they had procured in a trade deal. It was a slow, safe ride except for George's frequent stumbling, understandable at his age of twenty. Eventually, my brother-in-law gave George for me to keep, including a saddle.

The first time I took him for a long ride on our gravel country road, he was fine until I turned him around to head back home. He reacted as if he were literally on the racetrack's 'home stretch', going into a wild gallop. The saddle wasn't cinched tight enough to keep it from sliding down and around. I was in an almost upside-down position for the whole terrifying mile home until we pulled up at our barn door!

Lil never complained about her hard life, nor confessed about her hardships. She loved her husband unconditionally and lived for him and her children with the proverbial 'heart of gold'. I will never forget her laughter.

Maybelle never turned off her desire to teach. Whenever she was home, it was 'school time'—cutting sharply into my play time with our dogs and cats, for at least an hour at a time. It was boring to work on spelling and arithmetic. By the time I entered first grade at the little red schoolhouse, adjacent to a cow pasture, I read the whole first-grade primer on the first day of school. I validated the fact by reciting some excerpts, sarcastically, to prove my point.

After enduring that boring first grade, the school board decided to approve the teacher's recommendation for me to skip second grade and start my second year in third grade. As I started to collect memorabilia to include in this book, I found my very first report card. I was surprised that my behavior wasn't perfect. Back then it was called 'deportment'. I recalled being very bashful, yet I see the comment in the card 'whispers too much'.

Being promoted from first to third grade proved to be disadvantageous. It made me feel that school was easy so that I never developed good study habits. Also, I was two years younger than my peers so that I was not able to behave socially as they did, such as wear make-up, go on a date, or drive a car.

I chose to live at home and attend high school in my home town of 654 population. In high school there was a combined total of 85 students, from freshman through senior classes. In my junior and senior high school days, I felt that living on a farm was a disadvantage socially as well as academically. All of the town kids spoke a strange language about 'hanging out at the drug store' or attending a 'coed' party. Later in life I realized that the farm environment was not only more interesting, but it kept me out of the trouble that the town kids got involved in.

I participated in Serious Declamation, German Club, Band, Chorus, Basketball, and Cheerleading. I was successful in winning local, tri-county, and regional competitions—bringing home a variety of trophies. I also learned to drive a car with my mother as teacher. She would pick me up after school and let me drive home—first, on the country roads; later on the highway.

In spite of the accomplishments to my credit, I still lacked self-confidence and was extremely self-conscious and self-deprecating. It seemed incredulous that, in a school-wide popularity survey, I was voted to have the most beautiful eyes. That still amazes me. I'm sure that none of the students knew how much that compliment meant to me.

The most effective deterrent in avoiding questionable behavior was the ever-present thought: would my parents be embarrassed if they found out about it? I was always concerned about honoring their good name and making them proud of me.

Now, more than sixty years later, I subliminally still try to bring honor upon them.

Maybelle and I bonded with downright silliness. We had nicknames for each other taken from the Bob Hope radio show: Brenda and Cobena but, over the years, we've forgotten which tag fit either of us. We had a kind of gymnastic routine in greeting each other; now in our elderly years, it hurts just to think of that!

During the last years on the farm, when we were together in the summer months, we cooperated in cleaning the chicken eggs and packing them in the crates for Ma to sell to her clients. The eggs that had stains on them had to be gently wiped with a vinegar-dampened cloth. When that routine got boring, we'd spice up the chore by playing catch with the raw eggs, moving further apart with each throw. It got exciting, but we never dropped the 'ball'. (I told Ma that I was 'egged' on!)

We also had a weird snack that we originated but have never made since those days: two slices of toasted homemade bread, buttered, then add a piece of cheese, and some honey. Neither of us remember how that concoction evolved.

I most appreciated that she taught me ballroom dancing. She and her husband, Frank. were amazingly smooth, coordinated, professional-looking dance partners. In fact, they met at a public dance at a firemen's picnic in the small town outskirts where he was a farmer and caring for his elderly parents.

During the eight years they dated, they never missed the New Year's Eve ball in the Schwartz Ballroom in Hartford (WI). Maybelle would come home and slip into bed and put her ice cold feet on me. Frank's car, "Ophelia", didn't have a heater. The next morning, I coaxed her into telling me all about the evening. Ma would get impatient, calling me for breakfast and listening to my excuse for delaying, "Maybelle is lying on my pajamas." I would make Maybelle laugh when I quipped, "Can I be "Frank" with you?"

I was always conscientious, honest, and naïve. Like Tess, I had also married a closet alcoholic who inflicted mental and physical abuse on me. But I was too far from my parents to run home to mother, and I never wanted them to know how unhappy I was. Other similarities I shared with Tess was that I graduated from the same business college as she did; worked in an office all of my employment years; also divorced in the tenth year of marriage; and remarried twenty years later.

To this day, I thank Tess for encouraging me to take business courses in high school, especially typing. It was a life-saver that I was able to do home typing to support my small children and myself after my divorce; later as an executive secretary in the business world, and now on the computer in this cyber age. How technological advancements and language have changed in the latter part of the 20th and the beginning of the 21st century: a blackberry is not a fruit, an iPOD does not contain peas; a mouse is not a rodent; and gay is not always happy.

From Lil I learned that a girl can withstand and survive really hard physical labor, to serve in my stead to cope with future challenges: working in the fields for my father in driving hay-loading wagons with either a team of horses or a no-frills tractor; bending over all day picking potato bugs off of row after row of potato plants in the field; then later picking up the potatoes from the dug-up vines. Picking off the bugs or harvesting the potatoes in a bent-over position for hours at a time always brought on a horrific backache.

Another back-breaking job was to clear a field of crop-choking mustard, one plant at a time. I traversed the eight-acre field, having to pull out the individual plants with roots intact, place them in a gunny sack, then bring them back on foot about a mile to our house. There I laid them out on the lawn in piles of ten, earning me one cent for every pile. It took me ten summers to diligently eradicate the mustard. After all that work and time, my folks had to sell the farm because of their advancing age. The new owners sold the land shortly thereafter to the highway department and that plat of land is now known as 'Highway 41'.

Some of my other fun jobs: carrying heavy buckets of milk (as the cows were being milked); shelled hundreds of cobs of corn to feed the chickens, ducks, and pigs; took our dog to a far corner of the farm to round up the cows to come home for the evening milking; walked beside my father as he sat on a horse-drawn mower to bring the pea vines vertical that were flattened by the mower; salvaged a load of hay from an approaching thunderstorm, by driving a team of horses while I stood in the hay wagon while pulling the hay loader—a tricky and scary kind of caravan.

Pa stood at the rear of the wagon to distribute the hay around the wagon as it came off the loader's conveyor belt. I had to drive in a straight line, with only lightning to guide me, but making a wide turn at the end of each row—the kind of turn called a 'farmer turn.' Poor Ma worried about our safety the entire time we were out in a storm.

I try to imagine how children of urban, middle America would act today, if they were asked to do any of the tasks that we girls did. It never entered our minds to hesitate, let alone refuse, to do the chores expected of us. On a farm, each member of the family is part of the team and responsible for making the living. Our rewards were the satisfaction of being a help and enjoying a good night's sleep.

Great to Be Last

Speaking from true-life experience as the last in a 'litter' of four daughters, I was a kind of anti-climatic surprise to my forty-something parents. As a veteran dairy farmer, known for miles around, Pa endured good-natured ribbing that, even in his fourth try, he could not produce a hired man. To that I say, "Thank you, all you jokesters for helping to shape my life as a kind of intern for my father."

I loved being my father's little helper by following him around, waiting for any opportunity to help. I pretended to like feeding silage to the cows (as bad as fermenting chopped corn stalks smelled), waiting to carry buckets of milk after the cows that were stripped (that means 'good to the last drop'), and grooming a horse with a curry comb.

By the time I was old enough to be given the responsibility of completing these chores, my sisters were married or away at school. It was, therefore, like growing up as an only child. I had the luxury of knowing my creative parents in a relaxed environment with no one else vying for their attention, spending one-on-one hours with each of them.

Having already survived many crises in the preceding years, my parents had mellowed. They said that I kept them young. I not only enjoyed the special attention from them, but from my older, doting sisters when they did come home.

However, it also meant living in their shadows of things they did— whether right or wrong, but I also profited from the knowledge of their experiences passed on to me.

The academic challenges I was faced with put definite pressure on me. By the time I reached school age, I knew that I was destined to travel the same path: initially, going to the little red schoolhouse through the fourth grade, and then transferring to the parochial school in town through the eighth grade under the tutelage of nuns. I knew I would be compared with my predecessors which, in turn, means I would have to behave well and get good grades. I was fortunate, though, to have mentors like that.

THREE SISTERS: NUN-RELATED

The parochial school that my sisters and I attended was located in the quiet hamlet of Lomira (WI) where the population of 654 was mostly German, and quite evenly divided among three religious sects: Methodist, Lutheran, and Roman Catholic. My family attended St. Mary Catholic Church and parochial school which was run by three nuns of the Order of St. Agnes. They lived in a white frame building that held two schoolrooms with living quarters between them.

Sister Dolorita, a beautiful young woman, was in charge of the 'small' room for first through fourth grades; and Sister Carlotta, a sharp middle-aged woman, was in charge of the 'big' room that served fifth through eighth grades. Sister Ursala, a charming, older, kindly nun tended to the housework and meals which gave her the German label of 'koch schwester' (meaning 'cook sister').

I entered that school as a fifth grader—a shy, well-behaved child. It was, therefore, a mortifying experience when, on my first day in this strange surrounding, Sister Carlotta ordered me to kneel in front of the room because I had been 'rubber-necking', which meant I had turned around to talk to someone in the seat behind me. I was too scared, and knew it would do no good, to explain that it was a deliberate attempt on the part of those 'city' girls to get me in trouble.

My sensitive nature precluded my forgiving those two girls for setting me up like that and then laughing about it. Imagine my embarrassment having to kneel in front of all those strange classmates, so much so that my body started to tremble. I fought off the feeling of fainting. It is easy for me to understand why adults recall things that happened in their childhood, especially if they believe they were unfairly treated. This incident happened to me more than 70 years ago, yet I recall it very clearly.

Despite the strictness and holiness of the religious environment, bullies existed there as they did in the rural school. I dreaded the thought of having to deal with overt actions again. The bullies found great sport in taking advantage of the nun's brief absences from the room, attacking us girls with a barrage of blackboard erasers or their dirty boots (bearing traces of mud or manure) across the room, definitely not clean dirt. A couple of crude farm boys brought to school little bottles of a yellow liquid resembling nail polish remover, taunting the girls who had forgotten to remove the forbidden nail polish before coming to school. However, the liquid was not acetone, it was cow urine.

It got worse. It involved the small enclosed entrance to the room. There were two rows of coat hooks on each side. Coming in from outside recess, we had to hang up our coats in a hurry to avoid being body-slammed against the coat hooks and victimized with the bullies' sexual gyrations while we struggled to get free.

Sister Carlotta asked if the boys ever said naughty words. I nodded 'yes' but couldn't bring myself to repeat any. Somehow, I quickly made up a stupid 'code' for one of the words: Father, Uncle, Cousin, Kate. I don't know if she caught it, but she didn't pursue it any further. My mother thought it was funny, in a serious way, that I spontaneously came up with that configuration.

Those days were not funny to me until, many decades later, there were musical comedies that poked fun at Catholic schools' goings-on: "Do Black

Patent Shoes Really Reflect Up?" and "Nunsense". In our small farming community, I don't think anyone could afford to buy patent leather shoes.

We didn't have uniforms in those days, but we did have a dress code of sorts: we had to wear dresses or blouses and skirts, absolutely NO pants, not even in winter. I was worried when I got a snow suit for Christmas one year, consisting of a jacket and pants. My dear sweet mother 'straightened out' the nuns so that I could wear it to school. She explained that it was necessary to keep me warm and, more importantly, it was much more modest when playing outside at recess, especially when bending over or falling down. The nuns changed the rule accordingly.

Ma contested some other edicts, such as no girl could wear a sleeveless dress in church. She had bought a beautiful dress for Tess's eighth-grade graduation ceremony to be held in church: a pale, peach-colored chiffon/crepe A-line sleeveless dress with all-over glass beading. She had been advised that it would not be acceptable. Ma seldom consumed any alcohol, but on this occasion she admitted imbibing a little courage before commandeering the family's 1928 mohair-upholstered Oakland sedan and aimed it toward Lomira—specifically, toward the church's rectory to affirm with the priest that Tess WOULD be wearing the beaded chiffon/crepe sleeveless dress to the graduation ceremony.

Permission granted.

Ma returned home in the Oakland sedan. That's when she noticed it exuded a burned rubber smell. She realized then that she had made the 'assault and pepper' trip with the hand brake on, while making the gallant effort to reach 25 MPH!

I always looked forward to Mondays—the day that Sister Ursula did the laundry. She hung the nuns' clothes on a kind of carousel clothes line that went from their back porch to a pole in their backyard. It was intriguing to see what they wore under their floor-length black habits.

Especially interesting were the white wind sock-shaped garments. They looked like single leggings, about a yard long, wide at the top and tapered to ankle size at the bottom. I still don't know how they were used. I do remember the goose pimples I felt whenever a nun's habit touched me as she brushed against me, walking down the aisle in school.

Sister Carlotta was an excellent teacher, particularly of grammar and arithmetic. I became her ace student, always basking in the prestige of being the one selected to go to the blackboard to spell, diagram a phrase, or work an arithmetic problem. In my heart, I still thank Sister Carlotta for emphasizing those subjects. This foundation, constructed with the early help from my sister, Maybelle, gave me an edge in high school where the English teacher, Mr. John Burke, used me as his 'reliable' source whenever there was a grammatical question.

Later, in business college, it helped me win many 'battles of the words' with our Business English instructor, Ms. Eileen Barrett—a University of Wisconsin graduate and prodigy of *the* Professor Robert Aurner, head of the English Department at that time and author of our textbook.

I knew she was fond of me but, when it came to a personal duel, she would throw down the gauntlet and expect to be the victor. Despite the fact that I knew she was brilliant, I had the nerve to challenge her in class if I suspected she had used a word in an incorrect tense. She would retaliate by picking up the phone on her desk and dialing the local library for a decision. The classroom was filled with dead silence while my classmates waited for her announcement of who was right. Most times, it was I, and that would evoke a wild hoot and applause.

In 1978, forty years after I graduated from parochial school, I married my second husband, a police sergeant I had worked with in a Chicago police district. We often went to Fond du Lac to visit my 90+ year-old father and my sister Tess and her husband. On one of these visits, Tess told me that she heard Sister Carlotta was still living and was now in a retirement home there.

It was exciting to see her after all those years. I hoped that she would remember me. I phoned the facility to make an appointment to see her. She greeted us in the waiting room and suggested we visit as we walked with her to the chapel. She walked briskly and eerily looked as well as I remembered her from eighth grade. My husband couldn't wait to interrogate her, "Do you remember Joan as one of your students?" She quickly reassured him, "Oh my, yes!" Then "Did she get all A's?" I held my breath waiting for her answer, "Yes, she was a very bright girl." With that, I gave my husband a nudge in the ribs as if to say, "See, I told you so." I marveled at the fact that she remembered me at all.

Parochial students were rewarded for their good grades or good deeds, with holy pictures and medals. My collection of such holy pictures had notations on the back that were made by the nuns, "for horseradish", "for a case of beer", "for a dozen squabs". The latter was a delicacy, to be sure, but the thought of it now reviles me.

How does one raise squabs? In our instance, my father built nesting boxes, attached to the walls inside the upper level of the barn. There was a hole on the exterior side of the wall for the adult pigeons to enter, lay their eggs, and then hatch their young.

There was a hinged cover on the nesting box to monitor their growth and to 'harvest' them when they reached market size. I had to walk a narrow barn beam to get them, then individually hand them to my father standing on the hay below.

My parents would dress them, give them as gifts to friends or prepare them for our own consumption on a special occasion. Each diner would have an individual roasted, stuffed squab. In retrospect, it disgusts me to even think about it which others touted as a gourmet experience. But, then, I guess it's comparable to dropping live lobsters into boiling water, and yet enjoying a surf-and-turf dinner.

(Joan-as a toddler sitting on a lawn with 2 puppies)

"Joan with two puppies on the farm's lawn"

Inside the "little red schoolhouse"

"Bernice Steiner, Teacher - (last person, last row)
Joan - (second from right, middle row)

Jakob Joos Steiner
(circa 1865)

J.J. Steiner's family

Campbell Hotel
1700-02 S. State St.
Chicago World's Fair
1933-1934

Mrs. Campbell, Joan Steiner, Susan Steiner

Ma and Pa in 1958 on their 50th
(Golden) Wedding Anniversary

Pa astride, "Thunder," registered
Holstein bull, (Gus Richter, handler)

"King", purebred Percheron stallion,
Pa's wedding gift to Ma

Ma in longjohns circa 1902
(very risque in her time!)

The George Steiner family (pre-Joan, 1925)

Pa and Ma sitting with (left to right, Maybelle,
Tess (standing) and Lillian

Lil and Walter's Wedding
Sister Lillian, bottom, right
Sister Tess, top, right

Typical 1930's pose

The Flapper Sisters

Tess

Lillian

My High School Graduation

Valedictorian-May 22, 1942

Heidi, the wonder dog! 1969-1982

Teddy, Belgian police dog

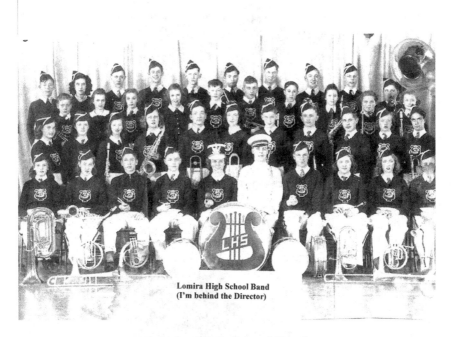

Lomira High School Band
(I'm behind the Director)

Lomira High School Band

(I'm behind the Director)

Rebuilt Farmhouse in 1912 after
Christmas morning fire

Maybelle and Frank Adashun standing in
front of our house in Lomira

Beautiful daughter Barbara at age 36

Joan at age 18

My favorite role "Honey Bun"

Husband: Sgt. Willard E. Kleppe
19th Chicago Police District
Last day on the job
1952-1985

RICHARD J. DALEY, *Mayor*
JAMES B. CONLISK, JR., *Superintendent*

30 March 1972

Ms. Joan Wellander
1922 West Patterson
Chicago, Illinois 60613

Dear Ms. Wellander:

May I first apologize for not contacting you before you left the department. Needless to say, it is from a very selfish standpoint that I and many others are sorry to see you leave us.

However, it is easy to recognize that advancement, economics, and all the necessary things that go into making a comfortable life, has preference over anything else.

The Chicago Police Department has grown in its ability to address itself to the social problems that exist in all of our communities. One of the most important factor that is necessary to prove to the public, is our credibility, rather than rhetoric, in our concern for all levels of our citizens.

You, Joan, have been one of the leaders in helping us attain that goal. In your years of involvement, over and beyond your regular assignment, your effort has been one of the highlights of this department, and especially the Bureau of Community Services since its inception a few years ago.

As you are aware, much more so than I, there were many, many instances of your unselfishness in your time, and the spending of your personal money, and effort in showing those fine young men of the 019th District the many ways in which they can better their lives, and assuredly their own careers. And our city and its leaders benefited in the appearances of those youngsters under your direction in the many exposures given.

I will always be grateful to you, and wish you the very best of success that goes with your new employment. I must add that unless you come to visit us occasionally, we would be very disappointed.

With best regards.

Sincerely,

Samuel W. Nolan
Deputy Superintendent

SWN/n

152L

Letter from Chicago Police Superintendent Sam Nolan

Barbara and son Zachary (age 10) ringbearer
at Tom and Pam Wellander's wedding:
November 10, 1995

Barbara with sons Josh and Jake at
same wedding (November 10, 1995)

"Do It Yourself Sousa" Concert
in Mount Prospect, Il.

Joan, John Bourgeois, and Tom
Aboard Carnival Cruise Ship
Community Bands at Sea

"Gorillas in our Midst"

(Joan on the left, surprising the
'real' gorilla-gram guy!)

Harry Stuhldreher--
All-American Notre Dame
University Quarterback-1924

The Four Horsemen of Notre Dame,
Harry Stuhldreher, Elmer Layden,
Jim Crowley, Don Miller

The young Stuhldreher "Backfield":
(clockwise, starting from upper left)
John, Michael, Skippy, Peter

Joan and Albert Wellander
Married June 1950

Tom Wellander, Prince Ernst, Pam Wellander
Buckeberg Castle, Schaumburg, Germany

Spring Valley Concert Band
Krainhagen, Germany Music Festival
1996
With John Tenuto and Joan Kleppe on Trombone

Joan's Second Marriage
Willard Kleppe and Joan
September 17, 1978

My grandsons Josh, Jake and Zach
2002

CHICAGO POLICE-FIRE
THRILL SHOW

at Soldier Field

19th Police District Junior Patrol
A Capella Boys Choir
Joan directing the choir

Spring Valley Concert Band
A Community Band with a Mission

Tom and Pam's wedding reception
November 1995

Granddaughters Hayley and Morgan
(with their cute pup, Chloe!)

A Man Called Pa

Everyone who knew him called him "PA".. If anyone had a bloated cow or sick horse, or needed to build a fence called on Pa for help. He assisted his brother, Fred (commonly called "Doc") in castrating pigs. It was believed that pigs would gain weight and therefore would bring more money at the market.

Pa rotated his crops, adding minerals if the soil needed anything. Whenever I visited him with my children, he always had a project in progress that the boys could work on. One thing in particular was 'how to pound a nail'== something basic that would always come in handy.

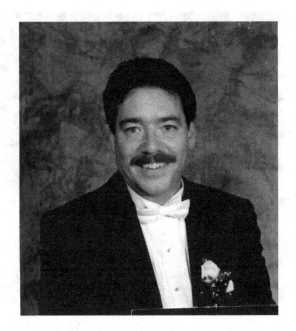

Tom, the groom

Al, the Best Man

Joan's homemade "alligator" coffeecake
Centerpiece at Fall Celebration

Majestic lion at Game Farm
in Brandon, Wisconsin

Fishing at Lake Puckaway in the '80's
Tom with a prize Northern Pike

Al-with a string of Walleyes

Tom and Joan, original founders of the
Spring Valley Concert Band

WORLD WAR II: EXCERPTS FROM
AN ENGLISH GIRL'S LETTERS

I don't recall with certainty where I got the names of pen pals, including a girl from Grantham, England and a young man from Sao Paulo, Brazil in the 40's.The only periodicals we received, while living on the farm, were the Sears catalog and a farm-oriented monthly magazine called "The Wisconsin Agriculturist." The following excerpts were taken from letters received from Marion Brooke, Grantham, England:

May 1941:

Our school system is different from yours. We attend an elementary school until we are 10 or 11, and then we go to a high school. A mistress is the same as a teacher, but a teacher can be either male or female, whereas a mistress is only female. A headmaster is only male. Also, we use "form" instead of "class". What is an honour role, please? ... I have never heard of playing catch with eggs. I suppose it was just an idea of yours, though!

July 1941:

You seem to be quite accomplished in music. You are a busy person, aren't you? Do you use a propelling pencil? I do, and I like them. A fortnight ago, we had a talk on French music by a Free French officer. Every now and then he would give a short summary in English which was nearly as hard to understand as the French.

September 1941:

I received the birthday card and lovely presents this morning. Goodness! You must be a genius. The apple pip necklace was a jolly good idea. Your last letter only took 1 month to get here (because it wasn't censored.) Letters from America have been censored and have taken 5 weeks. I did not have a party for my birthday, to not be extravagant in war time.

November 1941:

I'm sorry that I cannot send you a present, but we are not allowed to send Christmas presents to America or Canada. I was getting yours ready when the order was issued. Your letters to me are a family and friends affair. Everyone is interested in your letters.

February 1942:

I'll tell you a yarn about the Nazi regime:

> Hitler and Goering were driving along an Austrian road and ran over a pig. To create a good impression, Hitler told Goering to go to the farmer, apologize, and pay him for the loss of the pig. A half hour later, Goering came out of the farm house, laden with farm delicacies/Hitler asked him how he got all those things. "Oh, I just went in and said 'Heil, Hitler, the swine is dead', and this is what I got!"

Here's another:

> A bruiser went into a public house and asked, "Anyone here by the name of Jones?" A little fellow stood up and said, "Yes, that's my name." The bruiser instantly knocked him out, and left. After about 20 minutes, his

pals brought him 'round. He said, "Has that bruiser gone?" His pals said, "Yes." The little fellow said, "Ha, ha, I put one over on him. My name isn't Jones!"

July 1942:

You don't know how much I enjoy hearing from you. I wish I could send you a little gift like you send me, but all unnecessary articles have been banned or controlled. There is a list of them in today's paper. There is also an article about what American troops will be doing in England today, and one photo shows an American soldier from Milwaukee.

August 1942

I am enjoying office work. I do the filing of ration cards, entering all details. Next week, I'm going to a place near Gloucester for a week's holiday where the scenery is very beautiful. It is a cathedral city in the west of England. Listening on the wireless, there is an account of a woman who captured a Nazi who came down by parachute in her garden. I'm listening to a broad-cast of "Warsaw Concerto." They said you haven't heard it much in America, so do watch for it.

The narrator said that you American women are fighting this war for the future as well as us.

November 1942:

Mrs. (Franklin D.) Roosevelt does get about. In our paper, she wrote her usual column, "My Day", all the while she was here. She was so conscientious about everything. She would not take anything because she said it would be taking things away from us.

How is college going? Tell me all about it.

<u>June 1943:</u>
"One of Our Aircraft is Missing" is a jolly good picture and was filmed about 40 miles from here because the country resembles Holland where the film was supposed to have taken place.

What a tragedy...the death of the Duke of Kent was...in England! The Duchess of Kent certainly had the war brought home to her, as hundreds of women have. It is very sad, especially leaving the eight young children fatherless. It gives us great pleasure when we hear that Americans have begun to take part in air operations from England.

<u>October 1943:</u>
Your distances are staggering. Fancy going 600 or 700 miles for 6 days. In England, we think a 200-mile journey is bad enough. It just shows you that your transport must be very much faster. Yes, our shoes are rationed. We have just so many clothing coupons allowed us, and we have to surrender a certain number of coupons for each article of clothing bought, which includes shoes as well.

A friend of mine, who lives in London, came to stay 10 days with me. On Saturday, we sold flags for Red Cross Aid to Russia. Dorothy and I went to the Peak District of Derbyshire for our holiday. I've never seen such beautiful country. Two scenes stick in my mind.

Last Sunday, England had a "Battle of Britain" when we thanked God for our victories in the winter of bombing that we endured. There were processions and special church services. Our parade was a jolly good turnout of Air Force, R.A.F. Regiment, Army, all Civil Defense services, youth services, etc.

January 1944:

Query: What exactly are sweet potatoes? I've heard of them but have never really discovered what they are.

July 1944:

I'll still keep writing, Joan. Never fear that I'll stop, even if you don't hear from me for a time. Our friendship is too grand a thing to let slide. Who knows? We might meet one day. How I'd love that! (Author's note: We did meet in September 1975, only 30 years later, when daughter Barbara and I flew to England.)

"D-Day"—what a day in my life. I had imagined we'd all be crazy with joy, but no such thing happened. Everyone was terribly quiet, subdued, and occupied with their own thoughts. Everywhere seemed dead. There was scarcely any military traffic on the roads, and the air was void of the familiar hum of planes and, furthermore, the weather was very dull and rainy. The wireless programs were very touching, and I heard the most beautiful Church of England sermon ever, that night. Everyone sang with such fervour, and the prayers came from the depths of their hearts.

November 1944:

How lovely for you to be at the University of Wisconsin. Do you still like it? All the things you do, such as working and attending college as well. It beats me! I have enough to do with one job. Here's wishing you and yours a Happy Christmas, and may God grant us a victorious New Year.

April 1945:

Isn't the news wonderful?! The Allies linked up right across Europe. The Russians are in Berlin. Himmler has offered peace terms to the Anglo-American powers. Italian patriots are rising in northern Italy. The Pacific war is going well, and the San

Francisco 'Peace' Conference has begun. I've seen quite a few prisoners of war back home, released by the advancing Allies. That certainly must be a wonderful feeling, especially after being treated in the way they have by the Germans. The horror camps that have been brought to light are ample proof of what utter beasts the Germans are.

August 1945:

Apparently, you're under the impression that the mail still takes a month or more to get here by sea, whereas it's a matter of 2 or 3 weeks now. I'm afraid I'm not conversant with the American language. Just what are "duds"? I won't tell you what I think they are, in case I make too much of a bloomer!

I've managed to write all the much before mentioning the really good news. I still can't believe that the WAR's really over! Wow, did we lose some sleep over the V-J Days! The main event was a huge torchlight procession through the town of Beacon Hill (where huge beacons were lit in days gone by) to light a terrific bonfire. There were thousands of people up there, with fireworks exploding everywhere, community singing and dancing. It was great fun!

September 1945:

I had a very nice birthday, useful gifts and pretty cards. Presents included a smashing pair of silk pyjamas (pajamas, to you). Last weekend, I went up to London—saw a lot of really interesting things, including the fly-past of hundreds of fighters in commemoration of the "Battle of Britain", a big all-Services parade, and a German rocket (a V-2). Goodness, Joan, they are immense. I also saw London lit up at night. It was lovely!

Both of us were 16 years old when we started our 'pen pal' communication. As I reviewed her letters, extracting bits from them (always 8 pages long), I was still impressed with her perfect spelling, grammar, and, above all, her vocabulary and conversational style.

LETTER AND SONNET
FROM SAO PAULO, BRAZIL

During the same era as above, I received an articulate, literate, beautiful communication from a 20-year-old young man from Sao Paulo, Brazil—consisting of a beautifully penned letter in nearly perfect English and grammar, along with an eloquent, and romantic sonnet written in Portuguese and translated into English. The envelope had five 'examined by' inked censor stamps on the envelope. This was the first and last communications ever received from him:

The Letter:

February 12, 1942

Dear Joan,

I wish this letter may reach you in health and happily. I am well. How is your family?

Joan, you can't guess how glad I was when your letter reached me. You sent me a nice letter, a very nice one! Such dates. I can never forget, no! I can't! Never! (Author: *I have no idea, then or now, what dates he refers to—social or calendar?*)

Joan, now I am having school holidays. Are you having them, too? The classes will begin on next 10th of March. We have three months of school holiday. Have you the same? Joan, I want to thank you for the adjectives that you called me by. I thank you very much! I think I am not worthy.

It's a kindness from you.

Joan, now Carnival is "about to come". Carnival here in Brazil is wonderful! In Rio, it's very funny. It begins on 15th next. Carnival in Rio is the most beautiful of this world. Dear Joan, it is, indeed, very beautiful.

Joan, I've two sisters. I'm the only boy. My older sister is 20. and she's already married. She has a beautiful child. It's a girl. She is called Maria (Mary). Her child is called Etel. My youngest sister is ten years old. She is very beautiful. She has great black eyes, brown hair. She is brown of color. She's a very beautiful girl! Hear me, Joan. I am not saying this because she's my sister but, as we must say the truth, I said it!

Herewith, I send a little picture of my sister. It was taken by me at home when she'd had her First Communion, so that it does not look so beautiful.

I send another "soneto" to you, written in Portugese and in English because I don't remember which one I have sent you. Moreover, I have written so many, and it's very hard to find 'such one' out! Right now, I send the translation of this one; however, I can't make them rhyme in English. As you know, it's very difficult "to make a rhyme" idiomatic phrases which belong to "such a language"—there will not be any sense. However, I translate better English into Portugese than Portugese into English.

Here, included, I send a postal (postcard) from Sao Paulo to you. When I go to Rio, I'll send postals to you. I won't forget it. This time yet, I send my latest picture to you. I am writing that you send me another 'snapshot' of you, will you?

You're quite right in saying so. We must feel proud of our nationality. I agree with you. Joan, I wish you a happy year in your study and in everything that you may desire! As for your eyes, they are, indeed, very beautiful as you must be beautiful, too. (Author: I never got another letter after sending him a photo!) You must be "The Queen of blue eyes." You must put many hearts down! Will it not be so?

Joan, you ought to study singing. You already know how to sing, but you must study it thorough because singing is wonderful. It's a divine gift which not all persons have it. I like singing very much; however, I have a horrible voice. My voice does not help me. My congratulations to you! If you have an ambition, you must "take it" always up. Singing is wonderful. It's a divine gift which never all persons have it.

I like singing very much; however, I have a horrible voice. My voice does not help me! My congratulations to you! If you have an ambition, you must "take it always up", dear Joan.

Do you like to attend balls? I, from time to time, like to go to balls.

You are right again in saying that we are very far, and we are strange, too; but, as you know, it seems to me, I know you a long time ago!!

We had the same wishes—it was to have correspondence, and now, I feel very happy because, one dream of mine became true. I feel very happy.

You said you don't know how to swim. Would you like to learn, with me? I'd heartily teach you!

Joan, you said that your letter would be boring to me. On the contrary, I thought it was very nice and interesting. I read it over and over. Joan, your day must be a very clever one, is it not? I understand what you say. Unhappily, I can't say the same because I have none.

Joan, we celebrate Christmas in the same way as you do: "All in all, a gay time for all." However, we have not any snow, but a hot weather because at this time, it is summer.

Joan, you must lead a beautiful and nice life. Moreover, you live on a farm which is yours. There you may contemplate nature, and it's so beautiful. I do like riding horses, but here it's very hard because I live in the city; however, when I go to the country, then I have no time.

Joan, may I ask you any questions? Have you a sweetheart? What do you think about love? Love, for me, is the most beautiful and abstract thing of our life, is it not?

Joan, I am going to finish this letter; however, I am thinking about you. Eagerly, I am waiting for your reply. Remember me to your family. My kindest regards to you.

Sincerely, a Friend from South America, J. P. Guedes

* * * *

LIFE-CHANGING YEARS

A Time of Challenging Decisions

<u>1941:</u>

Like most people who recall where they were on December 7 of that year, I remember exactly where I was and what I was doing. Our friends, the Richter family, had come from Milwaukee to spend the day visiting us on the farm. The father, Gus, was a most pleasant person who loved my parents as if they were his own. He had arrived from Germany a few years earlier to escape the Nazi regime and worked as a hired hand for my parents until he married and moved to Milwaukee.

On that fateful day, he and my father decided to go into town for some supplies, and I tagged along in the back seat of our 1938 Chevy sedan. We were driving down the country road when the news came over the radio that Pearl Harbor had been attacked. I remember the exact spot on that road when we heard the shocking news report. We were stunned with disbelief. I thought of my cousin, Gertrude, who was married to a Navy Lieutenant Commander, living in Oahu with their two small daughters. She arrived in the States soon after to stay with her parents (my Uncle Joe and Aunt Mary) in Mayville (WI).) Every day, when that town's noon siren was blown, the little girls thought it was an air raid warning and ducked under the kitchen table.

<u>1942:</u>

I finished my senior year as valedictorian and won a coveted scholarship to Fond du Lac Commercial College. I had my first real job that summer as a waitress to earn room and board, and living away from home for the first time, at age 16. Those were challenging days to morph into adulthood overnight. I panicked when a bus load of Army recruits invaded that small restaurant called "Happy's", and I was the only waitress to handle that crowd.

When I turned 17 on August 22 that year, I left Happy's to work at a larger, well-known restaurant, "Schreiner's", on the other end of town. They had the best home cooking in town: Mrs. Schreiner came in early every morning to bake cloverleaf dinner rolls from scratch. Marie Tennyson was the pie baker as well as a chef. Doris was another full-time chef who prepared everything perfectly: especially the 'spare kraut and sauer ribs' as one old-timer called it, and who always ordered 'p-y-e' for dessert. I was the speediest waitress they had—because I never used a pad to write down orders. I had a knack of memorizing each order according to the customer's face.

<u>1943:</u>

I graduated Magna cum Laude from the commercial college in July 1943, thereupon going still further from home, taking a secretarial position with a corporate office in Milwaukee.

<u>1944:</u>

In the summer of 1944, after a year of secretarial work, I decided to attend the University of Wisconsin. Again deciding to work for room and board, the housing bureau confirmed that I could have such a position at the home of Harry Stuhldreher, legendary quarterback of the Four Horsemen of Notre Dame, and his family—wife Mary, and sons Harry "Skip", Jr., Michael, Johnny, and Peter, who became the loves of my life. Academically, I chose Journalism as my major.

<u>1945</u>:

At the start of my second year, I changed my major from Journalism to Music Education. In November, my sister Tess finally divorced her abusive, drug-addicted alcoholic husband. It was a 'first' in the family and would have been more difficult for my parents to cope with if it wasn't a physical hazard for her to stay with him. Being Catholic delayed her decision but, after humiliation and threats of bodily harm, it was time for her to start a new life. It had been years since she had worked as a bookkeeper, but she found employers who admitted being fortunate to have her in charge of the office—the books and finances for the next 30 years.

<u>1946</u>:

That summer, my parents moved from the farm to the city of Fond du Lac, where they bought a two-story "Fond du Lac Square" style house. It had a bedroom and half-bath on the first floor for their convenience, plus four bedrooms and full bath on the second floor. It had a finished attic and basement, at $6,500. The price was reasonable, but the house needed deep cleaning. It had previously been rented to a family of ten (three generations), and it was the third generation (a four-year-old girl) who did the cleaning!

When Ma and I washed the walls before moving in, we tied rags around our forearms to catch the rivulets of mud that ran down our arms. All of the hardwood floors were obviously water soaked. When we got settled and all cleaned up, remodeled, painted, floors sanded and varnished, my dad decided to have a garage moved in from the country, up our driveway shared with a neighbor, to be placed beside the existing one-car garage.

There were only inches to spare on either side between the two houses. I was amazed that my dad could engineer such an impossible feat, backing it up and putting it in place. My mother and I couldn't watch the tricky move. We said, "Just let us know when it's done."

The city looked a lot different living there instead of just visiting it during the past twenty years. I was anxious to find a job. I went 'cold' to the office of a manufacturer of tents, awnings, soft-side luggage, and cheerleader uniforms. I walked in and said I would like to apply for a secretarial position. It kind of 'threw' the office manager since she knew no such job had been advertised, but she gave me an application form anyway. A bespectacled, gray-haired, well-dressed gentleman emerged from his glassed-in office. He didn't ask any questions, except for my name, and escorted me to his office. All of the employees in that wide-open office stopped working and looked at the two of us with wide-open eyes. It was as if E. F. Hutton had spoken.

He was the president of the company who said he had not had a secretary for the past twenty years because, admittedly, no one ever met his requirements. He went on to say that he started out as an errand boy for the company and worked his way up to president of the board. He said he needed someone who knew grammar and how to spell to 'make him look good' to the board of director 'big wigs' who come from Milwaukee once monthly for meetings. (Like the line in *"Chorus Line"*) I said, 'That I can do." I started there the next day.

The company sold wholesale and to individuals, and also had a direct mail operation. Girls in the 'boiler room' spent their whole day addressing envelopes. He asked me to work with them for one whole day, to show them that I wasn't just 'frosting' on the cake, that I could work as hard as they did. That meant I would have to address 1,000 envelopes in one day. I met the quota and went home with the worst backache I ever had—even worse than when I had to pick potatoes all day in a stooped position in the field. Pa volunteered to give me a rubdown with his favorite potion: horse liniment. It was just what the doctor ordered!

1948:

A year of travel—in February with my parents and soon-to-be fiancé to Florida; in July with my sister Tess to the East Coast. In December, a surprise engagement to my first husband, Al Wellander--father of my three children.

The Courting Period and First Marriage

Al and I dated for four years, alternating a commute between Fond du Lac where I lived and Chicago, his home town, every two or three weeks. Although he had spent four years in the Navy, as a radio operator/decoder aboard a destroyer in the South Pacific, he never spoke about anything related to his tour of duty or action in WWII. He also never spoke about his habits and experiences before and after the war.

As I was thinking about marriage, I believed that, if you have a happy childhood, brought up in a home with loving parents, you expect that's the way your marriage will be. Although this was the kind of background both of us had, I never imagined our marriage would fail. It wasn't until after our wedding that I learned he had been an alcoholic since he was fifteen years old. His relatives avoided any mention of his drinking behavior, thinking that marriage to me would change him. Back then, alcoholism was not treated as a disease. It was believed a person could easily quit drinking.

The Ill-Fated Wedding

I had misgivings about getting married as the date came closer. I thought it might be just a case of the 'altar jitters'. All arrangements had been made. The invitations were mailed; the bridesmaids were chosen. As suggested by my Matron of Honor, my sister Maybelle, the female attendants would wear their previously-worn bridesmaid dresses of pastel color. I didn't care enough to object.

The hall was reserved which included a bartending service for a total of $15. Al and I completed the pre-Cana counseling at my local parish. My mother suggested that she and I look for a bridal gown downtown where ridiculously low prices were advertised to clear inventory. We bought one at $5 and one at $1. My mother combined them: the $5 satin gown with the $1 appliquéd lace one that had a long train. The night I finished sewing the satin-covered buttons down the back, I went downstairs to show my parents. Much to everyone's embarrassment, I opened their bedroom door to find them in a compromising position. (One's parents?!!) Oops!

My mother's sister, Rose, fashioned a flower girl's dress to match my bridal gown for her little daughter, Dorothy. She also hand-sewed a double-ring patchwork quilt as a wedding present. It was remarkable how she could do such painstaking sewing when, at the same time, she had to do all the farm work—plowing, planting, spreading fertilizer, doing the morning and evening milkings, plus cook for her family of 5 children and husband.

Her husband, Jake, wasn't able to do the farm work because of losing his left arm in a freak accident the previous fall. While using a corn shredder to cut up the cornstalks and blow them into the silo, his arm got caught in the stalks and was pulled forward by the machine's worm gear. He could not reach the mechanism to shut it down. It had already shredded his arm up to his elbow. He reached in his pocket with the free hand and used the pocket knife received as a Christmas gift from Maybelle, his godchild, and severed his own arm close to his shoulder.

June 10, 1950

Al and I were married during a High Mass at St. Joseph Catholic Church in Fond du Lac. Our reception was held at the American Legion Hall, starting at noon right after the ceremony, and lasted until past midnight, treating the guests to three meals—noon, evening, and late evening. Alphonse Buerger and his orchestra played all evening, after the evening meal to midnight.

My mother did her own catering for the all-day reception: chicken and trimmings for the noon meal, and baked ham with fixings for the evening meal, and left-overs for the late night snack, for about 150 guests. Even though she insisted on doing so, I should never have let her. She did all the cooking and baking but had some women friends do the serving.

My parents also provided the overnight accommodations at their house for the groom's parents. Their sacrifice, especially Ma doing all that work at age 65, was undoubtedly the carry-over from the Depression era and the many years they were in frightening debt due to tragedies over the years on the farm.

I always felt guilty knowing they deprived themselves of the niceties in life, yet gave so generously in helping their children.

The Honeymoon Sweet?

I had made reservations at a resort in Door County right on the bay. I knew within the first twenty-four hours that I made a great mistake in marrying Al. Besides drinking heavily, he ridiculed my virginity in public the second night, telling an older woman at a bar about my sexual inexperience. All I could think was: *I saved myself for this?*

At the end of the week, we traveled to Chicago to make a temporary home with his parents and a young teenage brother who still lived at home. It was an uncomfortable arrangement. My husband stayed out every night after he left work at the drug store when it closed at 10:00 P.M., coming home during the wee hours after stopping at the local tavern after work until it closed.

I would have given up after one week but, being a Catholic, I felt I was married for life, with or without him, and optimistically hoped he would change in time. His family later admitted they had withheld information about his drinking behavior because they hoped he would reform, that marriage would change him. It never does.

After a couple of months, we moved into a one-bedroom apartment above a cigar store in the neighborhood. I got a secretarial job at Sears, Roebuck and Company headquarters at Homan and Arthington. Al was still working at the drug store for 50 cents an hour, or $20 per week. I earned $50 per week and paid all the bills because Al drank and/or gambled away all of his earnings at the neighborhood tavern. Friday night was poker night, probably because most people got paid on Fridays. One night, I decided to pull a 'Lucy Ricardo' on the men-only game by stopping in, and accepting an invitation from one of the guys to sit in.

I could hardly contain myself when I saw the expression on the guys' faces as I pulled up a chair, hoping they would not be able to see apprehension in my face. I was the only female to ever sit in with these cronies. I was lucky enough to win a few big pots, and left as unobtrusively as I had entered.

Sears Parent Offices:
<u>August 1950</u>

I rode the Kedzie streetcar to work, learning to jump up on the back step, grab a post, and pull myself up to the inside of the car—sometimes lucky enough to get a bench seat at the rear of the car. After a few trips, I noticed that most of the riders were on the same schedule as I. In fact, one man always seemed to find a spot to stand in front of me and tried to wedge his knee between mine. I cured him of that perversion by hiding a 6" long hatpin under a newspaper on my lap. He never sought me out again after running his knee into it.

The office manager of Plumbing & Heating parent department of Sears was Mary Rigney, sister of a former Chicago White Sox pitcher, Johnny

Rigney—husband of Dorothy Comiskey of the famous Comiskey Park family—now known as Cellular Field.

Mary was a sweetheart and appreciative of the talents I brought to the department. She was surprised that my husband's cousin, Evar Swanson, had also been a star White Sox pitcher some years previously. She volunteered to use her influence with the Comiskeys to hire my husband as a scout for the White Sox, knowing of his love and knowledge of baseball, but Al was not stable enough to even try.

Working in a Sears parent department was interesting to learn they had price checkers to compare their merchandise offerings with those of competitor Montgomery Ward. One such person, an older woman named Eva Cagle, was the right person for that job. She knew percentages. She walked around with a racing scratch sheet. Every time she got up from her desk, she called her bookie—and was so preoccupied that she would run into you, if you didn't dodge her.

The Move to Chicago's North Side

1952:

The opportunity to go into business on the north side of Chicago, to buy a home delivery branch of the Chicago American daily newspaper became available. My father helped to finance the deal. We bought it, hoping it would be a move to motivate Al. Accordingly, we moved to a north side apartment to be closer to the business. I continued working at Sears because I loved my job and the people I worked with.

There was a young, attractive girl in our department whose promiscuity resulted in a pregnancy with her married boss. She felt she had no choice but to abort it which, at that time, was illegal. At her request, I accompanied her to an undisclosed location on Wabash Avenue where there was a waiting room filled with girls and women who had appointments for abortions—literally, a 'butcher shop.'

It was an unwise decision, but I let her recuperate at our apartment. She told her parents that she was staying with me to help me. Thank goodness, there were no complications; she pulled through it all right. But the faces of all those brutalized girls haunted me for years.

1953:

In December, I organized entertainment for the department's Christmas party. I wore a beautiful white, hand-knit sheath dress. I was thin and shapely then to do it justice. Just as I was about to begin the show, I got unexpected severe cramps. It turned out to be a miscarriage, but I didn't tell anyone about it.

1954:

I couldn't believe what really had happened and didn't see a doctor. I was so ignorant. The next month I was pregnant again, contrary to what a specialist had advised earlier —that I would never be able to have children. In fact, he warned that a pregnancy could be fatal for me and/or a child. On October 30, 1954 I gave birth to my son, Tom, in Chicago's St. Joseph Hospital after almost twenty hours of labor.

The hospital's post-natal care was antiquated. There were no in-room bathrooms. We had to shuffle down the corridor to a community bathroom where there were big pitchers of a diluted bleach or Lysol mixture that we took to a stall and poured it over our stitches. Ugh! Such a delightful conclusion to the long walk where I nearly fainted from weakness and pain. In that era, new mothers could stay six days in the hospital. I needed every one of those days.

When I brought little Tommy home, I felt very isolated in the apartment. I knew no one on the north side, and my closest relatives lived 150 miles away. I didn't leave the apartment to go anywhere for almost a year. Tommy had colic and cried from about midnight to eight o'clock in the morning. His dad had the car all day and usually came home drunk about three in the morning, so he was of no help. In fact, he'd swear

at us from the bedroom as I paced the floor, "Can't you keep that d...
kid quiet?"

I was frazzled from no sleep, from the spousal abuse, and my ignorance
about taking care of a baby. I had never even held a baby before. I
carried a towel on my shoulder to wipe the nervous perspiration off
my face. I was so afraid of something happening to Tommy. When he
was awake, I'd put him in a buggy so I could bring him anywhere in
the apartment to be near me, whether it was the kitchen, living-room,
or bedroom. When I had to go to the bathroom, I wheeled him to the
door to observe if he was breathing. I couldn't stop looking at this little
miracle. I kept saying to myself, "Isn't he beautiful! Isn't he a miracle!"

He was nearly a month old when I finally called the hospital nurse,
admitting I had not given him a bath since coming home from the
hospital. She asked, "How old is he?" I thought she'd jump through
the phone when I answered, "a month". She showed up the next day
and was helpful in a comforting, consoling way. From then on, I had
confidence and delighted in giving him a daily bath.

The days were sweet, but the nights were long and weary. Television
signed off at 1:00 A.M. Nothing helped him from crying. There was
no one to talk to; no one to help. There was nothing to do but walk
the floor all night. I became depressed which I now believe was post-
partum depression, although it was not recognized or labeled back then.

<u>1955</u>:
Tommy was six months old when I realized I was pregnant with my
second child, again disproving the Fond du Lac doctor's prognosis. My
father insisted we look to buy a house because he said, "an apartment
is no place to raise a child."

The House at 1922 West Patterson

<u>1956:</u>

I was apprehensive about buying a house, considering my husband's on again/off again drinking bouts—knowing my father would be investing his life's savings on our behalf. We couldn't find a house in a decent residential neighborhood for $10,000 or under, the ceiling established by my father, but he okayed $16,000 for the purchase of the Victorian frame house at 1922 West Patterson—a street of first and second generation owners.

It was the second oldest house on the block, built between 1900-1910. It had hardwood floors on the first and second stories, a 14'x 32' living-room, 14'x 20' dining-room (which we shortened to 14'x 14' to accommodate a full bath on the first floor), and a 10'x 10' kitchen. There was a large hall on the second floor, hosting four large bedrooms, a full bath, and an enclosed stairway to a finished attic. It had a full but unfinished basement.

We moved in during a blizzard on January 26, 1956. My second son, Alan, was born a month later on February 27—a whopping 10 lbs. 2 oz. darling of the nursery.

He could hold his head up without support shortly after his birth. The nurses put him in a flowered kimono to easily identify the largest baby in the nursery at the time, for fathers who asked, "Where is that little football player?"

Al visited us once at the hospital when I could tell he was drinking more heavily than ever—too far gone to realize that he was given another beautiful son.

I couldn't sleep at the hospital. All I could see in my mind's eye was Tommy's face in the front window, waving to me as I left for the hospital. I couldn't wait to go home to show him his beautiful brother.

Alan was only a few months old when his father stayed away from home for days at a time. He said he had stayed at a fellow's house for an all-night poker game. My father-in-law decided to get to the truth of what was going on. He took me along to visit the tavern frequented by my husband, located across the street from our newspaper branch office. I stayed in the car, shaking with nervousness. My father-in-law learned that my husband was involved with a woman patron. When my father-in-law told me the facts, my whole being seemed to turn to ice—a feeling of numbness I had never known before. My life collapsed in that moment. It felt like I had just been thrown off a cliff. Foreseeing a future of being a single parent, I prayed for the strength to take care of my children.

As I took stock of my personal appearance, haggard from worry and lack of sleep, out of shape from having babies too close together, not having help with the children, nor finances to have my hair done or buy becoming clothes, my self-image was at an incredible low. I imagined that my husband had found a beautiful, shapely blonde, who could give him the attention that I couldn't. I might then understand why he strayed.

1957:

The year that followed was one of turmoil, promises, reconcilement, permission for a legal separation, and the news that I was three months pregnant with a third child. I felt worse when I met Al's paramour, a foul-mouthed woman who prostituted herself to support both of their alcoholic habits. She was older than he. She was ugly and coarse. It was humiliating that he gave up his family for that. When she found out I was pregnant, that he had *cheated* on her, she retaliated with a physical confrontation with Al, in a jealous fit that spilled over to my house.

The two of them broke down my front door. I was nearly strangled with a drape that my husband ripped down and threw around my neck, while I struggled to protect my two young sons as both of the assailants threw glasses at the wall that shattered and landed in their playpen. Then Al lit matches that fell into my little sleeping sons' cribs. As I literally pushed the drunken pair out of the front door, I called the police. I proceeded with the divorce allowed by the Archdiocesan office on the promise I would not remarry while my ex-husband was alive. It was twenty years before I even considered it!

<u>1958:</u>

I received my prenatal care at a Chicago Park District branch where one of the nurses took a special interest in me and arranged for my delivery at a new northside hospital, still in the process of being built but finished through the sixth floor where the maternity wards and nurseries were located.

My baby was due on March 17 but, fortunately, arrived on March 16 which may have saved the lives of my two boys at home and my mother-in-law who came to stay with them while my young brother-in-law 'dropped me off' at the hospital.

When my father-in-law arrived at the house later that evening, he found his wife and my boys vomiting and headachy due to carbon monoxide fumes. He opened the windows and, investigating the clean-out door on the furnace, found a dead bird blocking the vent and a pile of soot that had been loosened in the chimney over time--the result of the furnace's earlier fuel conversion from coal to gas. I immediately called a company to install a stainless steel liner in the chimney.

I had a lustrous obstetrician, Dr. Bernard, who volunteered to deliver my baby while waiting for a pregnant mother of expected twins to be ready to deliver (the woman's husband being a partner of Roy Rogers.) How lucky was that, to have a luxury hospital where lobster was on the dinner menu, and the services of a noted obstetrician?!

The next morning, a nurse came into my room and said, "The father is here." My ire temperature rose as I was livid to think that my husband had the nerve to appear. I walked to the lounge area, prepared for battle, when I saw it was my favorite parish priest, FATHER Schackmuth. He had counseled me through some difficult times and had found a wonderful young girl, Christine, who wanted to live at my house as soon as I would come home from the hospital with baby Barbara.

A couple of days later, I visited the twins' mother who confirmed that Dr. Bernard was a really good obstetrician. Everything at that hospital, Louis Weiss Memorial, was first class. No more bleach or Lysol rinses for our stitches; we had sitz baths. I asked a nurse, "What is a *sitz* bath?" She explained, "We fill a bath tub with warm water, and then you SITZ in it!"

I began to feel strength in knowing my life was turning around. There is security in making and sticking with difficult decisions. I knew I could depend on myself.

Surviving the Darkest Hours

I tried to ignore the scary reality of my doomed first marriage as early as the second day of the honeymoon. When my newly-wed husband and I arrived at our Door County cottage, there was still evidence of winter: SNOW, in the middle of June! But that was more bearable for me than the icy treatment by my husband.

That night, after unpacking our clothes and taking a nap, we looked for a place to eat. We found a bar within walking distance of our cottage where we could get a sandwich. It was the only place open for business in the area. There was only one other couple in the place—a man and woman who appeared to be in their 40's.

The place was quiet. We sat at the bar and, as we waited for our hamburger, we ordered a beer. My husband went over to the jukebox to play a few tunes. As he came back, the woman reached out to him and beckoned him to sit next to her. I couldn't help hearing their cutting remarks about my sexual inexperience, my virginity, and her sarcastic advice that 'she (meaning me) will probably get better with time.' I hurtfully thought, 'I saved *it* for this, to be ridiculed?!'"

Her husband came over and sat next to me. I tried to ignore him as I cried inside. I felt mortally wounded, but I carried the pain silently for the years that followed, until this day, more than 50 years later. That pillar of pride that set me apart from many of my peers was smashed in a moment.

With not much to do in the area, Al suggested we take a ride in the rowboat that came with the cottage. It wasn't much fun for two reasons: the weather was really chilly, and the boat gave me chills because of the hole in it and the amount of water it was taking on. Would my fate be like Shelley Winters' in "A Place in the Sun"?

We cut short the honeymoon and went back to my parents' house en route to Chicago to settle temporarily in his parents' house. My mother confided in me that she had been concerned about an offhand remark made by Al's mother the day after the wedding: "We got the better part of that deal." My mother sensed there was truth in that statement. And there was.

Al and I lived at his parents' house for about six weeks as Al continued to work in his friend's drug store for 50 cents an hour and continued to stay out drinking every night until at least 1:00 A.M. I foolishly thought he would change when we found an apartment of our own in the neighborhood. But the few dollars he earned were spent on booze and the poker games at the same neighborhood bar.

We needed income for rent and food. I found a secretarial position at Sears and Roebuck's parent buying department headquarters to which I could take a streetcar. I thought I would have that job on a long-term basis, having been told that I could never have children but, if I would miraculously become pregnant, I would not be able to carry it full term.

THE DIVORCE: A POSITIVE NEGATIVE

The divorce marked the beginning of a new attitude and perspective on life. I appraised the situation as a jeweler might appraise precious gems. In this instance my three beautiful, healthy children were the precious gems—dearer to me than anything or anyone else on earth. When I looked at them, I realized what a tremendous responsibility I had assumed as a single parent: to nourish them with more than food, to raise them as loving, caring children to grow into adults of integrity.

I could have thought of my job as a burden; I thought of it as a blessing. I vowed to make the journey, as serious as it was, as much fun for me as it would be for them. I enjoyed every milestone in their lives; I was openly interested in everything they said and did. Listening to what children have to say is as important as is listening to adults. It serves to create lines of communication. I can honestly admit that I learned a lot from, and about, my children by listening to them.

There were poor but peaceful days and nights ahead. I stopped blaming myself for the failed marriage; I knew I had made every effort to salvage a marriage which should not have taken place at all. I rationalized that my children would be better off in *being* from a broken home than *living* in one where they would have been exposed to violence. For me, there was no more lying on the floor at the top of the stairs to protect my children from anyone breaking in. At last, there was peace.

Loving My Children and Their Friends

My door was always open to their friends. I got to know them and observe how my children treated them. We shared whatever food was on the table. My daughter's girlfriends were allowed to go through my boxes of costume jewelry and play 'dress up'. I catered to my sons' friends, for instance, by making a pair of stilts using an oak broom handle, and a right-angle iron to hold the footboard. Instead of drilling holes to attach them, I tried pounding a nail to hold them—not realizing the broom stick, being oak, was not penetrable. The nail went in crooked and, as I tried to pull it out with a claw hammer, the hammer slipped and came back to break my nose. I didn't black out from the pain; I had a 'white out'—not able to see but able to hear the voice of a little neighbor girl say, "That never happens to my daddy."

I resisted the urge to answer that. I recovered and proceeded to use a hand drill and finish the job successfully. It was the 'hit' of the neighborhood as my 10-year-old son, Alan, stood on the stilts, carrying a lightweight friend on his shoulders who wore a full-length raincoat that fell down to my son's shoulders—making it look like a tall man walking on stilts. They cleverly mastered the act very quickly.

I built a high-jump set-up in my backyard that could be adjusted for height. I was lithe enough in my 40's to easily clear any height the kids could make.

The neighborhood kids, I was told by the precinct captain (who opened $5 savings accounts for each one of them) that there were 47, would put on circuses. I helped by making clown costumes and furnishing my children's fire truck.

There were activities always going on at or in our house. As a den mother for Cub Scouts, I recorded their skits and silliness with my 8mm movie camera. We did a reverse-action comedic skit: whipped cream would jump back into the canister, spaghetti would exit their mouths in a stream to their plates, and a peeled banana would zip itself closed again.

I took some boys to an apple orchard to pick apples and eat apple cider doughnuts. A few weeks later, my old station wagon emitted the fragrance of a wine cellar. The boys had stashed and forgot the apples they secreted under the removable bench seat.

Kids came to our house to play piano, or would ask me to play for them. When my sons were studying the Mass in grade school, I made vestments for the class. One morning, a first-grade nun telephoned to ask if I could donate things for her to put in her Easter baskets (using discarded strawberry cartons). I made 70 popcorn balls, wrapped each one in waxed paper, twisted the ends and delivered them to her the same day.

There was one family on our block who let their young son and daughter out to 'graze' during the day. We were the poorest family on the block but always had food made from scratch. These two children would press their noses against the back screen door, "Zoanie (Joanie), what's you cookin'?" Invariably, I would invite them in for a bowl of chicken soup or a sandwich.

Children's Theatre

I wrote, directed, and costumed two original comedies: "Let Freedom Ring", based on Revolutionary days with a large Liberty Bell (fashioned out of an old lamp shade) hung high above the stage in St. Andrew auditorium where it was presented. The Patrick Henry character stood beneath it until he uttered the punch line which released the bell, dropped and enveloped him.

The other comedy, "Fractured Fairy Tale", a warped version of Rumpelstiltskin, incorporated scripted bloopers and a sheriff who spoke in rhyming lines. It was inspired by a south side preacher's sermon I heard on the radio: "What's all the hassle and rassle in the castle?" It was a successful shtick, with built-in flubs that children usually make on stage, plus a subliminal reference to the nerdy prince's sexuality. Surprisingly, I didn't receive any criticism, considering it was performed in a Catholic venue.

When a business area on Southport Avenue was being revitalized, and a parade held to bring attention to it, I happened to drive through the alley behind our church where I saw a pile of green satin stage curtains that had been thrown out.

I took them home and made a long dragon costume out of it, with a lamp shade for the dragon's head. My three kids were kind enough to walk in the dragon outfit while I led the parade as a prehistoric guide in a pith helmet. Entrants wishing to compete for prize money had to have a slogan. Ours was, "Southport won't be draggin' any more." Corny, but we won a prize, and in that costume I knew where my 'captive' children were at all times (and another lamp shade recycled!).

Young Barbara's birthday party at my house was creative but inexpensive. On one such occasion, I prepared a batch of bread dough, shaped aluminum foil into little loaf pans, and gave each guest a ball of dough—ready to rise—in the pans. When these miniature loaves had doubled in size, I put them in the oven to bake.

I sewed a white chef's hat and a blue vinyl apron for each child personalized with his or her name on it with a black marker. While the loaves were baking, I set up a cookie decorating table with little bowls of varied color frostings and sprinkles so they could 'paint' the cut-out sugar cookies I had baked for the occasion. Three boys from one family, who wouldn't eat bread at home without all the crusts removed, would not share their little loaves (brought home with them from my house) with anyone, not even their parents. That was a most successful event.

When my daughter was five years old, I read an announcement of a circus being sponsored by a civic organization. I went to buy the inexpensive tickets for my family. I observed the organization had a very inefficient way of handling ticket orders. On a whim, I wrote to the organization, suggesting a solution. I got a call from the board president of the organization who, coincidentally, was personnel director of WGN-TV. He offered me free tickets to the circus as well as a part-time job at WGN-TV.

That was the beginning of my return to the business world after a ten-year hiatus. It was wonderful to feel I was part of the outside world once again.

The Lake View Citizens' Council

I bought a '56 Ford for $50 (my very first car, at age 40) so that I could work half days, then pick up Barbara at kindergarten. The next year, when all three children were in school full time, I could pick them up after school and bring them to my office at the LVCC office. There they could do their homework or help fold flyers and seal envelopes. As a reward, I'd let my sons visit Woolworth's Five-and-Dime store to buy model cars to put together while they waited for me to finish my office work.

If I had to work past 5:00 P.M., the boss took all of us out to dinner. One time, he treated us to a dinner at a well-known Swedish restaurant, Ann Sather's, which is still operating today. It was wintertime. The boys hung up their heavy jackets on a coat rack at the entrance. When we claimed them on leaving, there was a puddle of water on the floor. Alan had 'saved' a snowball for future use that had, of course, melted in the pocket.

In 1967, when the funding for the LVCC started to dwindle, forcing my boss to leave, I was put in charge. I faced the possibility of receiving no salary. One of the board members, Commander John P. Fahey of the nearby police district station, came to my rescue. He said there was an opening at his office but required my taking a Civil Service exam. In spite of a horrendous migraine headache on exam day, I passed with flying colors and became his secretary.

Life at the 19th District (Town Hall) Police Station

I did not know what to expect in working at a police station. I had to deal with the 350 police officers, as they rotated on the three shifts. They were the finest men I ever met, and it was the best all-around job I ever had. I was in charge of the commander's correspondence, occasionally wrote speeches for his community appearances, checked police reports to commend civilians' cooperation, composed commendations for outstanding police work, sat in on interrogations to take statements, typed accountability reports for the vice squad and tactical team members.

The list of luminaries whom I met, and could refer to as real friends, during my tenure at the police station:

State Representatives John Merlo and Arthur Telscer
Chicago Aldermen John Hoellen and Joe Kerwin
Fathers Tom Byrne and Lucius Delire, pastors of Our Lady of Mount Carmel and Saint Bonaventure, respectively
George Mazarakos, Principal, Lane Technical High School
David O. Taylor, Personnel Director, WGN-TV
Judge Kenneth Wendt, Presiding Judge, Narcotics Court
Rev. George A. Rice, Pastor, Addison Street Baptist Church, Chairman of the 19th Police District Youth Committee, Chicago Police Department Chaplain
James B. Conlisk, Jr. and Samuel Nolan, Superintendents of Chicago Police
Pete Klein, Assistant Superintendent, Chicago Park District

When I had to deliver to, or pick up materials from, the board president at WGN-TV, I'd send little Barbara in as my messenger. The staff loved to see her and would give her left-over prizes from the Bozo's Circus program contests.

Best of all, I had the privilege to assist Officer Friendly 'Uncle' George Zaranti as he made the rounds of schools. I was privileged to answer the hundreds of letters he received every week from the first-through-fourth graders of schools he visited. Excerpts from those letters form the bulk of my "Kids 'n' Cops" book published by iUniverse, Inc. in 2006.

As could be expected, there was never a dull moment, especially with my special colleague, Regina Bryant, the only other girl in the office, who happened to be African-American. She gave me a dose of courage and self-confidence I never knew before. We were a pair of devilment co-conspirators. She *made my day*, every day.

She seldom drank anything alcoholic, but, if she did, it was Green Chartreuse—not for sissies. She brought a bottle of it to my house when my relatives visited from Wisconsin. One sip choked them.

Reggie had lost three fingers on her right hand, between her thumb and little finger, in a factory shop accident when she moonlighted to help support her son, but that didn't alter her beautiful, sweeping, artistic penmanship nor her sense of humor.

Both of us had to sign out of the office one afternoon to see an X-rated movie out of curiosity because we would bring disfavor upon ourselves and the Department if our identity as police department employees was publicized. The movie, "Wide Open Copenhagen" had been shut down a number of times but was now appearing once again at a local theatre. We gave in to a stupid urge to see how bad it really was.

The theatre was completely dark when we entered. We couldn't see where to sit, but we could hear the heavy breathing of men. We kept moving until we found a quiet spot. When our eyes adjusted to the darkness, we could see the small audience of men. Occasionally, during a torrid scene, we'd hear some groans. To sum it up, we could describe the whole movie as an oral encounter, so disgusting that we left after about twenty minutes.

One day, when our male co-workers stepped out of the office to go down to the first floor, Reggie lit an M-80 she took from her purse and whipped it down the corridor where it landed under an old-fashioned radiator with a resounding boom. They must have heard it downstairs in the squad room, but no one came upstairs to check on it. We were not as well-protected by the 'troops' as we thought we were.

Some mornings, both of us would arrive at the station at the same time and jockey on the street for the lone remaining parking spot across from the office. We'd get out of our cars and fake a shouting match. People in the nearby apartments would hang out of their windows to witness the action between the Black and White girls. It was hard to keep a straight face. I'd usually back off and find a different spot.

Reggie invited me and my children to visit her at her parents' home to see her collection of exotic pets, all confined to her bedroom: two 3' lizards and a giant African bullfrog in cages behind glass walls; a 6' Boa Constrictor and a Prairie Dog free to roam at will. She cleaned all cages every day so they were in immaculate condition. Her father finally gave her an ultimatum to get rid of the animals after the two lizards got loose one day. He tried to shoo them away with a broom, but one of them climbed right up the broom after him.

She related that, one night when she was in bed, there was movement in the mattress under her. On investigation, she discovered that the Prairie Dog had burrowed a hole in the under-side and, apparently, the Boa

Constrictor was trying to share his living quarters. Her parents were not happy about the new mattress getting ruined.

Reggie called the Lincoln Park Zoo and was allowed to donate the Prairie Dog, but somehow the Boa Constrictor had escaped to the outside world. She never found it. Imagine the surprise when someone did find it. Sometimes Reggie would come to work and show me the little skinny, sharp teeth of the snake imbedded in her arm.

While she still had the Boa, she kept a supply of live hamsters and white mice on hand to feed him. One noon, on our lunch hour, I accompanied her to a nearby supermarket to buy hamster food. Reggie was at the checkout counter, with a little old lady behind her. I was behind the little old lady who, seeing Reggie's purchase of hamster food, said, "My, my, how nice, you're buying food for your hamster."

Before Reggie had a chance to answer, I peered over the lady's shoulder and said, "Then she feeds the hamster to her pet snake", causing the little old lady to let out a squeamish scream "EeeeeUUUU".

It was a rare day when Reggie missed a day at the office. Without Reggie, the day was dull and seemed twice as long. She literally stirred up the dust of routine and, when the dust settled, something hilarious had occurred in the interim. Each day always played out in unexpected scenarios.

COMMANDER JOHN PATRICK FAHEY

Commander of the 19th Police District in Chicago, affectionately referred to as "Father" Fahey, became an outstanding mentor and advisor when I was in his employ in the 1960's—not only to me but also as a male role model to my three fatherless young children.

He was a most respected law enforcement official, honored with a brotherhood award by an ecumenical coalition of all religious denominations in the district and representatives from all indigent groups because of his unilateral attention given to the multi-ethnic population he served.

He was a loving husband to his 'bride' Veronica, and caring father of daughters,

Nancy and Mary, and son Patrick. Although it took some work on his part and mine, he eventually instilled a much-needed trait of confidence in myself. I had always thought of self-confidence as conceit. My 'conversion' to the real meaning made a great positive difference in my life.

A change of heart in his life, choosing to become a police officer instead of a priest was a blessing, indeed, for all whose lives he touched and protected. His mother may have been disappointed that he had chosen a different vocation, but, if she had lived to see the man he became, and the good he had done in his 38 years as a police officer, she would surely have approved his decision. His image and philosophy emulated that of a relationship between a shepherd and his flock.

He joined the Chicago Police Department in 1932 and was promoted to Sergeant in 1947 after serving with the Army in Panama during World War II. He was promoted to Lieutenant in 1954; he made Captain in 1959 and was assigned to the 19th (Town Hall) Police District as Commander. He passed away in April 1986.

During his tenure at Town Hall, he conducted classes in the public schools on police work and became actively effective in the community through innovative programs he established, "Bringing Up Father", stressing the importance of leading, not driving, their teens; and the "Junior Patrol" program for elementary school children (later adopted city-wide) to encourage youth to learn about and respect law enforcement. He said of his work with young people, "If I've kept one boy from stealing a car or one girl from shoplifting, the whole program has been worthwhile."

His advice to the men under his command who came to him with marital problems began with the suggestion that they should always refer to their wives as 'my bride'. It bodes better than referring to her disrespectfully as 'my old lady' which is negative and demeaning.

Speaking to young people in a language they could understand, he advised, "When another boy or girl dares you to commit a crime lest you be called 'chicken', tell that boy or girl that you'll still be a 'free' chicken when they are in the 'chicken coop' to stay!

Commander Fahey was a brilliant, honest and humble man, devoid of prejudice or pretentiousness. He was soft-spoken but firm, with a convincing countenance, persuasive manner, and a good sense of humor. His posture was that of a benevolent cleric, reflecting the years he spent in a seminary where, just prior to committing to final vows for the priesthood, he decided he might be better suited to be a husband and father.

The door to his office was always open and his heart ready to listen to anyone who entered, be it a child or an adult. Typical of most police officers, he had a special love for children, as evidenced by the innovative programs he created on their behalf, by the groups of children who visited him every day after school, and by his support of a boys a cappella choir which I founded as a volunteer. It gave him great joy to 'audition' grade school boys and then send them to my office to confirm their acceptance as a choir member.

He was a 'father' figure to these young admirers, many of whom came from single- parent or dysfunctional family homes, and that included my children and me as a single parent. My three pre-teen youngsters finally had a stellar role model in him as did I. He approved my eldest son's participation in the Department's 'Explorer Post', and arranged for my other son's gratis guitar lessons. Both boys also had an opportunity to make a training film for the Department. My daughter and I had a special privilege to have ballet lessons from his daughter, Nancy, a professional ballerina.

He was the anti-image of what a civilian might expect of a police officer. It was true that the only time the public meets law enforcement personnel is always under negative conditions—for a wrongdoing that. guilty or not, the civilian seldom wants to admit his or her own fault. They always find an excuse for their misdeeds and try to label the incident as being unfair. That's called 'human nature'—not wanting to own up to any infraction of the law.

My years at the police station, working among the 350 men, enlightened my children and me to the sides of police personnel never before realized. They have problems the same as any other citizens: bills and money worriesk illness of family members, problematic children, sleep deprivation, having to work a second job to make ends meet, arguments with family members or neighbors, or their own lack of rationality--the one issue that cannot be tested in the police academy training.

When civilians' salaries were frozen, I left the Department for the corporate world to seek a higher income to support my three children and myself. I left with the blessing and understanding of the Department and a healthy attitude toward men.

Years later, in a letter dated June 23, 1982, from retired commander Fahey, he sent me a copy of the biographic entry he submitted to a national publication in the search for a "Wonder Woman." This is what he wrote:

> *"More than one thousand boys of grammar school age were recruited by the personnel of the Town Hall police station. These boys participated in baseball, basketball, and football under the supervision of policemen. The purpose of organizing was to teach respect for the law and make them understand that no person is above the law, no person is below the law, and that every person has the duty to obey the law.*
>
> *Ms. Joan Kleppe worked in the Commander's office as a secretary. She was outstanding. She had a hunch that something was lacking in the Junior Patrolman organization. A hunch is nature's way of telling a person something, and it can provide creative insight. Very often, hunches are collections of facts stored in the subconscious mind. Who would expect a stenographer working for the City of Chicago would prove to be the most creative, innovative, and talented person in the community?*
>
> *She asked permission to organize an a cappella choir on her own time during after-school hours. Thank God, I possessed the foresight to realize the asset the choir would be to the community.*
>
> *After three months, the twenty-five boys who started on a singing career grew to a roster of ninety participants. The news that the boys choir was singing unusual police songs (parodies of popular standards) reached police*

headquarters where the boys sang at a special holiday program; also before Christmas Midnight Mass at St. Andrew Catholic Church; and at the Police/ Fire Thrill Show at Soldier Field—to name a few of the venues— in uniforms like those of patrolmen. This was the first and only choir in Chicago Police history. Ms. Kleppe tailored some of the songs to tell the community what to do when a crime is suspected or committed. Ms.Kleppe is to be commended

For her perseverance, forbearance, and foresight.

She is truly a noble person.

IMPROV AT CHICAGO'S SECOND CITY

This experience was so uniquely different and impressive that it deserves a chapter of its own. Barbara began taking improv lessons at Second City as part of her acting career progression. She made it sound so fun and challenging that I decided to join a class myself. We racked up some memorable times in the days and nights spend at Chicago's legendary improv theater, Second City, in 1977-78. Barb eventually completed four semesters there, and performed onstage in their Sunday afternoon children's show with other classmates. I filled in as a piano accompanist for the initial rehearsals of the children's show, but mostly enjoyed participation in the live improv classes. My teacher and director of the children's show was Jo Forsberg and Barbara's teacher was her daughter, Linnea.

What a feeling of euphoria to stand on the very stage where comedic giants honed their craft: the legendary John Belushi, his brother Jim Belushi, (who took a fancy to my beautiful daughter!) Shelley Long, David Steinberg (who I saw many years earlier and fortuitously told him he would be famous) Fred Willard, Bill Murray, Steven Kampmann, Tim Kazurinsky, George Wendt, Alan Arkin, and many more who went on to fame and acclaim. Amazing experience!

Barbara was invited to attend the farewell party for Shelley Long when she left Second City to audition in Los Angeles for a pilot TV series. The next time we saw her, it was on a little show called "Cheers".

Although I was 52 at the time, I didn't feel self-conscious about being twice the age of others in my improv group. That's what is great about improv--its being a common denominator for actors, where acceptance is taken for granted, regardless of age, color, ethnicity, or physical appearance.

In one incident of our being invited to a cast member's apartment, Barbara looked wide-eyed as I was offered a 'joint'. I tried not to look surprised, and took it into the kitchen where I found eager 'sharers'.

The most humorous fellow in my group was Steve Beshakis (John Belushi's best friend, frequently referred to in John's SNL skits) who seemed to enjoy partnering with me in outrageous vignettes. He broke the ice as he came into the building, dribbling an 'air' basketball. He told me that he had a night job as a server in a unique, themed restaurant in a western suburb called, "Aunt Teaks and Uncle Junques". Barbara and I went out there one night for dinner and where surprised to see that each booth's décor was different: one was a bathroom where the seats were toilet seats, for instance, and one was an open setting called 'the library'. That is where we sat, at a library table and the surrounding walls had shelves to display hundreds of books. It's the first time I ever left a $20 tip. That was considered generous in its time, in the 70's. I hoped that Steve would appreciate that we took the time to come out and support his 'other' career!

A LIFE LIVED WITH LOVE AND LAUGHTER

This is an overview of thoughts and events that could not be easily categorized and assimilated in any of the other chapters.

Growing up on a Wisconsin dairy farm was not dull. The daily drama of living so close to nature made life uncertain but exciting. There were no two days alike—some holding gloriously happy moments, some presenting life and death situations.

The Eclectic Visitors

We had a wide range of visitors. I am thinking of two far-removed characters who came to see us one summer:

> The 'goat man' who could be heard (and smelled) a mile away as he drove up in a wagon completely adorned with hanging pots and pans. It was a mystery how he found our remote location farm, or why he would want to. We couldn't ascertain how old he was. We felt sorry for the goats pulling the wagon and for the ones tied behind it. Although he didn't ask for a hand-out of food or money, my parents gave him some of each. He didn't hang around very long, and we never did know what his purpose was.

It reminded my father of a joke: *"A fellow stopped at a hotel with his goat, seeking an overnight accommodation for himself and his goat. The manager asked, "What about the smell? The fellow answered, 'Oh, he's gotten used to me.'"* That's what I thought of, how bad the goat man must have smelled, but I wouldn't get close enough to find out.

The other visitors were the millionaire owners of a department store with whom my parents exchanged social visits. I went along on visits to their house, occupying the time by playing with their dog while eavesdropping on the adult conversations. That couple met in the 30's when she was a buyer at Marshall Field's in Chicago, and he was a stock 'boy'—a step up from hauling manure in a wheelbarrow at the Chicago stockyards. He was happy to be doing any menial work, just to be in the United States, escaping the wrath of the Hitler regime emerging in Germany.

They were people of refinement and interesting conversationalists who made the visits enjoyable, even for me because ... I liked their dog!

Imagine how embarrassing it was for my mother and me when they showed up at the farm unexpectedly one summer afternoon. We had had a violent rainstorm the day before, knocking flat the rows of sweet corn in our garden. In order to save the crop, my mother and I worked barefoot in the mud, barehandedly packing mud around the base of the stalks to bring them to an upright position.

Just as we were finishing, a black Packard pulled up, bearing Mr. and Mrs. 'Perfect' and Corky, their dog. Ma and I looked at our grotesque mud-covered hands and feet, and our smudged faces. There was no way to clean up before greeting them. We would have to pass their car to get to the house entrance.

Before we had a chance to explain what we had been doing, little Corky escaped from their car and came running toward me in spite of their frantic pleas to come back to their car. They were obviously more concerned about the dog getting dirty than they were about appearance.

Sunday, the Best Day of the Week

On a dairy farm, there are always chores to do—beginning and ending the day on a schedule. Cows must be milked on schedule, morning and evening—Sundays and holidays included. Life revolves around that commitment. Sometimes we took time out to visit friends and relatives but, most times, spent the weekends at home—going to church on Sundays, hoping to have guests drop in for dinner, no reservations needed. The Sunday dinner usually featured roasted chicken, mashed potatoesl and gravy, gourmet-quality stuffing, home-made rolls, and angel-sunshine cake—an original creation concocted by my mother.

For me, it was a day I could wear a dress instead of over-alls. It was one day I didn't have to clean chicken barns or chop wood or mow the lawn. I did all that on Saturday. My peaceful times were spent teaching myself to play piano, crocheting doilies or a rug, embroidering pillow cases or decorating a blouse, or just lying on the lawn watching the clouds roll by.

Excitement ranged from weathering a cyclonic storm; having to ride four miles to school in a horse-drawn sleigh during or after a blizzard, bundled up under a fur blanket; getting to pet a newborn calf or a wiggly-legged foal; staying in the house while Pa grabbed the shotgun above the pantry door to shoot a rat in the chicken barn or setting off dynamite to clear a field of stumps.

A Time to Remember

Looking back, it was a time, when we had time, to enjoy the best things in life that were free. There was no television, microwave oven, automatic washer and dryer, no cell phones or computers, no internet or e-mail. Communicating was done by telephone, radio, in person, or by rural delivery mail.

How hard was it for women years ago to do laundry with a washboard in a large copper tub that also served as a bathtub? Ma made her own laundry soap using fat rendered from a butchered pig, combined with lye in a large black cauldron and boiled outdoors over a fire. She continued this dangerous chore for many years. I remember watching her stir the big black pot out in a field. When the mixture was 'ready', she poured it out, let it harden, scored it, and later broke it up into bars—the end product resembling Fels Naptha bars in color and density.

There were no cake mixes, no pizza, no fast food places. Many farmers did not have indoor plumbing or electricity as we did. Everything took longer and involved hard work, yet we had time to enjoy life and each other and, as is said, develop the fine art of conversation.

From DC to AC

In 1939, we received what was called the 'high line'—electricity supplied by a utility company rather than our Delco power plant operated on batteries. We had two such plants, no longer needed, which we advertised and sold to lake resorts in northern Wisconsin: one at Three Lakes and one at Lost Lake near Eagle River.

Pa, Ma, and I made two trips in a pickup truck, a little red 1933 Chevy half-ton, to deliver these units. I sat outside on an old car seat, securely snug with my back against the cab, enjoying the fresh air, and the scenerly we had just passed through.

We had such a good time with the owners of both resorts: the Blaeloch's at Three Lakes who entertained us in their residence and at local spots for fish fries. At Lost Lake, there were cabins as well as a big lodge house where there were family style dinners. At night, there were planned activities: Keno one night, parlor games on another, and nocturnal sight-seeing in a guide's vehicle. We saw plenty of deer and a porcupine whose quills stuck in a piece of wood that our guide tapped it with.

Our change to electricity source meant a change of all appliances: a Maytag wringer-washer to replace the washboard, an electric iron to replace the heavy solid ones heated alternately on the wood-burning kitchen range, a flip-flop toaster instead of removing a lid on the range and holding the bread with a fork over burning embers, and electric lights turned on with a switch instead of kerosene or gasoline-fueled lamps with wicks and lit with a match.

<u>A Puzzling Prejudice</u>

There was one thing that puzzled me as we traveled through the resort country but, at the time, I never asked what it meant. Many resorts that we passed had signs posted along the highway that read "Gentiles only". I thought they just wanted *gentle* people, no rowdies. I had never, ever heard that term before. It wasn't until years later that I learned it was anti-Semitic. How crude was that prejudice?

<u>Home Delivery</u>

When I gave birth to my first child, I thought of my mother having given birth to us four daughters—none of which were born in a hospital. We were born at home, perhaps with the help of a mid-wife, but now it seems incredible—considering the risks involved without professional help and resources available in a hospital.

There is another strange practice that I remember from my childhood: family members were waked at their home. My maternal grandmother lived on a farm with her daughter, my mother's sister. I recall going into the house and seeing my grandmother in a coffin in the parlor. That was scary to me. I imagine that's how children feel when they see any deceased person in a casket. In March, 2008, I attended the wake of my daughter's ex-husband, Chuck, who had died suddenly. He lie in an open casket. My four-year-old granddaughter's reaction made all of us smile as she asked her father, "Who's the guy sleeping on the couch?"

When Ma went visiting, to church, or to the doctor, she went by horse and buggy. Pa gave her a fiery, independent horse as a gift. It had been part of a pair, used to walking in one of the double tracks in the muddy path. When my mother used her singly on the buggy, the steed insisted on walking in one of the tracks. The buggy came close to tipping over several times as it clipped bushes and shrubs, and ran over boulders on the edge, while my mother was pulling hard on the reins and hanging on for dear life.

The Great Fire

When tragedy struck on Christmas morning in 1911, seeing their house on fire as they returned from church services in town, they dropped off baby Tess, nearly one year old, at the nearest neighbor. Ma saved her sewing machine by pushing it out of a second-floor window, accounting for the hole in the cabinet's back-side. She pushed out the upright piano on the first floor along with the wedding dishes and silverware. Everything else was lost, including her wedding dress and wedding photos.

My parents slept overnight at the neighbor's. In the morning, Tess's wet diaper was frozen to the wall. That's how cold the houses were in those days, with no central heat, just a pot-bellied stove in the parlor which did not radiate much heat to the rest of the house.

Cause of the fire was determined to have been caused by sparks emanating from the chimney, incinerating the roof. Pa and a crew of workers immediately cleaned up the devastation and began construction of a new house—designed by my father. It was a large two-story Colonial-style house (to me, a mansion) completed in 1912 as noted with completed date painted in large letters and numbers on a rafter inside of the attic. I looked at that marking every time I had to take things to or get things from the attic.

The first floor had a large kitchen, a small cloakroom with a lavatory to wash hands before meals, another small room called the 'kleine kammer' where we put cakes and breads to cool (also where behavioral lectures were given if we misbehaved.) On the other side of the kitchen was a large pantry with a sink to wash dishes. There was also a large den (where we had the piano, radio, sofa, and rocking chair) and a closet for 'good' clothes. The front half of the house hosted a large dining-room, living-room, and enclosed porch.

An enclosed stairway led from the kitchen to the second floor where there were four bedrooms with hardwood floors, and a full bath. From there, a closed stairway led to the attic.

My mother kept the house 'company ready'. Every surface that could be dusted was dusted every week. The floors were either washed or waxed, and the woodwork was kept in perfect condition with regular varnishing and polishing. When the stairway was varnished and had to dry overnight, it was an adventure to climb a ladder, walk across the porch roof, and enter a second-story window to go to bed.

Ablutions and Solutions

My parents espoused simple solutions for ills, without pills. My father's regimen for healing cuts, scrapes, and infections was Carbo Salve. For aches and pains, it was horse liniment. To cleanse one's body and soul, he started off each day with the juice of a lemon added to a cup of warm water.

No one liked my mother's soothing elixir as much as I did. I was almost happy to get sick in order to get a bowl of bread soup: her homemade bread sliced and toasted over the embers in our wood range, then cut in cubes sautéed in butter, adding enough hot milk to fill the bowl—seasoning it with a pinch of salt and pepper and a chunk of butter to melt on the surface.

For immediate relief of a toothache, Ma brought out a little bottle of kummel (caraway whiskey) from her closet, poured a little on a piece of cotton batting to dab on the tooth and gum. To relieve indigestion, she had me walk on all fours around the dining-room table a few times. It always worked. No staying home from school!

The best antidote for the frequent headaches I suffered as a child was my mother's gentle massaging of my head while telling me a tale or two—sometimes fiction, sometimes a true story. There was one vintage fairy tale I could listen to, over and over—her original mix of Snow White and Sleeping Beauty called "Genna-fayvah".

My parents gave me the greatest gift parents can give to their children; the ability to view even the darkest situations with the light of a positive attitude. I learned at a young age that a spoonful of humor helps the embarrassment go down. Whenever I stumbled into awkward situations, I discovered the magical reversal was the ability to laugh at myself instead of shrinking in shyness. Remember the line from the movie "Some Like It Hot" when Joe E. Brown said "Nobody's perfect."

GETTING HIRED VS. GETTING A HIGHER EDUCATION

A 'Split' Decision

I did both simultaneously, as my father had done: work in a restaurant while pursuing a business education. I worked part-time as a waitress while pursuing a prescribed secretarial course at an accredited business college.

Although my father was formally educated, having graduated from a business school and a short course at the University of Wisconsin, it was not he who encouraged his daughters to pursue higher education. It was an era when rural women were assumed to marry farmers' sons—only needing to know how to cook, clean, and have babies.

It was my mother, who had suffered her whole life from the stigma of not being able to attend school beyond the third grade, because of farm labor demands, and who insisted that we four girls should have the option of choosing to go to college. My choice could have been the University of Wisconsin which awarded a free first year of tuition to valedictorians—a whopping $96.00. Instead, I opted to take an exam to compete for the sole scholarship offered by the Fond du Lac Commercial College—a complete business course valued at $240.00.

I won the scholarship and, with the help of my mother, proceeded to make arrangements to find a place to live in Fond du Lac and a job to pay for the room and meals. It meant that, at age 16, I would be living away from home for the first time in my life—only 11 miles from the farm, but a world apart.

Ma and I checked the local newspaper ads to find a place within walking distance of the restaurant. My eldest sister, Tess, accompanied us when we decided on an advertised room-to-rent at a church parsonage. Sounded like a safe place to live. When we settled and were accepted on that choice, we were escorted by a gray-haired, soft-spoken minister to my quarters—a bedroom on the second floor. The minister was friendly and accommodating. As we walked to the stairs, we passed a small organ in the hallway. The minister said that I could play on his organ any time I wanted. (I was embarrassed with myself for turning that into an obscene thought.)

Upstairs in the bedroom, I unpacked my toothbrush, alarm clock, and a satchel full of clothes. My sister was busy installing a hook-and-eye to secure the door to the frame as there was no lock on the door. She insisted it was a necessary precaution to ensure my privacy and virtue. She didn't want me to have a scary experience as she had had when she was a young housekeeper for a country priest, awakened during the night by his intrusion into her bedroom.

After my mother and sister left, I secured my bedroom door and settled down for a good night's sleep. Ah, I sighed, I had become an adult at last.

My First Night Away From Home

Some time after midnight, I was awakened by chilling screams of what sounded like a young girl's voice, then sounds of slapping, and the minister's voice coming from across the hall. I didn't know that anyone else was living on the same floor. I looked at the hook-and-eye locking device on my door with a little more respect and affection.

Suddenly, all was quiet, and I heard a girl say 'thank you'. I bravely opened my door a crack, hoping to not be confronted by anyone or any thing, but prepared to run for my life. The minister came out of the girl's room, quickly apologized for the racket and hoped I hadn't been alarmed. (Alarmed?) That hardly described my panic. He explained that a bat had gotten into the other girl tenant's room and that he had been swatting at it to get it to leave through the screenless window.

I did have a lovely big bedroom for which I paid $3/week. It included a telephone, and it was close enough to the restaurant so I could easily walk to work.

<u>My First Real Job</u>

I was excitedly apprehensive about my first job: waitressing at 'Happy's', a small restaurant with a horseshoe-shaped counter, catering to breakfast and burger crowds. The very first customer had me stumped when he asked for 'dry' toast. I thought, "Isn't all toast dry?" The chef understood the strange term and explained it meant 'not buttered'. 'Boston' coffee was a tricky one. I thought, "Why not just drink hot milk?" What is a 'hamburger steak? Is it a hamburger, or is it a steak?

'Hold the onions'. How? 'Soup to go'. Where? 'On the side.' Of what? What's that all about? Wow, these city people have a strange language all their own.

I earned 50 cents per hour plus occasional tips of a nickel or dime. That's what tips averaged in those days because meals averaged about 39 cents.

My Motorized Man-date

Every day, as I walked to work, I passed a taxicab office where I got to know the friendly, flirtatious young cab drivers who were usually sitting outside. We exchanged little remarks which gradually grew into longer conversations. I finally accepted a date to go to a movie with one of them, Louie.

The evening he showed up at the parsonage to pick me up, the minister announced his arrival, "Joan, your young man is here." I wondered what his car looked like, or would he pick me up in a taxi—I had never been in a taxicab. (What a sheltered life I had led.) But there was Louie, and his MOTORCYCLE ! A wild beginning to my first date.

I had misgivings about the adventure, but Louie assured me he would drive very slowly and carefully. He said I should give him 'three pinches' if I wanted to stop. There I was, climbing on this dangerous contraption, bashfully putting my arms around a man for the first time in my life, my face against his back, risking my life—just to go to a movie a few blocks away. *What was I thinking?*

As we putt-putted down Main Street to the theater, I saw in an oncoming car—none other than my sister, Tess, the one who installed the locking device on my bedroom door to protect me from all harm. A lot of good that does now. Here I am astride the most dangerous vehicle on earth, with a man I hardly know, at the tender age of 16! I don't think she saw me; she seemed to be looking at the theater marquee that we were passing. My date and I went to the other theater in town, but I was so shaken up by that close call that I didn't recall anything about the movie.

The Summer of 1942

World War II was in full swing, and soon my taxi driver friends were all drafted into military service. When the commercial college session began in fall, I left Happy's to work at Schreiner's, a family-owned full-service restaurant at the other end of town where I could work a few hours after school, all day Saturday, and a few hours on Sunday evenings, to earn my suppers and the conservative but welcome tips. I got to spend Saturday nights and Sunday mornings at home on the farm.

I was inducted into the Pi Rho Zeta sorority. Initiation was conducted just for me, the lone pledge, by five older sorority sisters—beginning with a scavenger hunt, then drinks in the Schroeder company's upscale Retlaw (Walter spelled backwards) Hotel lounge. I didn't know what to order, but I heard one of the girls say 'CC and seven'. Sounded harmless enough. I said "the same" to the bartender and just swigged it down. Wow, I thought I suddenly went blind. Everything was out of focus as the room swirled around. I couldn't even feel the stool I was sitting on.

My consciousness returned in time to hear that our group was moving across the street to a rather fancy restaurant. At our table, the sorority president announced we had arrived at the finale and produced a raw egg for me to swallow in a liquid of my choice. I was still queasy from the "CC and seven" intoxication, so I could think of no good way to down the egg. I put it in a glass of water and, somehow, it went down as I tried to think only of the good food I was going to order at the sorority expense. By comparison, it made castor oil taste like a fine liqueur.

The next day, Tess's boss, a refined businessman, told her that he had been at the afore-mentioned restaurant the night before and saw a group of silly girls, laughing and 'egg'-ing on another girl to do something. He understood when she explained it was I in an initiation ritual—the price I had to pay for the glory of winning the scholarship.

My Friend, Gregg

The education offered at the commercial college was more varied than I expected, and standards were higher than I had experienced in the small rural high school I had attended. I took every subject offered: shorthand, typing, bookkeeping, business English, and the dreaded Parliamentary Procedure which focused on Roberts Rules of Order. That's the only subject I hated and couldn't get interested in—the only one for which I got an A-minus. I excelled in all the others with A's and A+'s to graduate Magna Cum Laude.

In shorthand, I got my speed up to 200 wpm, 85+ in typing—the latter score bringing my grade average above 'self-labeled genius' Mer Rue's which really triggered his competitive spirit. Whenever we had a speed test, he'd run to the typing room to get a seat behind me and just start pounding the keys erratically, hoping to unnerve me; or rip the paper out of his machine to possibly further annoy me. He soon learned that I work well 'under pressure'.

The President of the school, LaVelle Thompson Maze, was a taskmistress (her name alone struck fear into all of us students) who strictly enforced the policies of 'no fingernail polish' and the dress code of wearing office-appropriate apparel which included nylons (not a readily available shelf item in those WWII years) and heels. Her humble, flat-footed and bowlegged Mr. Maze, was as lovable as he was brilliant. He taught math, interspersed with 'rapid calculation'—an oral, brain exercise which I loved.

Mrs. Barrett, instructress of Business English, was a formidable opponent—a protégé of Professor Aurner who headed the University of Wisconsin English Department and the author of our current text book. When I challenged her, the whole class held their breaths as she would pick up her desk phone to check with an authoritative source at the local public library. She was a good sport, however, when I'd get the class's cheers for being correct.

Somehow, two guys in the class and I learned of Mrs. Barrett's fondness for Manhattans. One day, at the end of the lunch period, we three went across the street to the Rathskeller pub, got a Manhattan, and sneaked it to her in the assembly hall after everyone had gone to their classes. She enjoyed our little gesture of affection, but it always remained a secret—until now. She and I kept in touch for many years, always encouraging me to attend the University of Wisconsin, which I eventually did after spending a year employed as a secretary with the Schroeder Corporation in Milwaukee.

Schreiner's Home Cooking

I waitressed at Schreiner's Restaurant for the entire length of my business course. The sad part of waitressing was being rewarded with small tips, However, at that time, coffee was a nickel, hot sandwiches fifteen cents, and meals ranged from twenty-five to thirty-five cents. I was so elated when I got the biggest tip ever: two half dollars! It was a testimonial to the good service as well as the good food. When I proudly told the owner's wife (I'll never forget her backhanded compliment), she blurted out, "What a lucky fart!" I knew she meant well, but I thought it was crude.

I was the youngest waitress there, yet the owners trusted me to oversee the cash register when neither of them could be there. They had a huge clientele as the food was known to be the best for miles around. There were home-made cloverleaf rolls and pies baked every morning. It was the only restaurant fare that ever came close to my mother's cooking and baking. The kitchen was immaculate as was the entire restaurant.

My Saturday morning shift started very early, so early that some of the Friday night drinkers came in to sober up on almost-raw steaks. I was used to seeing cereal or bacon-and-egg breakfasts, so it was difficult for me to look nonplussed when serving a bloody steak to some liquor-breath lush, slopping it down with a raw-egg-in-tomato-juice chaser.

The owners, Albert and Regina, were wonderful, and their son, an only child, was a six-foot-four redhead. His parents called him by his baptismal name, BERnard, but many others, including myself, called him "Pinky" because of his red hair, of course.

He and I began to date during the time I worked at the restaurant, and my home was still on the farm. On our very first date, he picked me up where he could meet my parents. It was my mother who invited us to join her in our seldom-used living-room. She sat on an overstuffed chair while Pinky and I sat opposite her on a sofa.

He was very sociable and entertaining as he rambled on about his interests and comical incidents relating to some of the restaurant's customers. My mother appeared to be listening, but her eyes kept moving back and forth, from left to right and back again—not really looking directly at either of us, but more like she was watching a tennis match.

Of Mice and Man

When I came home after that date, Ma explained that, while Pinky was talking, a mouse came out of nowhere and kept criss-crossing back and forth behind us on the top edge of the sofa. She was wondering what would happen if it decided to walk onto one of us. What kind of impression would Pinky have of us if he saw a mouse in the house, especially since his parents' restaurant was free of vermin? Eventually I had the nerve to tell him of this incident, and he laughed hysterically—appreciating my mother's consternation.

He did have a great sense of humor, a slick Pontiac coupe, loved music (always played Harry James' *Ciribiribin,* Tommy Dorsey's *Boogie Woogie.* and *Heartaches* which he would translate to German *'Herzen Schmerzen'* because he loved the guttural sound of it. He was always a gentleman, a brilliant engineering student, and tireless worker. He made Saturday mornings interesting as we went about our menial tasks. He mopped the floors while I washed every inch of the wooden booths.

Drinking Beer Through a Straw

One Saturday morning, with no customers in the place, the cook, pastry chef, and Pinky all dared me to drink beer through a straw. I had no idea that this method would make it more intoxicating, but I remember getting really giddy after a few sips. I went back to my chores, walking right over a chair instead of going around it. I wasn't halfway finished before I was finished! How my audience applauded and laughed hysterically, somewhat like Ma must have laughed as she watched the drunk actor in a theatrical production.

Magna Cum Laude Graduation

I completed the Commercial College course in July 1943, a month before my 18th birthday, graduating Magna Cum Laude—second highest in my class. I excelled in typing, shorthand, and business English which included vocabulary and correspondence.

Also, in July 1943, Pinky enlisted in the Army and was stationed at Camp Campbell, Kentucky. On July 17, my sister Maybelle married Frank after a four-year courtship. The reception was held at our home on the farm. The day after, I traveled with Pinky and his mom down to Camp Campbell in his green Pontiac so he could have a car at camp. It was quite a boring visit, staying in barracks with no air-conditioning in that humid summer heat. The one memorable part on the base was seeing the movie, *Stormy Weather,* starring Lena Horne.

I know Red (aka Pinky) and his family had thoughts of our getting married some day, as did I, but I had to expunge all such thoughts as my sister Maybelle had me promise that I wouldn't get serious about anyone until her husband Frank's nephew, Al Wellander, would come home after the war. He was a Navy radio operator aboard a destroyer in the South Pacific during WWII.

The commercial college building was owned by the Schroeder Corporation of hotel and insurance fame in Milwaukee. They were also known for offering employment to the college's top graduates, and I accepted their offer—much to the disappointment of the college's instructor, Mrs. Eileen Barrett. She had been a student of the University's head of the English department, Dr. Robert Aurner, and wanted me to follow in her footsteps. I chose to utilize my secretarial skills on the job I accepted in Milwaukee.

<u>Working at Schroeder's in Milwaukee</u>

Being hired at the Schroeder Corporation was its own recommendation. They hired only the top graduate from their tenant, the Fond du Lac Commercial College. I hung out with two girls there who graduated before me. My immediate supervisor, Janet Carey, also had graduated from the same school many years before. She was the office manager and what a sweetheart she was—one of the most intelligent and moral persons I have ever known.

Once again, my dear mother helped me search for living quarters, close enough to the Schroeder offices so that I could walk to work. By coincidence, we came upon a rooming house run by a friendly, trustworthy older couple, Mr. and Mrs. Frank Palm. The wife was someone that Ma had known back home when they were young girls. It made us feel comfortable that I would be living in a place where the landlords would be looking out for me.

I paid $8/week rent for just a bedroom. I had to use a shared bathroom down the hall for nature calls and baths. It's hard to believe I was only 18, along in a big city, but there were nice, interesting people to work with. One perky widow, Helen Hanzlich, had a crush on the bachelor owner, Walter Schroeder, and paid me to ghost write poems for her to give to him—letting him know of her romantic interest. What a delightfully animated, eccentric woman. She had an odd habit of hanging an assortment of her shoes by their heels around the rim of her waste basket.

There was an errand girl, Candy Barr—a startling double for Judy Garland—who acted as a courier between our office and the elegant Schroeder Hotel that housed the legendary Empire Room where all the big bands played. You name 'em, they played there. I got to sneak in some nights to see many famous entertainers. Across the street from that hotel was a popular 'watering hole' called Muddy Waters, a great scene for live jazz.

In the year I worked in Milwaukee, I met many interesting people: the young members of St. Michael's youth group whose priest often babysat for young couples to have a night out. There was Franny, the 'merry mortician', who owned a funeral home. My co-workers and I made a weekly trip to hear the jazz pianist at a club called Easttown who called herself 'Big Fat Mama'.

Although I wasn't legally old enough to drink alcohol other than beer, they always served me with the other two girls. After a couple of months of this night life, my parents noticed the dark circles under my eyes. It took only one cautionary talk from them for me to discontinue handing around with the bad-influence girls.

I met fellows from all branches of Service when the youth group hosted dances and dinners for the men of Great Lakes Naval Training Center and Fort Sheridan.

One afternoon, a girlfriend and I went to see Hedy Lamarr, famous for a nude scene in the much publicized 'forbidden' movie, *Ecstasy*. We felt conspicuous standing in line outside the theatre at 3rd and Wells Streets, hoping no one from work would drive by and see us. Now, it would be considered 'tame' in comparison with what is even shown on television.

I bravely entered competition to sing on stage with Frankie Carle's orchestra at the famous Riverside Theatre on Wisconsin Avenue. The original 'Blackstone, the Magician' was on the same bill, whom I met, along with some of his animal stooges backstage including a huge white goose. I sang "It Had to be You". I remember Frankie asking what key I wanted. I said "Gee" as in "gee, I don't know", but he took it literally as the key of G. Thank goodness, it was a comfortable key. I had always sung songs from sheet music but never noted what keys they were in.

After a year in Milwaukee, I decided it was time to go to the University of Wisconsin at Madison. Tuition was only $48/semester for state residents. It was room and board in a dormitory or sorority house that was financially out of the question. To attend, I would have to work for room and board.

THE HOUSE OF STUHLDREHER

Through the University's student placement office, we learned that a position to earn room and board was possibly available at the home of the athletic director/

football coach, none other than Harry Stuhldreher of Notre Dame Four Horsemen fame, 1924 All-American under Knute Rockne.

On further inquiry, we were told that the vacancy had been filled by a Japanese girl. However, Mrs. Stuhldreher reconsidered, perhaps choosing me because I was a farm girl, and the family had had a good experience with having a farm boy from the same area in Wisconsin that I came from.

Stuhldrehers lived in University Heights where many faculty members resided. The 'pink palace' (so named because of the color of its exterior stucco finish) was a sprawling house with five bedrooms and baths— one of each for me, located at the rear of the house above the garage, accessed by a stairway off the kitchen. I chose to live there, expecting it to be the challenge of my life. The four sons, from the youngest to the oldest: Peter (6), Johnny (9), Michael (11), and Skippy (13) were quick to inform me that they used to back their maid up against the wall.

I decided to immediately establish my position in a positive light, so I rolled up the sleeve on my right arm and invited them to pound my firm bicep as I 'made a muscle'. I can't imagine that I really did that spontaneously, but I had to pre-empt any suspicion that I might be vulnerable to boys—which I was! I figured it would be suicide if I let them know my trepidation. Each one had a unique personality. We became great friends with no conflicts. I dearly loved each one.

To help me get settled in, my mother and 'security expert' sister, Tess, drove the 90 miles from home with me and my sparse belongings and, of course, armed with a hook-and-eye for my bedroom door. After Tess made the installation, she and Ma drove home.

The very first night, I was awakened by footsteps that were approaching up the back stairs. They stopped suddenly right outside my door. What is it, I thought, about these first-nighter scares? I heard the footsteps descending the stairs and breathed a sigh of relief. The next day, I found out that their supply of P.M.Deluxe was kept in a small closet outside my door.

Mrs. Stuhldreher cheerfully welcomed me the first day and informed me that she would prepare dinner that first evening: roast leg of lamb. I had never eaten lamb before. On the farm we ate the meats we raised: pork and chicken. She said that she would never allow pork in the house. She associated the smell that was always present in the home of their Black servants back in Pennsylvania when they took them home.

Game Daze

One Saturday afternoon, after a home football game when they always had a houseful of guests, including an Army general, I heard Skippy tell him, "You gotta come in the kitchen and see Joan's muscle!" Thank heavens, the general paid no attention to him, especially since I was busy making platters of hors d'oeuvres (cucumber and watercress canapés, bread cutouts with pate or bacon and water chestnuts.) They hired a bartender to fix drinks. For me it meant to shine as a 'maid' and work feverishly (with an antiquated stove broiler) to avoid burning the sardine/cheese/mustard combo on cocktail rye bread appetizers.

The guests included wealthy alumni, reporters, politicians, military personnel, coaches, and other faculty members. There were phone calls, too, from sports reporter Arch Ward of the Chicago Tribune, and celebrities like Joe E. Brown and Bing Crosby whom they knew from the making of a movie in Hollywood about the Four Horsemen.

<u>Maid to Order</u>

My duties were to be home from school every day by 5:00 P.M., to prepare dinner for the seven of us, ready to serve between 6:00-7:00 P.M., depending on the menu. I served the family in the dining-room, following the formal etiquette of 'serve from the left, take from the right'. This was especially important when Mary's father (who called her 'Mrs. God') would visit. The first time he came, as I went to serve him, the honored guest, there on the white linen tablecloth lay his denture.

Mary came from an affluent Philadelphia family. Her father, and her brothers Jeff and Michael were lawyers. Her brother Jim taught Latin and Greek at a Catholic college, with time out for a stint with the Army in World War II. Mary was a graduate of Trinity College in Washington, D.C. followed by post graduate studies at Columbia College in New York City.

Mary was a talented, prolific writer. She was working on a mystery novel during my last year at the house. She read chapters to me as she progressed, inviting my critique. Among her writing credits was an award-winning article: "They Were After His Scalp" which detailed the problems over Wisconsin's 1946 losing season, followed by the turn-around of the 1947 season. Other articles were: "The Tender Touch" published by Saturday Evening Post, November 1954; and "The High-heeled Recruiter" which appeared in Sports Illustrated in September 1963. She also authored the biographical book "Many a

Saturday Afternoon" about the family's lives which was published in September 1964.

Harry wrote a number of articles for magazines, including three for Saturday Evening Post and two well-known books: "Quarterback Play" and "Knute Rockne: Man Builder", published in 1931 by Grosset & Dunlap.

Their four sons followed divergent paths after graduating from high school: Skip, a hockey player at Michigan; Michael, a diver at Yale; John, a tennis player at Notre Dame; and Peter, who died in 2001, earned his fame as a designer of costumes for Broadway and television theatre.

Mary wasn't anti-Semitic but, in her facetious vernacular, she referred to Jewish students as "Heebs". Young Peter apparently stored this term in a mental cubicle because, one afternoon when I took him to the Union (quad) to have a hot dog and meet some of my friends who hung out there, the first thing he uttered was, "Where are all the heaps?" I hoped no one had heard that remark or didn't construe the word 'heaps' to be anything denigrating.

I ate my meals in the breakfast room off the kitchen. If any of the boys misbehaved, they were sent to dine with me. I'm sure they occasionally deliberately got into mischief so they could sit with me where they could laugh and be informal instead of adhering to strict manners—not to mention they might be able to ditch their vegetables down the cold-air vent when I had to leave the room to wait on their parents. I loved having them at my table; they were wonderful company.

We had the best of everything to eat: fresh vegetables and the finest cuts of meat at a time when meat was rationed. We had beef tenderloins the size of pot roasts, wonderfully tender lamb chops, and golden-breasted fowl. I really developed an immediate taste for lamb and was glad we had that quite often. My parents were just happy that I never went hungry.

After dinner, I had to carpet sweep the dining-room, do the dishes, and make bowls of Jell-O for the next day's after-school snacks. By that time, it would be close to 10:00 P.M., curfew time for me so that I couldn't go out anywhere, and too tired most nights to begin studying my homework. When I did stay awake to study one of the boys would knock on my door for a little conversation or advice on puberty problems. I remember the teenager asking, "Why do I break out in a sweat when I get close to a girl?" (I can't remember what I answered, if I did.) I did enjoy their stalling at bed time, giving me some concentrated time with each of them.

Sometimes when the coach was out of town, Mrs. S. (as she called herself) would get weepy from loneliness and call up the stairs to me, usually about 2:00 A.M.—just about the time I'd wake up from a nap and begin to study: "Lamb-y Pie, come down and have a glass of milk with me." Those chats were of an adult nature, revealing personal frustrations as well as reminiscences about happier times, giving her a chance to vent her perplexities.

Compensations for my duties were, of course, what we had agreed to: room and board, plus fifty cents per week transportation allowance to go back and forth to the university. Bus fare was five cents each way. Often, I would walk the 1-1/2 miles home to save the nickel which would later buy a hot dog or a 3.2 beer at the Union on campus, or five handfuls of peanuts from the penny dispenser in the booth of a pub where my friend Glen and I would meet for a much-needed break. If I couldn't get out of the house before curfew, he'd come to the house and help me with the dinner dishes. Lovely!

I realized too late what a great fellow he was and how much he must have cared. He was a good dancer, endeared himself to me with his deep resonant singing of the Ink Spots' *"You Always Hurt the One You Love"*, and could make me laugh about ordinary things. His rendition of *"Honey dear, honey lamb"* always cheered me up. I probably should have gotten as serious as he was, but it always stuck in my mind that I had to save myself for my brother-in-law's nephew to be discharged from the Navy. (What a disastrous decision that would later turn out to be.)

Mr. Stuhldreher was hardly ever home, except for meals during football season, and then on to a series of speaking engagements the rest of the year. He dictated a regular alumni newsletter which I would transcribe and type for him. Sometimes I'd have to sew a button on a sport coat before he went out. When I returned from my home one winter weekend, I brought Harry a gift my mother crafted by hand: a fur hat, something he thought was amusing because many of the professors wore them. Harry became an instant "honorary professor."

Occasionally, he'd give me a ride to school in the morning on the way to his office on campus in the Annex. I was in such awe of him that I was nervous in trying to think of things to talk about, but it was always safe to speak well of his sons—especially of Peter who was always entertaining. He always thanked me for my work and for the interest and love shown for his boys. He could relate to my working for room and board just as he handled working his way through the University of Notre Dame.

Knute Rockne called him "a bright young man with a sharp mind". Harry had piercing bright eyes and an aura of absolute confidence about him. I could see why he was a legendary quarterback in spite of his size, 5'6" tall, weighing 157 pounds. In today's standards that would be small, but my football-savvy grandson advised me that quarterbacks don't have to be huge, just smart. And smart he was.

During football season, when the games were 'away', I was allowed to go home to the farm—a heavenly respite. I anticipated with joy the whole 90 miles back to Fond du Lac where my parents would meet me at the Greyhound bus station. My parents were the kind you missed, the minute they were out of sight.

The three older boys were sports enthusiasts, but young Peter spent hours in his room 'saying Mass', complete with gospels and sermons, on a makeshift altar. He was thrilled when I gave him my maroon satin bathrobe to serve as a priest's vestment. Much to his brothers' embarrassment, he wore it as he paraded about outdoors, blessing everything. That wasn't as embarrassing as it was to Mrs. S. when football party guests arrived to see a stripped sanitary pad on the library table in the front hall with Peter wearing the gauze as a veil or as a covering for a chalice.

Mrs. Stuhldreher thought it was time to turn his attention to more masculine interests and enrolled him in Saturday boxing classes at the field house, a few blocks away. Every Saturday, he'd be gone for about an hour. Everyone was happy about his 'conversion' until his mother visited the boxing coach to check on Peter's progress. Completely puzzled, the coach said he had never seen Peter. That devious kid had cleverly dodged the bullet by stopping in at a fraternity house along the way where his little girlfriend lived.

Queen For a Day, or Two

When both parents were out of town for the weekend, and I was in charge, the boys and I had a great time. I had permission to drive the family car: a four-door 1940-something white Ford. The boys named it the "Ghost" because, as they told their father, I drove really fast (which I didn't, in spite of Skippy's urging!)

At night I was authorized to sleep in one of the twin beds in their father's bedroom, in case the parents would call or if I needed it for an emergency reason. The boys would wrangle for the privilege of sleeping in the other bed. I kept a lot so each one would eventually get his fair turn. Peter usually won because he was th3e youngest, but, no matter which boy was my temporary room mate, he would talk non-stop most of the night. Those were unforgettable, and most happy times of my life.

Peter's Field Trip to the Farm

One weekend in spring, I took Peter home with me on the Greyhound bus to Fond du Lac where my parents met us en route to the farm. He loved seeing the farm animals and eating Ma's pork roast dinner. PORK? He had never tasted it before because it was never served at his home. My mother was concerned about his eating too much of something not in his normal diet. It might make him ill, but it agreed with him.

Peter brought the 'vestments' with him that I had made to say Mass for my family, complete with sermons. My folks loved every word, every action. My father suggested he take up a collection and gave him a tin cup. Everyone put money in it. Accordingly, the services got shorter and the collections more frequent.

I took Peter up to our woods that paralleled the Soo Line railroad tracks. As we were picking wild flowers, a freight train came along. I told Peter, "Wave, if you see someone standing in the last car (caboose)." Sure enough, there was a man standing and urinating off the caboose. Of course, this was the first thing Peter told his parents when we returned to Madison. In fact, he stormed past me to tell them, "I saw a man peeing off a train." How they laughed.

A Visit from 'General' McEnery

Mary's brother, Jimmie McEnery, spent an Army furlough visiting the Stuhldreher house. Mary teased that someday I'd marry the 'General' (actually a Private). He had what Mary called a 'Mick' (Irish) face with beautiful, twinkling blue eyes. I enjoyed his company and loved him as a wonderful friend. We had great talks every night while he helped me with the dishes or when I was doing my homework.

We never got physical, never held hands or embraced—just loved each other's company. It was seldom that I met any man so intelligent and educated—he was a professor of Latin and Greek in a college, and yet had an earthy sense of humor. We got along well though we really had nothing in common in our background.

We did keep in touch by letter throughout the war years and beyond. He wrote nearly every day—interesting letters, and photos. They would have been an excellent historical record relevant to WWII, but somewhere, during my many moves, I lost them. I do recall the coincidence that he shared my mother's birth date, July 4!

<u>The Four Horsemen of Notre Dame</u>

"Outlined against a blue, gray October sky, the Four Horsemen rode again." In dramatic lore, they are known as famine, pestilence, destruction, and death. These are only aliases, Their real names are: Harry Stuhldreher (quarterback), Don Miller (right halfback), Jim Crowley (left halfback), and Elmer Layden (fullback).

The words of Grantland Rice, a sportswriter for the New York Herald-Tribune, established the name that would aid them in achieving immortality. He derived the name from a halftime conversation that he overheard in the press box of the Notre Dame-Army game on October 18, 1924, of George Strickler, a student assistant, describing a movie that featured the biblical features of doom and disaster. Rice borrowed the terms to describe the four men who led to Notre Dame's 13-7 victory. The words Rice used to describe the men remain today as the most famous 'lead' ever written on a sports event.

These words have become a symbol and legacy to Notre Dame students. These four men led Notre Dame to a perfect 10-0 season and the National Championship in 1924, beating Stanford 27-10 in the historic Rose Bowl game on January 1, 1925.

Stuhldreher led the team as quarterback, not only utilizing his passing ability but returning punts and throwing blocks with the best of them.

He was cocky, ambitious, and feisty—all characteristics that proved to be assets to leading the team to victory. They became the most fabled foursome in college history and eventually became featured on a U.S. postage stamp.

In the 30 games the four men played as a unit, they had only two defeats—both to Nebraska. None of the four, incidentally, was taller than 6 feet or weighed more than 162 pounds.

From becoming starting quarterback midway through his sophomore year in 1922, Stuhldreher became All-American in 1924. In those days, it was a most special title because that honor was bestowed on only *one* person. His statistics that year showed he completed 25 passes out of 33 attempts for 471 yards for a .757 percentage.

The statistics do not accurately reflect Stuhldreher's athletic talent, however, as his son, Michael, confirmed: "The forward pass was used on a very limited basis at that time. He was considered a very, very accurate passer. Many years later, when he was a college coach, he would put a tire on a rope and could thread pass after pass through that tire from 40 yards away. That always impressed his players."

That early attitude toward the forward pass is evident in his statistics, as he attempted only 118 passes in three years. His primary talent as a football player was his speed on end sweeps.

In that historic Rose Bowl game, Stanford superstar Ernie Nevers was stopped by Stuhldreher at the goal line on the fourth down. For years thereafter, many Californians insisted that Nevers had, in fact, crossed the goal line and that Notre Dame had stolen the victory. One evening, Los Angeles sportswriter George Davis was arguing this very point when a stranger interjected, "I say he didn't score."

"Where were you sitting?", Davis challenged. "I was sitting on Nevers' neck," the man replied, "I'm Harry Stuhldreher."

Strickler later thought he would do anything he could to make sure that the name remained with the four men. After the team arrived back in South Bend from the Army game in New York, he posed the four players in their uniforms, complete with helmets and footballs, on the back of four horses from a livery stable in town. After the photo was released onto the wire services, the four men ensured the position as famous football figures of their time. That photo hung in Harry's bedroom.

There also were photos of Bing Crosby and Joe E. Brown whom Harry and Mary Stuhldreher got to know in Hollywood during the making of a movie and from whom they occasionally received telephone calls. Imagine my thrill when I would answer the phone in the library and hear their unmistakably identifiable voices. Another luminary, one who lived across the street, was Mrs. Phil LaFollette—wife of the former governor of Wisconsin who was then serving under General MacArthur in the Philippines.

When Harry returned from speaking engagement trips, he gave me gifts that he had received. That goes back more than sixty years, but I still have the two pairs of bookends he gave me: a pair of bronze lion heads, and a replica of Mount Rushmore. Harry died January 26, 1965, at the age of 63.

Matriculating and 'Curriculating

Matriculation at the University began with an open house for freshmen at the house of President Dykstra. I dressed in my favorite outfit: a black flared poplin skirt, a white blouse I had made with tight-ruffled trim at the neck and short sleeves which peaked out from under the black bolero. Peter's little friend, a daughter of a fraternity house janitor, saw me and exclaimed, "Are you Peter's maid?" Every time I wore that outfit after that, I felt I was en route to employment for a maid.

I started out the school year with a 16-credit load, although it was suggested that working students should carry no more than a 12-credit load. It seemed like I could handle that. The journalism course was disappointedly inadequate which made me switch to Music Education in my sophomore year with emphasis on vocal music. My voice teacher was a respected professional from Reykjavik, Iceland.

My English professor was a brilliant, colorful older woman named Helen White. No one could forget her, merely for the fact that she dressed completely in purple every day which prompted one student to quip. "Maybe that's because she looks like hell-in-white." She taught a whole year's course using the Bible as the textbook because, as she explained, it was a book that contained every act of human behavior that could be found in a whole library.

Back in the day, Catholics were not encouraged to read the Bible because, as lay people, its language might be misinterpreted. Therefore, it was suggested that we should rely on the clergy to discuss it in religious services. But, as a student, I had to purchase the King James version as our official textbook to Professor White's class. I took it with me on a visit home and read passages to my mother while she was working in the kitchen. Her curiosity finally caused her to ask, "WHAT are you reading?" It was a revelation to both of us that those sinful passages appeared in the Bible. Ma quipped, "No wonder the Bible is the most popular book ever printed."

Extra Curricular Activities

It was my good fortune to meet Jacquie, a native of Madison, a brilliant girl of Norwegian extraction, with an effervescent personality. She was a music student and an accomplished musician who worked in the school of music. She was one of two persons who played the carillon in the Carillon Tower on campus. She encouraged me to audition for the 50-voice University A Cappella choir, and join the Local Student Association for resident students and for those who lived in private homes. I sometimes stayed overnight at her house which was liberating and pleasant to be a temporary member of her family. She was the only child of wonderful Norwegian parents. Her father owned and operated a railroad car diner advertising "We can serve 10,000 people, 10 at a time."

I was accepted into the University choir as a *tenor* because, the day I auditioned, my voice was very low due to a case of bronchitis. That was okay as I got to rub shoulders with all the males in the back rows.

We rehearsed in a Presbyterian chapel on campus, under a tee-totaling conductor whom we respected and loved dearly. One day, before rehearsal, I had a hot dog and a nickel beer in the Union. It was a 3.2 beer, low in alcohol but still strong on the breath like real beer. That was the day our conductor offered a challenge about breath control. "Does anyone feel their abdomen expanding as the diaphragm tightens and breath is expelled?" Of course, I was the only show-off to raise my hand and, therefore, was invited to come up front to demonstrate. I had to exhale very close to the conductor's face and nearly blew him over. All he said was, "You may return to your space, thank you."

Jacquie organized a singing trio with me and another girl to entertain as part of a USO troupe at Truax Air Field outside of Madison. She suggested a classy, simple outfit would be appropriate: a navy blue skirt (which she loaned me), a navy blue sweater (which I would have to buy for about $5) and a string of pearls. I had never written home for money, but now I needed $5 for a sweater. A few days after mailing the request to Ma and Pa, I followed up with a post card that carried one sentence, "Did Pa come off the ceiling yet?" The humorous approach paid off. I received the $5!

We were part of a busload of girls who attended dances at that military base. Our trio was also asked to sing at the prom held at the University Union ballroom when Vaughan Monroe's orchestra played there. When Jacquie and the other trio girl became too ill to perform, I hung around the stage area and got to sing our trio's signature tune *"Always"* with the Vaughan Monroe band.

When the same girl quit school, Jacquie recruited two fellows, a bass and baritone, whose natural ability to harmonize made our quartet just perfect. We had no scripted music and could not afford to rent rehearsal space, so we often rehearsed going up and down in the Union elevator. How about that? Elevator music, LIVE!

One popular song of the day was *"Don't Fence Me In"* which I taught to young Peter Stuhldreher, driving everyone crazy in the house as he sang it day and night.

During my years at the university, I didn't date much. Working long hours left me no time for much social life except for Glen who was willing to share conversation and a few laughs over dishes. The fact that those war years created a ratio of females to males 26:1 left few desirable males at hand, and extreme competition for those who were available. I spent the time between classes to catalog species of fish for the State of Wisconsin Conservation Department for 50 cents per hour. Every little bit helped.

1948: A MEMORABLE YEAR OF TRAVEL

New Orleans – Pensacola – St. Augustine

In February, my father decided that the four of us—he, my mother, my fiancé Al, and I—should drive to Pensacola, Florida to celebrate the 77ᵗʰ birthday of his favorite sister, Amelia, who lived there with her daughter, Ruth.

My mother and I came up with the bright idea: why not leave early enough to swing by New Orleans for Fat Tuesday, the last day of Mardi Gras. Agreed. We drove as far as Chicago on the first leg of the trip to pick up Al who was interested in looking up his WWII Navy buddy living in New Orleans.

After spending the first night of our trip in Chicago at the home of Al's parents, we arose early the next morning and aimed my parents' 1938 Chevy sedan toward New Orleans. On that very first day, we ran into treacherous road conditions—a coat of ice, but my father insisted on moving along, if only at 15 MPH.

It was my mother's idea to stay in tourist homes on the trip, a popular accommodation in those days, and she probably figured they would be nice-looking ones as those back home. Motor trips were the popular mode of travel at the time, and every town's travel route was dotted with tourist homes.

People chose them because they were homey, didn't require advance reservations, maybe a chance to socialize with the residents about the area, and share a light breakfast of at least toast and coffee. They were exceptionally reasonable, usually $2 per night for a room with a double bed. They were available in almost every small town so that you didn't have to drive extra miles to find a big city hotel.

We arrived before nightfall at our first tourist home to spend the night in Flora, Illinois. It was a quiet little town where the lovely house was owned by two spinster sisters whose southern Illinois twang was as welcoming as it was amusing.

From there we hit snowstorms all the way to the South. I remember pulling into a gas station in Meridian, Mississippi with our car covered in snow, the attendant said, "You sure must have come a long, long way from up north."

When we arrived in New Orleans, we found Al's Navy buddy who drove us around the city, but his parents had no room for us to stay at their house. It was, of course, the last and biggest day of Mardi Gras, so it was no wonder there wasn't a hotel room, tourist room, or dorm room available.

We drove up and down residential streets including the Elysian Fields neighborhood where you could feel the ambiance of *A Streetcar Named Desire*. There actually was a streetcar named 'Desire' in New Orleans; we rode it while we were there.

There seemed to be no activity in that area except for one lone woman, probably about 30 years old, walking in a slow and easy saunter (not too many people saunter nowadays), dressed in a gypsy-looking long dress. Ma called out to her about sleeping quarters, and she said that she would try to accommodate us.

We parked on the street and followed the woman inside the quaint old house. We passed through the first big room where she said a few college boys were staying. Ours was the next room where there was one full-size bed with head- and footboards. We took the room, deciding we could lie cross-wise in the bed—better than sleeping in the car.

We put our suitcases in the room and headed downtown in time to see the Neptune parade, the biggest of all. We stood at the curb in front of a public restroom, puzzled by the door marked WHITE and another door marked COLORED. Hicks that we were, knowing nothing 'bout segregation', we figured it out as we saw which persons went in where. Then we also knew why we caused raised eyebrows and some muttering when we boarded a streetcar to go to the parade as we got on and sat in the back...*with the Colored!*

The people called 'colored' kind of smiled and talked to us, while the 'white' folks at the front of the car looked very disturbed. We were not aware of what segregation meant until we stopped at places while traveling through the South. We were appalled at the disparity of treatment for Black people by supposedly civilized Whites. In sincere friendliness, we struck up conversations with everyone we met. One little girl (in those days referred to as a pickaninny) at a street corner told us she could dance for us, for a penny. Ma said, "OK." That little child did a little jig. Ma said, "How would you dance for a dime?" You never saw any legs move that fast. Ma gave her the dime, and the girl was still dancing as we moved away.

The Neptune parade was, in today's term, AWESOME! The floats were indescribable works of art. There were people on them in outrageous costumes, or none at all—their bodies painted entirely in silver or gold. Beads were flying everywhere. The most memorable of all were the 'colored' torch bearers, walking close behind each other in a line on either side of the parade with their arms raised high, the tall flames framing and illuminating this hallowed procession preceding the many formal balls (admittance by invitation only) that followed.

The celebrations were halted at midnight, shutting down the entire city's partying as Lent began on the next day, Wednesday. The city was eerily quiet as 100,000 tourists had mysteriously disappeared. Hotel rooms were readily available on Wednesday, a bit different than the night before—four of us in one bed, listening to the college guys partying in the next room and the loud crackling of their fireplace.

I had an almost sleepless night as I lay between my mother and Al, hoping their hands across my body wouldn't meet. Because of the theatrical setting, I kept expecting Marlon Brando to yell out, "Stella, Stella." The next morning, it was quiet. The boys in the next room were already gone. Our gypsy hostess, whom I could only think of as 'Stella' offered to fix breakfast for us. Ma whispered to Pa, me, and Al, *"I think it would be safe to eat fried eggs because the hot frying pan would kill any germs, and the toaster would de-bug the bread."* We accepted the offer, sauntered into the kitchen, and sat down at the table. Our answer was, "Yes,

scrambled eggs, toast, and coffee would be appreciated." She reached for a large bowl on the shelf above the stove, when a large cat jumped out of it. Ma was hard-pressed to opt out of the offer, saying "You really shouldn't bother." Too late. Our hostess kept saying, "Oh, it's no botha." We had no excuse then, but kept looking at each other when we were eating...to see who was going to throw up first. Nobody did. But that phrase of hers became a running gag, so to speak, ever since: "it's no botha."

We spent Wednesday sightseeing in New Orleans: the museum of Mardi Gras costumes, Pierre La Fitte's cave where he hid out, some jazz places, the Court of Two Sisters restaurant, a gambling casino outside the city limits, a tour of the above-ground tombs where a typical jazz funeral procession was going on.

That evening, we left to make it on time for Aunt Amelia's 77th birthday in Pensacola. As we traveled along the Gulf Coast, we encountered a heavy fog—so thick we could hear the ocean waters slapping the shore but could not see the road. My mother and I were unsuccessful in convincing my father to stop and wait to finish the trip in daylight. With frazzled nerves, we arrived at our destination just before midnight.

Amelia's daughter, cousin Ruth, prepared the most delicious fresh red snapper dinner. The next day, she took us to see some beautiful flower gardens and to the Pensacola Naval Station where we had the privilege of boarding a large carrier through the courtesy of her friend, a Navy officer.

After Pensacola, we went to see the Bok Singing Tower, Cypress Gardens—its beautiful flowers and the beautiful water-skiing formations of beautiful girls. At St. Petersburg we stayed in a tourist home of a refined family and were entertained by a daughter who played the harp for us. Al and I went out to see the town and a movie. As we entered the theatre, we looked at each other and at the same time said, "There's no one but old people in here". We then realized that we were in the city known for being made up of retirees.

We proceeded further south to Sarasota where we visited the circus museum and the winter headquarters of the Ringling Brothers circus. There we saw the famous animal trainer, Gunter, work with the elephants and the 'big cats'. As we were having a snack at a refreshment stand, we had an uncanny experience of seeing a couple from Campbellsport (WI) whom we met at my sister Maybelle's home there the previous summer.

As we traveled through the South, we were made aware of the White folks' racial prejudice of the Colored people, and heard remarks like "you gotta keep 'em in their place." We never made any comments: first, because we just didn't understand their vitriolic attitude to another human being and, second, because my dad's father was a Union fighter for the abolition of slavery.

On our return trip back home, we stopped at several tourist attractions and small zoos, alligator farms, and one country tavern where a big bear was cruelly chained up to a stump outside where patrons were feeding him beers. We stopped at the oldest city in the nation, St. Augustine. We entered the city through a big arch and stopped at the first restaurant in sight. We were famished, ready for a meal, and the only thing we could afford was a bowl of soup. We spent the next day touring the city's points of interest: the oldest schoolhouse in the country, drank from Ponce de Leon's Fountain of Youth, and the military fort built in the 1600's but still in good condition.

I was the navigator and map reader for the trip. Leaving St. Augustine I chose to head home via a new route, and, since that city is fairly close to the northern border of Florida, we expected to soon enter Georgia. After driving hours and hours, how thrilled we were to suddenly be faced with a sign that read, "Welcome to Florida."

Everywhere we went in the South, grits wasn't listed on the menu as a choice 'side'. It came with your food (breakfast, lunch, or dinner) whether you ordered it or not. When I would expressly request that it not be included, I was never heard. After a few days, I got to like it; I actually missed it when we got back home.

TRAVEL: SOMETHING OLD, SOMETHING NEW

It was June 1998. Fifty years had passed since the first trip to New Orleans and Florida in 1948, when I traveled with my parents and fiancé. Now, I was a parent taking my daughter, Barbara, and her three sons, Josh, Jake, and Zachary to New Orleans and Orlando, Florida—not in a 1938 Chevy sedan, but by air in a super-jet.

New Orleans—A Beloved Old Friend

It was my grandsons' first air adventure. It was June, the weather was sunny but much too early to deal with the 100-degree temperature when we arrived in New Orleans. We had to deal with this high temperature and humid weather during our whole 10-day stay in the South. We had excellent accommodations at a Best Western motel from where we enlisted taxicab services to take us to the Audubon Zoo, the huge renowned aquarium, and the French Quarter.

We had a fabulous brunch at the Two Sisters restaurant where it seemed like I stepped back in time to the 1948 visit. I could not see any change in the ambiance or excellent quantity of food since that memorable first visit.

In the evening we strolled through the French Quarter and listened to door-after-door strains of jazz music until we camped at Preservation Hall to hear the legendary musicians whom I had heard and seen locally over the years. For me, that made the whole trip worthwhile. I'll admit that I expected the Hall to be larger and with permanent seating. Instead, it had a small stage, wooden floor, and just a few rows of benches up front. Most of the audience had to stand, spilling out of the single entrance door. But the music couldn't have been any more exciting than if it had been played in Carnegie Hall. My oldest grandson, Josh, at 12 was a budding trumpet player, and a good one at that. The look in his eyes as he stood transfixed watching those old, fabulous jazz musicians play their hearts out made the whole trip worthwhile. He shook those men's hands as they walked offstage and has never forgot the privilege of hearing true New Orleans jazz up close and personal.

We had an exciting, unforgettable experience having dinner in the Marriott's 40th floor dining room at dusk, overlooking riverboats moving in the bay, and the city lights as they sprouted across the romantic Big Easy. It was elegantly furnished. The food of gourmet quality including truffles was served by a charming tuxedoed waiter. My daughter, knowing her sons didn't want to miss the outcome of the Bulls' game in progress, asked our waiter (whom we didn't expect to be interested in 'our' team a thousand miles away) if he knew how the game was going. With only a few minutes left of the game, the waiter surprised all of us by whipping a little portable TV out of his pocket. He then ushered them into the dining room kitchen to see the Bulls win in the last minute of the game.

Wherever we went, we were treated like celebrities, particularly by the African-American residents—musicians, waiters, taxicab drivers, maitre d's, and the people on the street. Perhaps it was because we were two women with children, or because we were friendly and appreciative—I believe it was the latter. My daughter remarked, "How much we would have missed out on, all the friendliness, all the simple kindnesses of the people of color in New Orleans, if we were prejudiced."

<u>Orlando: A New Playground</u>

On arrival at the Orlando airport, we rented a mini-van to explore the area at our own pace. We confirmed the reservations I had made some months before our trip for Josh (nearly 13) and Jake (11 ½) to swim with the dolphins at Sea World. We had to arrive there hours before the place opened which meant getting up at 5:30 AM. Visitors don't actually swim with the dolphins. They stand on a sort of platform in the water and are shown how to direct the dolphins to perform various exercises like spinning and waving.

The grandsons opted to visit Universal Studios instead of Disney World. The park furnished a courtesy pick-up for us at the parking lot because it was too great a distance for me to maneuver because of hip pain. We saw a wheelchair concession close to the entrance and took advantage of the convenience because I knew I could not walk any reasonable distance.

Everyone took turns pushing me around, but after only fifteen minutes, my thighs were suffering from an intense burning pain. The stainless steel panel on each side of the seat was being rubbed by the wheel mechanism. My daughter bought a couple magazines and two tee shirts to insulate my hips from the hot side panels, offering minimal help.

When we left the park that day, my daughter berated Universal officials about the awful wheelchair conditions I'd suffered that hot day. They apologized and offered a free day of admission the next day and promised to pick us up in the parking lot the next day and bring us to the main entrance where they would have a motorized wheelchair waiting. There still were unexpected problems. The battery on the first one died out. Management brought me a different once as we were about to enter a show. When the show was over, I noticed the wheelchair was functioning peculiarly. The management furnished yet another vehicle because mine had a flat tire.

All of the shows we saw were amazing in construction and effect. The food and souvenirs were reasonably priced, and the management was attentive to our needs and requests. The most exciting part of our experience was trying to make our scheduled exit flight as we pursued faulty directions that led us miles away from the airport. We managed to unseat people who had assumed our seating. We stepped into the craft just seconds before it taxied across the tarmac.

I'm glad we had an opportunity to see New Orleans in its unique makeup before the ravaging destruction brought upon it by Hurricane Katrina.

Community Bands at Sea – John Bourgeois, Conductor

In August 1998, there was an opportunity for band musicians to travel aboard a Carnival cruise ship to Puerto Rico and the Virgin Islands for ten days at a greatly reduced rate in exchange for our services playing in the band. An upper-class stateroom for two, with two beds, closet, desk, bathroom, and exterior window was about $700.00, which included all meals. We had to pay our own flights, however, to and from the point of embarkation, Miami.

My son, Tom, and his wife, Pam, and I chose to be on the main deck because the dining and rehearsal rooms were on that level. As we walked to the rehearsal room, we passed the slot machines and a bar. While aboard ship, we spent about an hour each morning and afternoon rehearsing our band music.

The first day, I arrived a little early and saw a pleasant-looking older man placing music parts on the chairs that were set up for the band members. I thought he might be part of the agency that made the travel and concert plans. When rehearsal was finally called to order, the 'man' was none other than Col. John Bourgeois—himself, the legendary retired conductor of the 'President's Own', the United States Marine Band, considered to be the best in the country.

I was one of three trombone players, and Tom was outstanding in the percussion section. It was an experience to remember. The maestro appeared to be humble and subdued as he directed with no baton, just slight movements of his hands and commanding facial expressions. We played some of his classic arrangements and particularly liked "American's We".

We played on shore at several Virgin Islands and aboard on the trip. Our free time was spent playing the slot machines, swimming in the main deck pool or sunning ourselves. Our staterooms were comfortable, with showers and television, and huge picture windows looking out at the sea. We didn't get to make the first night stop at San Juan, Puerto Rico because we were delayed in rescuing a boat of people fleeing from Haiti, which I witnessed from my picture window.

Our dinners were delicious. We were told that the servers came from 19 different countries. They put on a show every night following dinner, going up and down the dining room aisles. The stateroom crew surprised everyone: every night when we were at dinner, they changed our bed linens and created a different animal or character out of our towels, which we found sitting on our beds when we returned from dinner. They were really clever and efficient.

We had no complaints about anything. Ed Pio of Salinas, California had made all the necessary arrangements through his travel agency, Community Bands at Sea, with Carnival Cruise Lines for great price reductions for all musicians and their guests.

THE LOVES OF MY LIFE

This is not a tell-all confession of hot and steamy affairs. I admit to sincerely loving people in general, some just more than others. Like most girls, I have never forgotten my first serious crush. A sailor from Manhattan was mine.

Charles Karmazin was a sailor I met in the summer of 1942. I was 16 years old, and had just graduated from high school. My parents and I were in Milwaukee to see the star-studded live entertainment at the Riverside Theatre. After the show, we stepped into Walgreen's next door to buy some scenic postcards. I had never been allowed to date during the high school years, but now that I had graduated, I felt 'liberated' and found myself flirting for the first time in my life.

There was a small group of sailors in Walgreen's and, as I caught the eye of the tall, cutest one, I said, "Hi, tight pants". (I had never seen a sailor before, but I remembered that line from a movie.) He laughed. We engaged in some small talk where he disclosed he was on weekend liberty from Great Lakes Naval Training Station. I was a little reluctant to admit to being a farm girl.

We exchanged addresses and wrote each other almost daily. I actually read his letters to my mother, which apparently influenced my parents to invite him to spend a weekend at our farm before being shipped out.

Having been brought up in Manhattan, he loved his first time on a farm. We took a walk up the lane where we both climbed up onto an old wooden gate. He gave me a sweet, innocent kiss. He later wrote, "I'll never forget what happened at the gate". (When I read that letter to my mother, it did raise her eyebrows a little!)

We continued to write after he shipped out, and he eventually proposed marriage. When I said I was too young to commit, he said he would volunteer for submarine duty. Suddenly, the letters stopped. Later, when my marriage to Al failed, my mother quipped, "You may have been better off marrying that sailor."

In 1944, my love was four-fold. Their names were Skip, Michael, Johnny and Peter, ages between twelve and six—the sons of Mary and Harry Stuhldreher in whose home I became part of the family while attending the University of Wisconsin. Each boy had a unique personality and a special place in my heart forever. Sixty some years later in 2008, with the help of the internet, I located Michael. It is a joy to reminisce about the 'olden' days, as young Peter used to say. (Sadly, Peter had passed before I could reunite with him.)

In 1945, my dear friend, Glenn, also a U of W student, showed he cared by always being there for me by helping with my household chores, just to be together—laughing while drying dishes; singing sweet and low Ink Spots lyrics in my ear on those rare times when we went dancing; or having a nickel beer and a handful of Spanish peanuts for a penny from a little dispenser in a neighborhood pub—always making me feel special and happy doing simple things together.

In 1967, my little black book could have included most of the 350 men I worked with at the 19th Police District. They were caring, thoughtful, respectful and helpful to me and my three children—a connection that was providential.

In 1970, while employed at the Police District, I founded and directed 90 boys in an a cappella choir. The volunteer activity was a labor of love. When I was with them—teaching in rehearsals or performing at some event—I felt I had encircled them and brought them close to my heart. I sensed they knew I truly cared about them.

In 1978, I married Sergeant Willard E. Kleppe, whom I met while employed at the 19th District. It was the 'second time around' for both of us. He treated me like my father treated my mother—with love, respect, and gratitude for anything I did for him. Even in his most painful moments of enduring cancer, he said, "I'd be happy to bear all of this, if I could only stay with you."

I appreciate having been blessed to experience love in many ways. It is sad that there are people who never know the fulfillment of love because they are mired in bigotry and selfishness when only a smile or a kind word can move mountains.

1967: A PIVOTAL YEAR

The winds of change were in the air, in my private live and in the public arena:

In January, fire destroyed McCormick Place, Chicago's jewel on Lake Shore Drive—a convention center and performing arts venue and site of the 1933-1934 World's Fairs. It ran the size of six football fields with 486,000 square feet of space on three levels, becoming the site of the U.S.'s biggest trade shows. It cost Chicago $35,000,000 to build. One boast was that it would be more durable than the Coliseum.

According to TIME magazine, "It was the victim of a blaze that in total money terms rivaled the fire of 1871". The fire, which started in a main exhibition hall's booth, became an inferno in fifteen minutes. The mayor appointed a panel to determine why the six-year-old exhibition center, built to outlast the Coliseum, had no fire walls or sprinkler system.

While 'Rome' (McCormick Place) burned on the south side, 'Nero' (our theater group) 'fiddled' on the north side as we performed highlights from five musicals (Oklahoma, South Pacific, The Sound of Music, The Music Man, and Guys and Dolls) titled "The Greatest Show on Mirth". It was my appearance in Oklahoma as Ado Annie that hooked me on community theater forever.

The theater group's cast party was scheduled for coincidentally the same weekend of the Great Blizzard, dumping two feet of snow in 48 hours which paralyzed the city and the expressways. I remember walking four blocks in knee-high snow bringing my food contribution to the party. One other actress brought a revolutionary new side dish, Green Bean Casserole.

It was the last time that particular cast performed as an ensemble. The beautiful auburn-haired single mom became a policewoman. Our lovely, talented piano accompanist succumbed to leukemia. The rest of us formed a group that took the show 'on the road' to perform at retirement/nursing homes, Great Lakes Naval Training Station, the USO, the VA research hospital in downtown Chicago as well as the hospital in Hines (IL), the rehabilitation Institute of Chicago, and Dunning Mental Facility on Chicago's northwest side.

I took over the roles of "Nelly Forbush" singing the "Honey Bun" duet with Orlando Menicucci as Luther from South Pacific; "Adelaide's Lament" from Guys and Dolls; "Second Hand Rose" from Funny Girl; and sharing the duet "Sunrise, Sunset" from Fiddler on the Roof.

My mother's passing on February 24 occurred a month after she returned from making the 150-mile trip to Chicago to see me perform in the various musicals' roles. She had insisted that the foursome (my father, my sister, Tess, and her long-time beau, Francis, and my mother) make the trip in spite of the bad weather. My sister said there was no trying to convince my mother against it. Their arrival surprised me as I was preparing to go to the performance site to get into costume and have my make-up applied. The visit was eerily prophetic as it was the last time I saw my mother alive.

My children will never forget the ominous phone call from my sister that my mother had died. It was 11:30 at night and the children were asleep in their beds when I answered the phone on the first floor and let out an earth shattering scream that lasted several minutes. I couldn't stop. The shock of that loss lasted a year. I couldn't think of her without breaking into tears. That was more than forty years ago, but tears are forming in my eyes as I write about it.

Twenty-five years prior to that devastating loss, I was a senior in high school performing a serious declamation in a state-wide forensics competition. When the judge prefaced his announcement of the winner, he said one contestant's performance was 'head and shoulders' above the rest, I knew it wasn't mine…but it was. I'm not sure if it was the body of literature that made me a winner; I'm sure it was the tears on command that 'got' him.

My mother wondered how I could do that. I said, "I think of something sad". I never told her that the tears would come if I thought of losing her. And how they flowed when that day did come.

In November, I passed a Civil Service exam which validated my employment with the Chicago Police Department in order to serve as a personal secretary to Commander Fahey of the 19th District and to assist Officer Friendly, "Uncle George" Zaranti. Besides handling correspondence for the Commander and Officer Zaranti, I was motivated to implement a boys a cappella choir. The best part of all, to realized in the distant future, was to meet the man I would eventually marry. It was the most interesting, enjoyable, and rewarding job of my life.

In December, my children and I were ecstatically happy to have our first dog, Heidi—loved by us for the next thirteen years.

TEETH FOR WHO, AND TOOTH FORSEE

What do these two things, girdles and dentures, have in common?
TEETH

I have had to call in the following incidents as honest-to-gosh legitimate excuses for 'going to be late' for work.

It was difficult enough to get to the office on time, with having to get three children ready for school and out the door to hook up with other kids on the block (for safety-in-numbers' sake), and then shower, arrange my hair, apply make-up, and get dressed. At that state in my life, I was quite slim but wore a girdle to anchor my nylons.

I slipped into my girdle and, as I zipped it up the side, the zipper teeth caught my skin. If I would move the tab either way, my skin would be further cut. I had to call the office before I could figure out how to solve the situation. I told the truth to the receptionist, but what an uproar it caused at the office—which I was subjected to on my return. I did manage to finally work up the nerve to detach the girdle from my hide, suffering pain and bruising, and a vow never to wear that girdle next to my skin. It was unconventional, perhaps, but I wore it over my underwear.

The other episode involved a dental bridge to replace some tooth extractions. The dentist told me to remove it at night to let my gum rest. So I put it on my nightstand next to the bed. The next morning, when I got out of bed, I couldn't imagine what I was stepping on that was sharp and hurtful. I turned on the lamp but couldn't see what these sharp bits could possibly. I knew what it was when I reached for my dental bridge what was not on the night stand.

I knew what an uproar it caused when the office gang heard my excuse that 'my dog ate my teeth!' It wasn't funny at all for me since the bridge was expensive and not covered by dental insurance.

My last experience involved teeth—my first upper denture. It happened as I emceed my first concert of the Spring Valley Concert band presented at the local prestigious performing arts center. It was decided that, at intermission, we would have a random drawing for door prizes. I called out to the audience, which included our mayor, for 'the young lad in the red shirt' to come up on stage to draw the winning tickets.

As the boy stood up, an adult gentleman beat him to the stage. I was distracted by that but told the boy to come on up and share the honors. Then, as I turned to the gentleman who was now in my face, I realized it was an ex-brother-in-law of mine who lived some distance away. I had not seen him in years and was not aware he was in the audience. As I gasped in surprise, my upper denture dropped—leaving me speechless. I turned my back to the audience while I adjusted the device to then call out the first winning number. Who was it? The mayor, of course!

MAGNA CUM LAUDE GRADUATION

I completed the Commercial College course in July 1943, a month before my 18th birthday, graduating Magna Cum Laude--second highest in my class. I excelled in typing, shorthand, and business English which included vocabulary and correspondence.

Also, in July 1943, Pinky enlisted in the Army and was stationed at Camp Campbell, Kentucky. On July 17, my sister, Maybelle, married Frank after a four-year courtship. The reception was held at our home on the farm. The day after, I traveled with Pinky and his mom to Fort Campbell, Kentucky in his green Pontiac so that he'd have a car at camp. It was a boring visit, staying in barracks with no air-conditioning in that humid, sweltering heat. A memorable plus was seeing the movie, 'Stormy Weather', starring Lena Horne.

I know Red (aka Pinky) and his family had thoughts of our getting married some day, as did I, but I had to expunge all such thoughts as my sister, Maybelle, had me promise that I wouldn't get serious about anyone until her husband's nephew, Al Wellander, could come home after the war. Al was a Navy radio operator and decoder aboard a destroyer in the South Pacific during WWII.

THE BABY YEARS: 1954, 1956, 1958

I was frazzled from no sleep, from spousal abuse, and my ignorance about taking care of a baby. I had never even held a baby before Tommy's birth. I carried a towel on my shoulder to wipe the perspiration of nervousness off of my face. I was so afraid of something happening to Tommy. When he was awake, I'd put him in a buggy so I could bring him anywhere in the apartment to be near me, whether it was the kitchen, living room, or bedroom. When I had to go to the bathroom, I wheeled him to the door to observe if he was breathing. I couldn't stop looking at this little miracle. I kept saying to myself, "Isn't he beautiful? Isn't he a miracle!"

He was nearly a month old when I finally called the hospital nurse, admitting I had not given him a bath since coming home from the hospital. She asked, "How old is he?" I thought she'd jump through the phone when I answered, "a month". She showed up the next day and was helpful in a comforting, consoling way. From then on, with my new-found confidence, I delighted in giving him a daily bath.

The days were sweet, but the nights were long and weary. Television signed off at 1:00 A.M. Rocking didn't help him stop crying; nursing didn't help either. There was no one to talk to; no one to help. There was nothing to do but walk the floor all night. I became depressed which I now believe was post-partum depression, although it was not recognized or labeled back then.

1955: He was six months old when I found out that I was pregnant with my second child, again disproving the doctor's prognosis when I was younger who said I would never be able to bear children. My father insisted that we look to buy a house because he believed that an apartment was no place to raise a child.

THE HOUSE AT 1922 W. PATTERSON AVENUE, CHICAGO

1956: I was apprehensive about buying a house, considering my husband's on again/off again drinking bouts--knowing my father would be investing his life's savings on our behalf. We couldn't find a house in a decent residential neighborhood for $10,000 or under, the ceiling established by my father, but he okayed $16,000 for the purchase of the Victorian frame house at 1922 W. Patterson--on a street of first and second generation owners. It was the second oldest house on the block, probably built between 1900-1910. It had hardwood floors, a 14 x 32 living room, 14 x 20 dining room (which we shortened to 14 x 14 to accommodate a full bath on the first floor), and a 10 x 10 kitchen. There was a large hall on the second floor hosting four large bedrooms, and an enclosed stairway to a finished attic. There was also a full unfinished basement.

We moved in during a blizzard on January 26, 1956. My second son, Alan, was born a month later on February 27--a whopping 10 lbs. 2 oz. darling of the nursery. He could hold his head up without support shortly after birth. The nurses put him in a flowered kimono to easily identify the largest baby in the nursery at the time, for fathers who asked, "Where is that little football player?" Al visited us once at the hospital when I could tell he was drinking more heavily than ever--too far gone to realize that he was given another beautiful son.

I couldn't sleep at the hospital. All I could see in my mind's eye was Tommy's face in the front window, waving to me as I left for the hospital. I couldn't wait to go home to show him his beautiful brother.

Alan was only a few months old when his father stayed away from home for days at a time. He said he had stayed at a fellow's house for an all-night poker game. My father-in-law decided to get to the truth of what was going on. He took me along to visit the tavern that my husband frequented, located across the street from our newspaper branch office. I stayed in the car, shaking with nervousness. My father-in-law learned that my husband was involved with a woman patron. When my father-in-law told me the facts, my whole being seemed to turn to ice--a feeling of numbness I had never known before. My life collapsed in that moment. It felt like I had just been thrown off of a cliff. Foreseeing a future of being a single parent, I prayed for the strength to take care of my children.

As I took stock of my personal appearance, haggard from worry and lack of sleep, out of shape from having babies too close together, not having help with the children nor finances to have my hair done or buy becoming clothes, my self-image was at an incredible low. I imagined that my husband had found a beautiful, shapely blonde, who could give him the attention that I couldn't. I could understand why he strayed.

<u>1957:</u> The year that followed was one of turmoil, promises, reconcilement, permission for a legal separation, and the news that I was three months pregnant with a third child. It made me feel worse when I met Al's paramour, a foul-mouthed woman who prostituted herself to support both of their alcoholic habits. She was older than he. She was ugly and coarse. It was humiliating that he gave up not only me, but his beautiful children for this woman. When she found out I was pregnant, that he had *cheated on her,* she retaliated with a physical confrontation with Al, in a jealous fit which spilled over to my house.

The two of them broke down my front door. I was nearly strangled with a drape that my husband ripped down and threw around my neck, while I struggled to protect my two young sons as both of the assailants threw glasses at the wall that shattered and landed in their playpen. Al lit matches that fell into my little sleeping sons' cribs. As I literally pushed the drunken pair out of the front door, I called the police. I proceeded with the divorce allowed by the Archdiocesan office on the promise I would not remarry while my ex-husband was alive. It was twenty years before I even considered it!

1958: I received my prenatal care at a Chicago Park District branch where one of the nurses took a special interest in me and arranged for my delivery at a new hospital by the lake, Weiss Memorial Hospital, still in the process of being built but finished through the sixth floor where the maternity wards and nurseries were.

My baby was due on March 17, 1958, but, fortunately, she arrived on March 16 which may have saved the lives of my two young sons and my mother-in-law who came to stay with them while my young brother-in-law 'dropped me off' at the hospital. When my father-in-law arrived later that evening, he found his wife and my boys vomiting and headache-y due to carbon monoxide fumes, which are odorless. He opened the windows and, investigating the clean-out door on the furnace, found a dead bird blocking the vent and a pile of soot that had been loosened in the chimney over time--the result of the furnace's earlier fuel conversion from coal to gas. I immediately called a company to install a steel liner for the chimney.

I had an illustrious obstetrician, Dr. Bernard, who volunteered to deliver Barbara while he was waiting for the pregnant mother of twins to be ready for delivery. How lucky was that, to have a luxury hospital and a noted obstetrician!

The next morning, a nurse came into my room and said, "The father is here." My temperature rose as I was livid to think my husband had the nerve to appear. I walked to the lounge area, prepared for battle, when I saw that it was my favorite parish priest, FATHER Schackmuth. He had counseled me through some difficult moments and had found this wonderful girl, Christine, who wanted to live at my house as soon as I would come home from the hospital with baby Barbara. Christine had a turbulent family life and the priest thought I could offer a place of refuge for her and Christine could offer help to me with the children. And he was right.

A couple of days later, I visited the twins' mother who said that her husband was the partner of Roy Rogers. She confirmed that I had had a really good obstetrician. The treatment and food received at that hospital was first-class, even having lobster for one of my meals.

I began to feel strength in knowing my life was turning around. There is security in making and sticking with difficult decisions. I knew I could depend on myself.

REMEMBERING THE 70'S IN
WORDS AND MUSIC

The exciting era finally arrived when my three children became teenagers. I had looked forward to experiencing this plateau with my children. Although I knew this period would be more difficult for them than it would be for me, I hoped I could assuage some of their apprehension. Reflecting on my own adolescent years, the teen years can be the most confusing, trying, and most scary of one's life--in one word, awkward. You try to impress your peers while you're no longer a kid and not yet an adult. As someone put it: you're too old to cry, too young to swear.

I made every effort to understand and enjoy my children. We learned much from each other. Even when they were little tots, I believed that what they had to say was as important to them as my ideas were to me. I promulgated the theory that children should be heard as well as seen. I remember a line from a sitcom many years ago, starring William Bendix who said he had a talk with his teenage children and said, "Boy, did I learn a lot!" I can vouch for that truism. If I wanted to know anything about contemporary music, new car models, the latest clothes fashions, or movie and TV trivia, I could ask them and get defining answers.

Beginning with the crushes that they had in grade school, I prayed they wouldn't have their hearts broken by someone who they felt was the real deal. It may be one of many infatuations, but, at that age, a break-up can be painful. They don't want to hear that the path of love is not always smooth, or long-lasting, or fair.

I know how devastated I felt when I was betrayed by their father, and how I vowed that I would never trust anyone nor fall in love again. The end of my first marriage felt like a mortal wound but, within the year, I experienced a reincarnation of body and soul. Instead of getting bitter, learn from the pitfalls and discover that there are people out there that deserve your love and trust.

THE COMMON DENOMINATOR: MUSIC

My teenagers were the most interesting people I knew. I enjoyed their company more than anyone else's. We had jobs, friends, and a social life that we could talk about. Our common interest was music. I listened to theirs of the 60's and 70's, and they were familiar with mine of the 40's and 50's. All of us were playing or had played musical instruments in a band: Tom on drums, Alan on euphonium, Barb on clarinet, and me on trombone.

When I had an opportunity to play trombone with the Ukrainian Cathedral Concert Band in Chicago, my son Tom was invited to join the percussion section. When that band traveled to Minneapolis to play at the national Ukrainian convention, my three children were allowed to travel with me, all expenses paid. We couldn't pass up that deal.

It was an interesting experience, to say the least. It was not a pleasant surprise when our bus broke down about 100 miles short of our destination. We were stranded in 100-degree weather, with nothing to do but sit in the hot sun by the side of the road for hours, waiting for help. When we arrived in Minneapolis, our hosts had a nice, most welcome meal waiting for us. But when we got to our hotel, there were no accommodations for us -- the trip organizer forgot to make reservations. We were directed to another hotel where Barb and I got a nice big room with a private bath that included a bidet. The boys bunked with some of the musicians in a dormitory set-up where they were 'educated' by their older roomies.

The next day, the band played on stage in an auditorium. When we were finished, we got to watch the other acts on stage -- the best being the Cossack dancers, in full dress. We enjoyed the ethnic food, generously spread out for us to partake -- it was much like Polish cuisine.

THE ST. ANDREW PLAYERS GROUP

Becoming a member of St. Andrew Church helped me break out of my shell that I had built around myself after the divorce was finalized. I joined the choir, worked part-time at WGN-TV, which led to the executive secretary position at the Lake View Citizen's Council for five years. When that organization faltered, I passed a Civil Service exam in order to be employed at the 19th (Town Hall) Police District station.

I was one of the founders of the Players Group which consisted of a dozen members: actors, singers, and dancers --all volunteers who performed comedy and classical for the USO and the Red Cross. We had a Park District drama instructor, Delores Masonick, who directed our annual musical performances in the St. Andrew auditorium as well as the park district facilities.

I can only describe those variety shows as absolute 'blasts'. We made our own costumes. Individuals had the liberty to choose their routines and were responsible for fine-tuning their acts before we had a pre-performance rehearsal. Some girls did a number wearing vintage bloomer-styled bathing suits; headbands and fringed dresses for the Charleston dances; three sisters sang familiar ballads in perfect harmony; a professional tenor performed classic arias as well as love songs, and versatile enough to be my foil in novelty comedy bits -- our most popular collaboration being "Honey Bun" from *South Pacific*.

There was also an opportunity to involve our children. My son Tom accompanied the pianist on drums. Son Alan wore knickers and tap shoes as boys did the clog to "East Side, West Side". After their first performance when the audience tossed money onto the stage, he didn't have to be coaxed ever again to perform their routine. Daughter Barbara had speaking lines in excerpts from "The King and I" and a Roaring Twenties comedy, "Charlie My Boy".

THE JUNIOR PATROL BOYS
A CAPPELLA CHOIR

It wasn't because I didn't have enough to do--raising three young children, a full-time secretarial job, playing trombone in the Ukrainian Cathedral Concert Band, performing with the St. Andrew Players group--I was inspired to volunteer to establish a boys a cappella choir for the Police Department. My superior, Commander John Fahey, was really supportive of the idea. He kept sending boys to my office to sing for me, or would have me come to his office to listen to the boys who invaded his office every day. It drove his male secretaries crazy, but I decided to pursue the idea, supported whole-heartedly by Department headquarters--both the administrative and the community service personnel.

I composed flyers which I sent to all public and parochial schools in the district, inviting boys ages 6-16 to join. I thought a choir would be perfect to augment the sports programs already in place. After all, not every boy wants to, or can, play sports; conversely, some sports participants might also like to sing.

Within a short time, I had 90 boys on the roster, from the working-class families to the affluent Gold Coast high-rise dwellers on the lake shore, representing every ethnic group in the Lakeview area: German, Irish, Filipino, Puerto Rican, East Indian, and Jewish backgrounds.

Excuses for tardiness or absences given me were not the usual "sick" ones. For example, one boy said he had to stay home with his little brothers and sisters because his parents were arrested for running bunco (a gambling operation.) Another one said he had to go to court because his father raped his sister. As you can tell, the boys felt comfortable confiding in me. When any of them said he didn't have black shoes to wear with the uniform, I assured them that my sons had only one pair of shoes at a time, either gym shoes or dress shoes.

Police headquarters personnel showed approval by furnishing patrolmen-type uniforms. Parents could shop at a local department store to get the black pants, blue long-sleeved dress shirts, and black ties--and the Department would pick up the tab. The brass nameplates engraved with each boy's first initial and full last name, plus sleeve patches were personally furnished by Superintendent Conlisk. Monsignor Quinn of St. Andrew parish allowed us to rehearse in the grade school basement where I also had the use of a piano. We were in business...an idea that bore fruit.

THE CUSTOMIZED REPERTOIRE

I prepared concert material, suitable for boys -- all with a subliminal message relevant to law enforcement--in advance of our first rehearsal. I never expected an avalanche of applicants from that first, the only, round of recruiting. Word of mouth did the rest. (I couldn't visualize the scenario of one boy asking another, "Hey, you wanna sing in a boy's choir?" I promised myself that I would not subject these boys to teasing by asking them to do something wimpy. The concept of a boys' choir was validated in a matter of weeks when there were 90 members on the roster.

Not everyone could carry a tune. Those who couldn't were drowned out by those who could. There was no discrimination of any kind. The Department furnished buses to take the group, along with parents, grandparents, or siblings, who wished to accompany the boys. I judged the boys' enthusiasm by the fact that they always arrived early at our meeting place--the police station roll call room, to board the bus for our field trips.

On only one occasion did I arrive a few minutes late. It was hilarious to see the on-duty Captain pace up and down in the squad room, completely frazzled not knowing what to do with the assembly of the adrenalin-pumped choir boys. As I entered the station, I could hear him frantically saying, "Where *is* she? When is she coming?" The

Lieutenant echoed the same questions. I thought, "These are the men with *guns*. All I have is a skinny baton." In retrospect, it was amazing that I did have control of the group--not with consistent patience and a lot of love.

My commitment to this extra-circular activity was on a volunteer basis. Not only did I direct them, I composed original police-oriented skits, parodies of familiar songs, created costumes, and furnished props appropriate for special numbers. For example, I tailored the District's number "Dear O-1-9" to the tune "Sweet Adeline"; the emergency phone number for the police at the time was "PO5-1313" was adapted to a song from The Sound of Music song "Doe a deer, a female deer"; a comedic version of "Old MacDonald Had a Farm"; a soft-shoe routine to the old song "Cecilia"; a serious skit exposing 'Stranger-Danger'; and the vaudeville version of Al Jolson's "Sonny Boy".

One of the boys, John Irwin, was encouraged to perform his clever impersonations of John Wayne and Jimmy Cagney. The three Sabaduquia boys added to programs with their trumpet trio--in fact, they were scene stealers. As they lifted their trumpets to their lips, one of them would hold up the act by bending down to tie his shoestrings. (Clever coaching by their family.) They also were members of the Nisei Drum and Bugle Corps--two actually played the trumpet, the third one faked it so he could march in parades with them.

After rehearsals, I loaded my bungalow-sized '64 Pontiac station wagon with as many boys as I could fit in it and drove to the nearest McDonald's where I had been given free rein to buy as much food as the boys could handle. Occasionally, I agreed to baby-sit one of the boys at my home to accommodate a parent's request, and sometimes I just invited some for an overnight at the suggestion of my children.

LIFE IN THE POLICE STATION

(as I saw it)

The environment of a metropolitan police station was not the rowdy, rough-talking place I had envisioned, nor was it the bustling, romance-laden venue portrayed in movies or television. The officers never used foul language around me and never disrespected me in any way. They treated me and my children as part of the 'family'.

The men in blue, whom I knew, had hearts of gold. They knew that I, a single parent and a lowly-paid civilian employee, really appreciated their kindnesses. About once a month, they would set up reservations for me and my children to dine carte blanch at an upscale restaurant.

They helped to make one of my happiest Christmases ever--one that began quite disastrously. The night before Christmas Eve, my young daughter and I took a walk to the local butcher with our little Red Flyer wagon. We put the packages of meat in the wagon and proceeded to the corner grocery for the Christmas dinner trimmings. Because of the cold weather, I brought my little daughter inside. When we came out, the wagon was empty. I was not only heartbroken, I was just plain broke, period. The next morning, when one of the Vice Squad men phoned to wish us a 'Merry Christmas', I blurted out what had happened the night before.

A few hours later, as my children and I were cleaning house, our doorbell rang. There stood the three "Wise" (Vice) men, who then handed me negotiable, 'gold, frankincense, and myrrh' in the form of three $100 bills! Talk about happy endings.

Late one afternoon at the station, extremely painful lower-back pains forced me to go home. When I realized that I needed to go to a hospital, but without money to call a taxicab, I called the station for help. A squadron was sent to pick me up but, en route, the squadron was dispatched to an official call on my street. The officers enlisted the help of a fire department ambulance to transport me to a hospital while they went to answer the call from the dispatcher.

Meanwhile, 'back at the ranch', the Vice squad checked with the squadron for an update, assuming those officers had picked me up. The wagon men radioed back, "Oh, that was a DOA." The Vice men panicked, "Oh no, not Joan! Now who's going to type our reports?" When I returned to work after painfully passing a kidney stone that fateful night, I teased them about keeping their priorities straight!"

Amidst the ever-present pathos of crime and corruption encountered by these law enforcement officers, they usually sought a nugget of humor in every situation in order to cope with it rationally. That brings to mind an incident involving multiple calls at the same address of a man threatening to jump from the second floor roof. The Tactical team that responded to act but, instead, called his bluff with "Go ahead, jump". The jumper indignantly shouted back, "You want me to *kill* myself?"--followed by his swift retreat into the building and down to the street to submit to arrest.

What's in a name? As I updated the station's personnel roster, I was amused by some of the names: there was a John Lennon, a Pizza with Basil, a Black and a White, a crossing officer with a weathered face that looked like tanned leather whose first name was Shirley.

Some had nicknames: Harry the Hip; Chicken Charlie because he worked security at the poultry processing plant within the District's boundaries, and the District Commander himself was referred to as "Father" because of his extensive seminary education before joining the police department and still continued teaching Christian doctrine to teenagers on Saturdays.

My two teenage sons, who had concession-stand jobs along the lakefront, occasionally got high-speed rides via Tactical Team members from home to work. The siren and flashing lights treatment trimmed their 30-minute travel time by bicycle down to about four and one-half minutes. How many kids can boast that kind of experience?!

My three children loved the police officers as their new friends and role models. My daughter was happy to have a ride from our Warrant Officer who picked her up after grade school hours and brought her to my office. Occasionally, I was chosen to do surveillance team to check out gambling activity that the Vice Squad suspected might be emanating from a restaurant or beauty salon.

One of the desk sergeants had an alcohol-related problem. He sat on a stool with a swivel seat, once resulting in his sliding off as he turned too quickly. His perch put him above the high countertop so that a little old lady, coming in to ask a question, had to raise her head to talk to him. As he spoke down to her, she immediately began fanning the fumes from her face.

I personally observed the look on a citizen's face as he tried to report a crime to the same sergeant and was advised, "Why don't you go home and call the police?" The man's expression seemed to take stock of where he was, *I thought I was in a police station.*

During the riots of '68, all the squad cars, except two, were sent to help quell the disturbances. No one could believe the two remaining cars accidentally ran into each other! One of the supervisors quipped, "I can't wait to read their accountability report."

When I first arrived at the 19th District, I did not know what to expect in working at a police station. I had to deal with the 350 police officers, as they rotated on the three shifts. They were the finest men I ever met, and it was the best all-around job I ever had. I was in charge of the commander's correspondence, occasionally wrote speeches for his community appearances, checked police reports to commend civilians' cooperation, composed commendations for outstanding police work, sat in on interrogations to take statements, typed accountability reports for the vice squad and tactical team members.

The list of luminaries whom I met, and could refer to as real friends, during my tenure at the police station:

State Representatives John Merlo and Arthur Telcser
Chicago Aldermen John Hoellen and Joe Kerwin
Fathers Tom Byrne and Lucius Delire, pastors at Our Lady
    of Mount Carmel and Saint Bonaventure, respectively
George Mazarakos, Principal, Lane Technical High School
David O. Taylor, Personnel Director, WGN-TV
Judge Kenneth Wendt, Presiding Judge, Narcotics Court
Rev. George A. Rice, Pastor, Addison Street Baptist
    Church, Chairman of the 19th Police District Youth
    Committee, Chicago Police Department Chaplain
James B. Conlisk, Jr. and Samuel Nolan,
    Superintendents of Chicago Police
Pete Klein, Assistant Superintendent, Chicago Park District

Best of all, I had the privilege to assist Officer Friendly 'Uncle' George Zaranti as he made the rounds of schools. I was privileged to answer the hundreds of letters he received every week from the first-through-fourth graders of schools he visited. Excerpts from those letters form the bulk of my "Kids 'N' Cops' book published by iUniverse, Inc. 2006.

As could be expected, there was never a dull moment, especially with my special colleague, Regina Bryant, the only other 'girl' in the office. She gave me a dose of courage and self-confidence I never knew before. We were a pair of devilment co-conspirators. She *made my day*, every day.

We always knew when she arrived for work, with her boom box on her shoulder blaring away as she came up the stairs to our second-floor office. She never went anywhere without her pearl-handled Derringer in her purse. (And this was *before* conceal-carry). Even though she was African-American, she was fearful of visiting her friends in black neighborhoods on the South Side. Eventually, she moved to the North side of Chicago.

She seldom drank anything alcoholic, but if she did, it was Green Chartreuse--not for sissies. She brought a bottle of it to my house when my relatives visited from Wisconsin. One sip choked them.

Reggie had lost three fingers on her right hand, between her thumb and little finger in a factory shop accident when she moonlighted to help support her son, but that didn't alter her beautiful, sweeping, artistic penmanship nor her sense of humor.

Both of us had to sign out of the office one afternoon to see an X-rated movie out of curiosity because we would bring disfavor upon ourselves and the Department if our identity as police department employees was publicized. The movie, "Wide Open Copenhagen" had been shut down a number of times but was now appearing once again at a local theatre. We gave in to a stupid urge to see how bad it really was.

The theatre was completely dark when we entered. We couldn't see where to sit, but we could hear the heavy breathing of men. We kept moving until we found a quiet spot. When our eyes adjusted to the darkness, we could see the small audience of men. Occasionally, during a torrid scene, we'd hear some groans. To sum it up, we could describe the whole movie as an oral encounter, so disgusting that we left after about twenty minutes.

One day, when our male co-workers stepped out of the office to go down to the first floor, Reggie lit an M-80 she took from her purse and whipped it down the corridor where it landed under and old-fashioned radiator with a resounding boom. They must have heard it downstairs in the squad room, but no one came upstairs to check on it. We were not as well-protected by the 'troops' as we thought we were.

Some mornings, both of us would arrive at the station at the same time and jockey on the street for the lone remaining parking spot across from the office. We'd get out of our cars and fake a shouting match. People in the nearby apartments would hang out of their windows to witness the action between the Black and White girls. It was hard to keep a straight face. I'd usually back off and find a different spot. Reggie invited me and my children to visit her at her parents' home to see her collection of exotic pets, all confined to her bedroom: two 3' lizards and a giant African bullfrog in cages behind glass walls; a 6' Boa Constrictor and a Prairie Dog free to roam at will. She cleaned all cages every day so they were in immaculate condition. Her father finally gave her an ultimatum to get rid of the animals after the two lizards got loose one day. He tried to shoo them away with a broom, but one of them climbed right up the broom after him.

She related that, one night when she was in bed, there was movement in the mattress under her. On investigation, she discovered that the Prairie Dog had burrowed a hole in the underside and, apparently, the boa constrictor was trying to share his living quarters. Her parents were not happy about the new mattress getting ruined.

Reggie called the Lincoln Park Zoo and was allowed to donate the Prairie Dog, but somehow the boa constrictor had escaped to the outside world. She never found it. Imagine the surprise when someone did find it. Sometimes Reggie would come to work and show me the little, skinny teeth of the snake imbedded in her arm This, although I tried not to show it, really upset me. I *hate* snakes!

While she still had the boa, she kept a supply of live hamsters and white mice on hand to feed him. One noon, on our lunch hour, I accompanied her to a nearby supermarket to buy hamster food. Reggie was at the checkout counter, with a little old lady behind her. I was behind the little old lady, who, seeing Reggie's purchase of hamster food said, "My, my, how nice that you're buying food for your hamsters." Before Reggie had a chance to answer, I peered over the lady's shoulder and said, "Then she feeds the hamster to her pet snake", causing the little old lady to let out a squeamish scream, "EEEEUUUUU".

It was a rare day when Reggie missed a day at the office. Without Reggie, the day was dull and seemed to take twice as long. She literally stirred up the dust of routine and, when the dust settled, something hilarious had occurred in the interim. Each day always played out in unexpected scenarios.

My work with the boys' choir earned me a recommendation from the Kiwanis Club and a plaque from the police department engraved, "The Most Valuable Civilian Employee in the Chicago Police Department". Before I left the Department, I had the opportunity at a luncheon honoring volunteers to thank my benefactors for allowing me to have the unique experience of using music to make positive connections between youth and the police. I was in the company of the highest ranking members of the Department at my table, including Superintendent James B. Conlisk, Deputy Superintendent James Rotchford, 6th Area Deputy Chief Robert Lynskey, Commander Samuel Nolan of Community Services and his lovely wife.

When Superintendent Conlisk searched his pockets but couldn't find his official invitation when they were being collected, I clumsily quipped, "There's always one in the crowd!" Deputy Superintendent

Rochford added, "Somebody better I.D. him." Everyone loosened up after that exchange.

Although awards were presented to me were appreciated, the most gratifying reward was hearing from the boys and their parents years later, referring to those days affectionately. On one occasion, when I checked into a beauty salon, a woman under the dryer heard my name--recognizing it as the retired director of the boys' choir. She made a point of telling me that her son, presently in the Marines, still talks about the days in the choir and the opportunity given to him to perform a solo, "I Believe".

My immediate supervisor, Captain John Patrick Fahey, Commander of the 19th Police District in Chicago, affectionately referred to as "Father" Fahey, became an outstanding mentor and advisor when I was in his employ in the 1960's--not only to me but as a male role model to m three fatherless young children.

He was a most respected law enforcement official, honored with a brotherhood award by an ecumenical coalition of all religious denominations in the district and representatives from all indigent groups because of his unilateral attention given to the multi-ethnic population he served.

He was a loving husband to his 'bride' Veronica, and caring father of daughters Nancy and Mary, and son Patrick. Although it took some work on his part and mine, he eventually instilled a much-needed trait of confidence in myself. I had always thought of self-confidence as conceit. My 'conversion' to the real meaning made a great positive difference in my life.

A change of heart in his life, choosing to become a police officer instead of a priest was a blessing, indeed, for all whose lives he touched and protected. His mother may have been disappointed that he had chosen a different vocation, but, if she lived to see the man he became, and the good he had done in his 38 years as a police officer, she would surely have approved his decision. His image and philosophy emulated that of a relationship between a shepherd and his flock. He joined the Chicago Police Department in 1932 and among his many accomplishments was establishing the "Junior Patrol" program for elementary school children (later adopted city-wide) to encourage youth to learn about and respect law enforcement. He said of his work with young people, "If I have kept one boy from stealing a car, or one girl from shoplifting, the whole program has been worthwhile."

Commander Fahey was a brilliant, honest and humble man, devoid of prejudice or pretentiousness. He was soft-spoken but firm, with a convincing countenance, persuasive manner, and a good sense of humor. His posture was that of a benevolent cleric, reflecting the years he spent in a seminary where, just prior to committing to final vows for the priesthood, he decided he might be better suited to be a husband and father. He passed away in 1986 after retiring in 1970.

I left the corporate world when civilians' salaries were frozen, forcing me to seek a higher income to support my three children and myself. I went away with the blessing and understanding of the Department, and a healthy attitude toward men.

Years later, in a letter dated June 23, 1982 from retired commander Fahey, he sent me a copy of the biographic entry he submitted to a national publication in the search for a "Wonder Woman." This is what he wrote:

> *"More than one thousand boys of grammar school age were recruited by the personnel of the Town Hall police station. These boys participated in baseball, basketball, and football under the supervision of policemen. The purpose of organizing was to teach respect for the law and make them understand that no person is above the law, no person is below the law, and that every person has the duty to obey the law.*

Ms. Joan Kleppe worked in the Commander's office as a secretary. She was outstanding. She had a hunch that something was lacking in the Junior Patrol organization. A hunch is nature's way of telling a person something, and it can provide creative insight. Very often, hunches are collections of facts stored in the subconscious mind. Who would expect a stenographer working for the City of Chicago would prove to be the most creative, innovative, and talented person in the community?

She asked permission to organize an a cappella choir on her own time during after-school hours. Thank God, I possessed the foresight to realize the asset the choir would be to the community.

After three months, the twenty-five boys who started on a singing career grew to a roster of 90 participants. The news that the boys choir was singing unusual police songs (parodies of popular standards) reached police headquarters where the boys sang at a special holiday program; also before Christmas Midnight Mass at St. Andrew Catholic Church; and at the Police/Fire Thrill Show at Soldier Field--to name a few of the venues--in uniforms like those of patrolmen. This was the first and only choir in Chicago police history. Ms. Kleppe tailored some of the songs to tell the community what to do when crime is suspected or committed.

Ms. Kleppe is to be commended for her creativity, foresight, and perseverance. She is truly a noble person."

There were many happy stories working in the Department, but there were sad stories, too. Personal tragedies that many of the men had to deal with, yet still having to be rational and level-headed while serving the public. Just a few of those stories surfaced that touched our hearts. I couldn't imagine the heartbreak suffered by one of the most conscientious, older, pleasant officers whose son committed suicide at home, asphyxiated in a running car in a closed garage. One young police officer never recovered from depression of guilt after accidentally killing a young woman crossing the street as he answered an emergency call. He was exonerated, but he couldn't live with the memory.

One of the tallest young men on the Tactical Team was assigned to a detail where there was known drug trafficking. He approached a vehicle in a 'no parking' zone. When the occupant rolled down his window but refused to exit the vehicle, the soft-spoken officer did the unpredictable. He reached in and pulled the suspect right out through the window, bruising nothing but the guy's ego.

One sergeant made it his mission to protect the well-being of youngsters who were found in the company of their parents in taverns. He would ask them to leave and suggest that *"next time, take your kid out for an ice cream cone instead."*

The same sergeant was honored as "Police Officer of the Month" by WGN-TV and received a Department Commendation for exceptional humanitarian service. While on routine patrol of streets in the industrial area of the District, a citizen waved him down. The man hysterically related a co-worker's fingers had been accidentally severed by a machine. The sergeant radioed for an ambulance to pick up the wounded employee, then rushed into the building to ask the office girls to give him some ice cubes in a plastic bag in which to place that employee's severed fingers. As one girl fainted, another girl kept her wits about her and came up with an ice pack. As the ambulance transported the man to the hospital, the sergeant arrived there with the iced fingers. Thanks to the sergeant's quick thinking and action, and hours of micro-surgery, the reattached fingers were saved and soon functional.

I was very proud of that sergeant, because he was the officer who became my second husband, Sgt. Willard Kleppe.

POLICE SERGEANT WILLARD E. KLEPPE

He was a police officer also assigned to Chicago's 19th District as a supervisor who worked the streets in the usual three revolving shifts: midnight to 8:00 A.M., 8:00 A.M. to 4:00 P.M., and 4:00 P.M. to midnight. Since I worked the day shift, the only time I ever saw him was on the rare occasion he came into the office to get a report typed. He insisted on giving me a $5 tip for my work. As a single parent of three pre-teen youngsters, I appreciated every dollar--always going for food.

Over the five-year period I worked at the station, I got to know him through his beautifully penned reports which had to be submitted in typed form to the upper brass. I was impressed by the understanding, compassion, and honesty revealed in his amelioration of the most controversial situations. His actions showed he had a special talent to think on his feet and calmly quash incendiary eruptions.

In his career spanning 33 years from 1952 to 1985, he started as a patrolman in a high-crime district, then later assigned to motorcade duty where he escorted high-profile dignitaries such as the wife of China's prime minister from her airport arrival and the funeral procession of Elizabeth Taylor's husband, Mike Todd. In 1968 he was promoted to Sergeant and assigned to the 19th Police District. He was loved and respected by the men he supervised and by his family members: four married stepsons whose collective efforts gave him fourteen grandchildren.

We kept in touch after I left the district station, still meeting to type his reports and keeping up to date about our respective families with emphasis on the children. I had been a single parent/widow for twenty years when he became a widower in January of 1978. It seemed to be a natural progression of our friendship to marry. In September of that year, officiated by a Department chaplain and a mutual long-time friend, Rev. George A. Rice, we embarked on a most happy journey: a second marriage. He wasn't the man I had observed over the years; he was even more of an incredibly caring and sensitive person than I ever imagined.

He never raised his voice. He was patient, tolerant, with a diabolical sense of humor and accompanying raucous, infectious laughter. He seldom talked about his job unless it was something comical. One incident comes to mind which I hadn't personally witnessed but that was picturesquely described by Bill. As a patrol supervisor, he was called by the two paddy wagon officers for assistance.

When he arrived at the scene, they were unsuccessfully trying to get two obese gentlemen into the wagon. It took the three of them to get the 'big boys' into the wagon. As they struggled, the fellows' dog came out of their yard looking for his masters and was overweight just like the fellows were--proving once again that humans and their pets eventually bear an eerie likeness to each other!

Bill left his stressful profession at work. When he came home every day, he would change into his work clothes, have a cup of coffee, and immediately start on whatever project was pending. He could do anything: carpentry, electrical projects requiring conduit bending, building a deck for the above-ground swimming pool, working with concrete to double the size of our driveway for off-street parking, and building a new 2 ½ car garage (lining it with pegboard, covering the building completely with chicken wire and then applying a thick layer of stucco by hand.) Occasionally, I could coax him to take time out to relax playing the organ or his slide guitar.

My children, two sons and a daughter, were now in their early 20's and loved by him. Ironically, he had never had a child of his own, but he had enough love in his heart to embrace all those who came into his life.

In 1983, we found the perfect hideaway in a cozy, airy cottage on the sandy shore of a 5600-acre fish-friendly lake in central Wisconsin, near Princeton, on Lake Puckaway. We bought a bass boat and shore lift, enjoying every minute we spent there--summer and winter, whether or not conditions were favorable for fishing. We had the perfect holding facility for our catches: a live well at the shore line, with constant-changing fresh water fed from an artesian well that initially serviced the house. It then continued underground to exit into the lake at the shore line. The water was always at 45 degrees which was warm enough in winter to keep the pump in the house's basement from freezing and a watering hole open at the shoreline for deer to drink.

It was a quite a pristine area, not commercially blemished with speedboats and water skiers. There were Sandhill cranes all around, and a hundred Great Blue Herons who made their nests in the tall, dead trees of a prehistoric-looking island at one end of the lake. When they and their offspring left the nests, the Cormorants took over as tenants. There were rare Terns that could dive like bullets straight down to the water at the speed of light to snare their swimming dinners.

MOVING ON IN THE 70'S

In 1972, when the City froze the wages of civilian employees, I reluctantly left the police department to accept a secretarial offer from Jim Koburi, (brother of a 19th district police officer) who owned and operated a polygraph lab, The Institute of Lie Detection.

His clientele included the corporate world as well as the private sector. Businesses ordered tests for pre-employment and for employee theft. Every situation was unique and definitely not boring. My duties were to do the initial interviews of the persons to be tested and then type up the results as elicited by the polygrapher. Jim occasionally hired other professional, licensed polygraphers to assist in the process when there was a need to expedite the testing of a group of people.

In going back to the corporate world, I would not have the time to volunteer the necessary hours to continue rehearsals and performances. I felt like a traitor in 'abandoning' those wonderful boys of the choir.

Sadder still was the fact that no one stepped up to continue the program that had such a great start which, I am sure, made a positive impact on those who participated in it. It was a life-changing experience for me, filled with warm memories, still held dear to my heart.

My boss, Jim, was sharp and intuitive. He was also an excellent cook and generous host. He often invited my family for cookouts and swimming at his beautiful new home with a mansard roof. (He made a point of emphasizing that construction feature.) His hamburgers were meals-in-a-bun. I've not had anything since quite like them. One of his corporate clients, Jimmy Jack, a former Chicago police officer--now in charge of security for Toys-R-Us, was a close personal friend. He used to call Jim's hamburgers "meatloaf on a bun" because of all the ingredients they contained besides meat. He also used to tease Jim that his poodle should better be used as a toilet brush. He obviously didn't think much of little dogs.

Jim lived in Schaumburg when the town was still a fledgling suburb. His children actually learned to ride horses at a small horse farm just a few doors from his house, on Roselle Road, which runs through the middle of Schaumburg.

Twenty years later, when I moved with my second husband, Bill, to Schaumburg, the two-lane road leading to his street became a four-lane principal artery; the horse farm had been replaced with a child care facility and some other commercial buildings. The lone White Hen store was now in the center of a thriving strip mall. Progress happens!

After finding a replacement for my position, I eventually left his employ to accept a better paying job with an electronics importer/exporter where I stayed for the next five years.

A HALF CENTURY MILESTONE

That's the label my children gave to my 50th birthday anniversary of August 22. Earlier in 1975, my ex-husband/my children's father had passed away on March 1, a blustery cold winter day.

I had not known of his whereabouts for the previous ten years. On that particular day, I got a call from my police sergeant friend who was curious about the identity of a body the wagon men had just picked up, with the same last name as mine. I asked, "Where was the pickup?" He said, "At the end of your block." In fact, we later learned that Al had lived there for several years, yet neither my children nor I had ever run into him. We probably wouldn't have recognized him, I thought, when we saw him in the casket. He was only 53 years old, but looked more like 83. The handsome face that I had known was now yellow and distorted. Typical results of liver destroyed by alcohol.

FIRST FLIGHT: ACROSS THE POND TO: LONDON, PARIS, AND MADRID

London

The year was 1975, and I spent my 50th birthday on August 22 finalizing plans to travel to Europe in September. With our share of $10000 from the VA insurance that I kept up for over twenty years, Barbara and I decided that it would be a good choice to spend it on travel, a trip to remember for the rest of our lives.

I called a travel agent previously used and recommended by my son, Tom. Together Barb and I planned an itinerary to cover as much as possible in ten days. I chose small hotels that were available in England and Paris as recommended by the agent. I was happy to also make reservations for private citizen travel guides in those two cities. In London, we had a college girl take us all around London; in Paris, we had a male medical student show us Paris. Both of them were pleasant, knowledgeable, patient, and accommodating.

We got a positive reply from John Cleese of Monty Python fame to attend a taping of an episode of John's new series, "Fawlty Towers" a comedy series and we confirmed a date. I sent a letter to the last-known address of Marion Brooke, my female pen pal I corresponded with during World War II. It happened that the town's postmaster knew Marion's sister, a local law enforcement officer. When contacting Marion, we received a huge welcome to visit her, her husband David (a member of the Conservative party in Parliament) and her son Nigel (who at 17 years old was the same age as my daughter and ironically, our kids were the same ages as Marion and I were when we wrote to each other during WWII).

I often said that I wouldn't do it: fly, rationalizing that I can't die in a plane crash if I never got on a plane. But now, the end results of seeing Europe was enough to block out my fear. We boarded a British Airways jumbo jet and, seven hours later, I looked out and saw a landscape of red-tiled roofs. It had to be London, and it was.

VICTORIA STATION

The next morning, we woke up to the clip-clop of a horse going down our street, followed by the familiar sound of the British police vehicles--making it real that we really were in London. We also remember hearing the name 'Victoria Station' on BBC programs. We were within walking distance, so we packed essentials in our luggage and headed for the train to take us to Grantham where my pen pal, Marion, would be waiting with her husband to pick us up.

As we walked to the station, a limo driver stood next to hi Rolls-Royce taxicab in a parking lot and motioned for us to come over. When we got close to him, he reached out and gave me a big hug. Barb teased me about getting more attention at 50 than she was at 17.

As we continued on, we were impressed by the sidewalk artists--people using the sidewalks for palettes, drawing unbelievably beautiful scenes with colored chalk. A shame that the foot traffic or rain would erase all their talented efforts. Before we got to the train station, I bought a big, luscious-looking pear from a walking vendor. I took a bite and, offered it to Barb who promptly screamed and threw the pear. Worse than finding a worm in a piece of fruit is finding half a worm!

We boarded the train and were on our way to meet the 'girl' I last wrote to in 1942 and her husband, David--a member of the Parliament's Conservative Party. As soon as the train pulled into the station at Grantham, I knew the refined-looking couple was them. It was a moment that I, as a teenage pen pal, never expected to experience. What a thrill!

After David dropped Marion off to fix dinner for us, and picked up his son, Nigel, he took all of us sight-seeing. As he drove the narrow, graveled country roads on the 'wrong' side, at what we thought was a bit unsafe speed, we appreciated his effort in showing us memorable historic sights: the town of Harrogate where there was the oldest drug store in England and featured in the television series, "All Creatures Great and Small"; and Knaresborough Castle built in the 11th century, where a caretaker took us up the worn-down stone stairway to what was once a dining area with a trough along one wall that, he explained, served as a urinal for the men to relieve themselves. The four of us stayed close to each other and were relieved to get out of there. We had visions of being locked in the place by the weird caretaker who had the key to the big concrete door at the bottom of the stairway.

At night, Marion went with us to the Fountains Abbey, a spooky-looking place in a desolate rural location where Gregorian Chant music was softly playing but loud enough to cover the flapping noise of bats or ghosts of an earlier era moving about.

The next day, Marion prepared a typical English meal of roast beef with popovers and (sour) apple pie with milk poured on it. Then we were soon on our way by train to Liverpool. The passenger crowd was very friendly, at least I thought so after having a couple of warm beers (no refrigeration on the train) and delicious sandwiches. As we passed through Manchester, there were sheep in the fields everywhere. No wonder, that's where they make the wonderful woolen sweaters.

LIVERPOOL

We arrived in St. John station in Liverpool where there were many shops, a sort of strip mall: candy, clothes, butcher shops, and the like. We walked down to its stairs and started looking for a taxicab. The first one that stopped wasn't interested, probably didn't understand, as to what we meant by a tour to find the homes of the four Beatles. The next cabbie was an older man who didn't fully understand at first but soon got the adventurous spirit himself. He knew where two or three of them had grown up but gladly stopped to ask some young fellows for the location of George Harrison's home.

Our mission completed, we headed back to the train station. People were running from it, due to a rumor that it might be bombed by the Irish faction who had been known to bomb dense locations in England. Everything was back to normal when we went to board our train back to London. When we got back to our hotel, the owner said he hoped we hadn't been in the heart of London where a hotel was bombed, resulting in casualties. He was relieved that we were alright.

"FAWLTY TOWERS" AT THE BBC

When we arrived at the BBC, there was a long line of people standing outside, waiting to go in. Barb and I got in line, about fifty feet from the studio, when a man came out of the building and asked us to accompany him to the taping site. We never figured out how he knew who we were. Maybe we looked so unmistakably 'American'. Or maybe it was how beautiful Barb looked in her 'lucky' red dress. He seated us next to the wife of the program's producer who was very friendly.

It was a hilarious episode. I couldn't help laughing so loudly that now, when we view that segment on television, we can hear my laughter. Some scenes had to be re-done, which made them progressively funnier. John Cleese's wife at the time was Connie Booth, a writer and actress for the show, and sang one of the numbers I had done when I was in a Chicago production of "Oklahoma": "I'm Just a Girl Who Cain't Say No".

After the taping was finished, John Cleese came out to the lobby to talk to us. We had no idea that he was *that* tall! And so down-to-earth, friendly, and interested in what we had to say. We have been in touch with him ever since. In fact, when the Monty Python group filmed the movie "The Life of Brian" in Tunisia, North Africa in November, 1978, John invited Barbara to visit and observe how film was made, as she aspired to be an actress/writer since she was three years old. Against my better judgment as a mother, I did allow her, at age 20 and by herself, to make the trip, after she worked several jobs just to save the money to travel overseas. John made sure to watch over her and answer any questions she may have had regarding acting and writing. A once-in-a-lifetime experience, to be sure.

On our other days in London, we visited the Tower of London, Trafalgar Square, drove along the Thames River, Piccadilly Circus, Buckingham Palace for the changing of the Guards and saw Big Ben,

Victoria Station, Hyde Park, double-decker buses, Downing Street and a side trip to Windsor Castle.

We stayed in a small, privately owned hotel off the beaten path as recommended by our travel agent. It was a plain little building where you had to be buzzed in at the front door by the owner. Breakfast in the large lower-level dining room was included which was okay except for the rancid bacon. John Cleese was right when he warned that English food could be horrible, especially the hamburgers. He said he longed for the big, juicy, greasy American ones.

The first night, we walked around the neighborhood of the hotel and found a lovely French café with outdoor seating. We were so lucky that September that the weather was truly glorious wherever we went. Sunny, in the 60's and 70's; great weather to walk around in. We ordered what we thought we knew--the menu was written in French and the waiter, formally dressed in a tuxedo, spoke only French. Of course, no French meal is complete without wine. Not being a wine connoisseur or speaking French, I simply pointed to what the couple had at another table.

The food was exquisite. Steak, cooked to perfection in a thin gravy, and thin pommes frites with tasty haricot verts was unforgettable. The profiteroles for dessert have never been matched, either in taste or preparation. Barbara and I felt a temporary status of celebrity as we sat there. Suddenly we were entertained by a movie-like comedy scene. A drunken passerby weaved up to a lamp post, hanging on with one hand while reaching to grab a wine bottle left on a deserted table. He finished the contents, then proceeded to another table but as he tipped over a partially full wine bottle, elegantly dressed maitre d' in tails ushered him away to oblivion. Now, that's genuine ambiance.

When we returned to our small hotel, we sat in our room and pored over some brochures, trying to search for interesting things we didn't want to miss on this once-in-a-lifetime adventure. I went downstairs to the owner, asking if he had time to make some suggestions. Oh he had suggestions, all right. He suggested that I step into his bedroom, as he approached me in a flying wedge attack. I actually had to fight him off, while wishing my daughter would somehow sense my danger and come down to rescue me. He kept saying his wife was out of town but finally he took my firm "NO" as a definite rebuttal. The breakfasts afterward were awkward but safe, as there were other people in attendance. It was such a shock because we had written back and forth for several months before we stayed in his bed and breakfast/hotel and he was such a gentleman and seemed so kindly. Never one untoward word or suggestive phrase was sent back or forth. We learned that ladies traveling without men must be especially cautious.

ON TO PARIS, WE? OUI!

Once again, we stayed in a privately-owned small hotel, the Hotel Duminy, as recommended by our travel agent, right behind the Paris Opera House. We had a huge room on the ground floor with windows facing an inner courtyard. We had a rather strange, cluttered hallway to navigate to get to our room, leading us to believe we were given a servant's quarters by 'accident'. What had our travel agent gotten us into? We had no telephone in our room, so we had to use a public one on the stairs between floors. Every midnight, we'd made a collect call home (which was about 7:00 P.M. Chicago time), not necessarily to talk to my sons per se, but to check to make sure they were taking good care of our beloved Shepherd-mix, Heidi. We insisted that they make her bark so we'd know she was still alive!

We were furnished a continental breakfast, but we were unable to communicate our wish to hire a cab to go to the Lido nightclub later that evening. Barb and I finally went outside that nigh to hail one ourselves. Finally we arrived at the Lido. The place was packed to capacity. The box office consisted of several men sitting at a table. I understood they would find room for us so I paid the cover charge and ordered a magnum of champagne. We were escorted to a tiny table for two against a wall far from the stage. Just as the floorshow was about to begin, a soft-spoken gray-haired gentleman came to our table. My first thought was that we were being removed from the premises. After all, this was a nightclub and Barbara was only seventeen! Instead, he led us to a long table, center stage, where we were seated with foreign-looking dignitaries. The magnum of champagne arrived, expensive at around $40 dollars, was about 1-½ quarts. That we could polish off!

The show was incredible. There was a sandstorm, camels, and sheiks in tents, a waterfall upstage that went completely across the width of the stage. All the girls were topless in every number but not too exciting for the male patrons, I would guess, as the girls were not well-endowed--in fact, they were skinny and bony. The costumes were more breathtaking, however, than I can describe. What an introduction into the French nightlife!

The next day we traveled around Paris. One simply cannot overreact to the Eiffel Tower. I knew it would be tall, but it was enormous! Any time I see it since in a newspaper or television coverage, I recall so vividly the reaction to seeing it in person the first time. There's no explaining it; it just IS. No matter where you are in Paris, it is always in view.

We met our guide at a pre-arranged place and time. He took us to the Montmartre where there is always a collection of outdoor artists. We walked around and looked at what they were working on and one of them quickly approached and began drawing a portrait of Barbara in charcoal. It turned out so well we bought it when he was finished. She still has it to this day, and it doesn't look really any older than when he sketched it up on the hills overlooking Paris. While there, we visited the Basilica of Sacre Coeur. Breathtakingly beautiful. Again, we were blessed with gorgeous, crisp, fall weather, which made our travels throughout the City of Light even more spectacular.

The next day we took a bus tour to the Palace of Versailles. The grounds were too magnificent to describe. As we waited to enter the palace, I remember buying an ice cream cone from a truck parked at the curb.

Once inside the palace, it was a surreal experience to walk down the Hall of Mirrors. Barbara and I were always impatient to move along, ahead of a tour describing every thread in a wall tapestry, so we peeked in a few rooms by ourselves. As we walked alone down the Hall of Mirrors we spotted a maid with a bucket and mop open one of the mirrored doors and cross the hall and enter another mirrored door on the opposite side. That was a sight we probably wouldn't have seen in the tour group!

MADRID

No small hotel here. We stayed at the Washington Hotel in the heart of Madrid. By this time, both of us were getting worn out and homesick. We did a little shopping, spending most of the time in a shop that sold hand-tooled suits of armor, made in Toledo, Spain. I would have loved to send one home, but the cost was $750 which would have taken all the money we had. Then there would be a costly shipping fee, so we forgot about that.

By the time we arrived in Madrid, our traveling stamina had ebbed. We spent a few hours in a busy town square, ate white asparagus in a lunchtime café, and window shopped in a few stores where we bought some leather belts and silk scarves.

We ate in the hotel dining-room the last night of our stay and were catered to by a bevy of wait staff: a maitre d' greeted us, handed us off to another gentleman who took us to a table, where a host gave us a menu, a different fellow took our order, and the fifth person served us. I could only start adding up mentally how many tips were mounting, knowing the protocol of having to tip each servant. I felt no pain, however, when they served the crepes suzettes swimming in brandy. I lapped up every drop like a thirsty puppy.

I was relieved the next day when we cleared the Pyrenees mountain range safely on our return trip to London's Heathrow Airport, and on our merry way back home.

CALIFORNIA, READY OR
NOT, HERE WE COME

In September, 1977, daughter Barbara and I flew Pan American Airlines to Los Angeles were we went to visit longtime friends, Shirlee Meier and Helen Kirchoff who had entertained with us back in Chicago with the St. Andrew Players.

Shirlee and her family greeted us warmly and took us to Universal Studios, her with her daughter, Susie, who was a couple years younger than my daughter, Barb, who was then 19 years old. We joined a tour group in a small open-air boat that parted the 'Red Sea'. As we moved forward along the shoreline, we heard the familiar warning notes of "Jaws" which was immediately followed by the appearance of a realistic-looking shark that emerged and lunged towards our boat, causing lots of screams to occur.

We spotted the house from "Psycho" on a hill in the distance. After that, we rode across a trestle, and when we looked back and the whole thing collapsed! Also, Shirlee introduced us to the Pacific Ocean and we spent a lovely part of the afternoon relaxing on the beach.

The salt air seemed to do wonders for our bodies and minds.

We left our generous hosts to accept an invitation from Helen Kirchoff to visit with her. She took us all around the area including Newport Beach where we had a sumptuous lunch aboard a land-based boat owned by the actor, John Wayne. We then went to some of the shops in the area and enjoyed the lovely weather, not too hot or too cold.

We left the Los Angeles via Tupanga Canyon and made our first stop at the city of Solvang, complete with windmills. A peaceful-looking place with the overall décor of blue and white more than hinted that this was a Dutch town. We planned to drive up highway 101 all the way to our final destination of San Francisco.

The highlight of our trip was the stop at San Simeon to view Hearst's Castle. To reach it you had to take a bus that zigzagged its way up a hill, passing the wildlife tenants that included zebras, giraffes, and others that I don't recall, and a huge grape arbor.

To briefly summarize the rest of this amazingly appointed landmark, the "house" has an Olympic-sized pool and a large theater. On the grounds were many statues and endless array of flowers and shrubbery.

From there, en route to San Francisco, the ride was white-knuckle driving. There were huge drops on either side of the two-lane road, with no guard rails. When we reached our hotel in Monterey, I held onto the desk, panting in relief as we registered. Did I mention that both Barb and I are terrified of heights? It was dark when we went to our room--that's when we appreciated a wondrous sight as we looked out our window: moonlight on the water!

We drove through Carmel but didn't see Clint Eastwood or even a place to park. So we kept on driving to San Francisco. We were greeted by Hare Krishna selling carnations on the street. We got cramps in the thighs, starting at the top of Lombard Street and walking down the steps. From there, we went to the Fairmont Hotel for dinner and a performance by Bernadette Peters. When we went to Finnochio's, a show starring male transvestites, and they were astonishingly beautiful and looked like real women!

We passed a hot spot called "Dance Your Ass Off" disco. We had our first sour dough bread here. It was spooky to eat in our restaurant in Chinatown…fortunately, we ate there when we did because the next night there was a big, random shooting in this tourist attraction.

We ended our vacation trip by having a wonderful lobster dinner in our hotel.

THE LAST HURRAH

I had the "luck of the Irish" when I accepted a position on March 17th at General Instrument Corporation, a Fortune 500 company, that was closer to my home than my previous position. It was exciting to be part of a large corporation again, even better than my experience in the 50's at Sears.

It was, indeed, a blessing to have the last place of employment be the best since leaving the police department. I was secretary to three personable, individualistic executives who were interesting to know and work for: the operations manager, the comptroller, and the director of human resources.

All of the employees were both talented and easy to get along with. The office manager got things done with gentle persuasion. Teresa, an older woman in the accounting department, had spent 53 years with the company--as long as I was old. She and her spinster sister roommate had a weakness for tomatoes and appreciated the 'love apples' I brought from my garden. She was the only one in the department who wouldn't give up her 'two hands on' comptometer for a modern calculator. She never used her vacation time, just allowed it to accumulate and took the money instead. I was privy to individuals' salary history and surprised to learn that, after all those years of employment, her annual salary had only reached $10,000.

During my years there, a couple of traditions were set in place. One was the 'good table' at Halloween: everyone on our floor donated food and drinks that took up a conference table the length of the meeting room--everything from apple cider to canapés to bread pudding to cheeses and cold cuts to salads. I always furnished the edible centerpiece: a two-foot shiny-coated fruit and nut coffee cake shaped like an alligator with short legs, pecans for the toenails, and a pink-frosted wide-open mouth with sharp white frosting 'teeth'.

The other tradition took place in another department during deer-hunting season: a warm meal with venison meatballs as the entrée. They were prepared in an unusual sauce made with the unlikely main ingredients of grape jelly, chili sauce, Lipton onion soup mix, a little barbecue sauce and seasonings. (Recipe available on request!) I would make that same recipe at home substituting ground beef for the venison and it was always a hit.

I noticed a strangely funny thing one day as I left the building to go home after work. Outside on the sidewalk was a newspaper dispensing stand, the kind with a clear glass door so you can see if there are any newspapers in it before you deposit a coin. This day, I did a double-take. There were two full-grown scraggly-looking chickens in it. I didn't want to be inhumane by releasing them into an urban environment. I decided to go home and find something suitable and safe to put them in. When I got home, a television newsman was shown covering the incident.

I found a crate at home and a screen to put over it. I drove back to the newspaper dispenser, took the chickens one by one and put them into the crate. I went back home to enlist the help of my daughter. We concurred on the idea to call Lincoln Park Zoo to see if they had a place for them. They said, "Yes, we'll feed them to the snakes." Ooohh, that sounded gross.

We decided we'd take them to the zoorookery section after dark, a fenced-in area where birds flew and roamed freely amid greenery. About 9:00 P.M. it was dark, but it was also raining really hard. Nevertheless, we parked on the back side of the farm area as close as we could get to the 10' high fence. I grabbed each chicken the way my mother used to do when she was ready to butcher one: grasp both wing tips along with the legs, forming a kind of bullet configuration, and threw each one like a football pass. They cleared the fence, landing almost next to each other, and went clucking on their merry way.

I got caught up in the swing of practical jokes which occurred on a frequent basis. My deed was inspired by eavesdropping on a plan to surprise one of the accountants on his birthday by one of his colleagues. He told me he had hired a gorilla-costumed deliverer of a singing birthday greeting. That gave me an idea: wouldn't it be funny if a second gorilla was on hand to greet the singing gorilla?!

I went home at lunchtime, changed into a black jumpsuit, black gloves, and a realistic gorilla mask. I had no time to explain to my husband why I had changed clothes, and why a swarm of fruit flies was following me out the door. (I had put a ripe banana in a bag with the gorilla mask.)

Returning to the office, I told the first-floor receptionist to alert me as soon as the singing gorilla arrived. She did. It gave me time to put on the gorilla mask, grab the banana, and head down the stairs to the front entrance. As I passed the second-floor receptionist, I said, "Don't be alarmed if you see two gorillas going by." Of course, she was duly puzzled. That was nothing compared to the look on the hired gorilla's face when I opened the front door for him. I know he thought someone else had beat him to this paying ($80) gig. He admitted it was weirdly funny, after he had collected the $80.

I was an accomplice to a diabolical deed dreamed up by the manufacturing personnel to impose on the sales manager. They removed his executive chair from his desk, replacing it with a toilet. I had the privilege of decorating the rim of the bowl with some disgusting-looking green fuzzy material. I also found a speaker box at a party goods store that (if anyone sat on the bowl) shouted: "What's going on up there?" or words to that effect. (You had to be there!)

THE SECOND TIME AROUND

The year 1978 marked the end of a wonderful 10-year friendship and the beginning of a beautiful marriage to a Chicago police sergeant named Willard Kleppe. We all called him Bill.

Turning back the calendar, with a little background music, Bill was appointed as a patrolman in September 1952; promoted to sergeant in 1960. His rookie years were spent on patrol in a rough west side district. Proud to wear the uniform, he thought it made invincible, until someone fired a shot at him. He was incredulous that someone would actually shoot at a person wearing a 'sacred' police uniform.

Shortly thereafter, when he was shot at again, he retaliated only after he had announced his station, ordered the offender to freeze, and killed the attacker. He felt terrible reporting it to his Captain. He expected repercussions, but all he got was, "Good work."

His next assignment was motorcycle duty which included escorting high-profile visitors to the city, such as Madame Chiang Kai-shek's cavalcade from the airport, and the funeral procession of one of Elizabeth Taylor's husbands, Mike Todd. He enjoyed the motorcycle duty, admitting it had its perks around the holidays when merchants would fill his sidecar with groceries to help feed his four stepsons.

When he passed the sergeant's exam in 1960, he was assigned to the 19th (Town Hall) Police District at Addison and Halsted Streets where I met him when I became employed there as the Commander's secretary in December 1967.

It was known that I typed commendations, correspondence, orders of the day, accountability, and investigative reports for the men. This pleasant, handsome sergeant timidly approached me to type a report for him. He was impressed that I spelled everything correctly, changed the grammar a little without altering the context, and had done it quickly. He showed his appreciation with a bottle of Chanel #5. After using most of it, I decided to leave an ounce in it--replacing the cap tightly. Now, exactly forty-seven years later, that ounce still remains.

He became my regular client, thereafter always tipping me with a $5 bill. The money and the cologne were luxuries for me. Having three children and myself to support, I appreciated every dime. He was a 'street' man and avoided coming into the office except for roll calls.

Even after I left the department we stayed on a friendly basis. After his wife died, it seemed only natural to continue our friendship and cement our partnership in marriage. So on September 17, 1978 we were married at Addison Street Baptist Church in Chicago.

My two sons were groomsmen, and my daughter was maid of honor. It was a beautiful ceremony performed by a mutual friend and Police Department chaplain, Reverend George Rice. If rain on your wedding day means blessings, we were abundantly blessed with such a downpour that some guests were unable to get from their cars into the church. We had a beautiful reception where all the guests were served champagne and family-style dinners of prime rib and chicken, and dancing to a live band.

My children, all in their 20's, loved having a father figure for the first time in their lives. After twenty years as a single parent, it was great for me to have a partner--someone to lean on, a loving, dependable man of the house, to always be there for me and my children. The merging of five adults under one roof was accomplished happily and more easily than one would expect.

Bill was loving, tolerant, and patient, but, as long as we knew each other in a working relationship, the first months of marriage involved a major adjustment for me. I never had to consult anyone in making decisions before, but we soon enjoyed having an actual family atmosphere and a happy home. Bill made it livable.

It was a great partnership for us. We were never apart, other than time spent at our jobs. We were always working on some project, or fishing, or taking three-day weekend trips. He was so grateful to have good home-cooked meals every day, the pleasantness of our house, and the respect of my children who adored him.

He built a 2 ½ car garage to replace the antiquated 'horse barn', finishing it with stucco to match the house. He rebuilt the driveway, had a custom-made wrought iron fence built by an ex-con, (a police officer hires an ex-con? Bill said convicts are good welders because they learn it in prison) to enclose the backyard patio. He had a 16' by 32' above-ground swimming pool put in with a large deck he designed and built. He bought Tuscany statuary and planters to add ambiance to the property. He enjoyed making these home improvements--making it truly his castle, and treating me like a queen.

When we found a dozen stained and leaded glass windows in the attic, he had them repaired by and Old World artisan and re-installed them where they had initially belonged--in the living room, dining room, and stairway windows. He built a maze-like entrance for our dogs to go in and out of the basement. He installed an alarm on the side entrance which we never used but which would be a likely target for an intruder--an alarm that shook the neighborhood in the first test of its activation.

Just weeks after our marriage, coming home from work, I opened the front door to be startled as a man stepped out from behind it. I let out a scream as his imaged appeared to be a ghost of my deceased husband. It was the hair. Bill had decided to surprise me with his daring purchase of a toupee. I had never seen him other than bald, so indeed, it was a shocker. He mistook my scream as disapproval. To the contrary, I loved it, and the fact that he felt free to be so adventurous after all those years of being self-conscious on the loss of his hair. He blamed the baldness from taking overdoses of quinine to ward off malaria while stationed in the Philippines during WWII.

He felt secure enough with my love to know that I trusted him and never distorted our relationship with jealousy. I contended that I could never live with jealous feelings as they would contaminate the good thing we had. Honesty, not jealousy, is a healthy, productive emotion--a foundation on which to build a happy life and lasting love.

I had never been so happy as I was with this wonderful man. Being tall, dark and handsome were the extra perks of a man so intelligent, loving, thoughtful, generous, hardworking and with boundless humor and laughter. He was unpretentious, always wearing old, almost threadbare, clothes--and satisfied with the simplest of foods, grateful for any attention paid to his needs, always working on a project around the house, and proud of his profession as a police officer.

In May 1980, my literal bundle of joy, daughter Barbara, was married. Bill was sad to lose "his little girl" as he gave his only 'daughter' away in the ceremony--walking down the aisle with her, wearing typical cop gear with his tuxedo: shades!

In July, our beloved shepherd, Heidi, passed away. She had loved me, but she was crazy about Bill. Any mention of his name and she would get excited. Bill, my son Alan, and I stood around the table at the animal hospital as she took her last breaths. I vowed to never get another dog, but two weeks later, I brought home a 5-month-old black Labrador Retriever--a bundle of perpetual energy, whom Barb named, "Misty". On Bill's suggestion, given him by a park district dog obedience trainer, Misty and I signed up for a course at a nearby gym. We lasted one session. The mayhem of 20 dogs barking, yelping, and jumping around was unsettling for both of us. The trainer also advocated a more physically confrontational method with our pup than we liked.

AWKWARD MOMENTS--STUCK
AT STUCKEY'S

My husband, Bill, and daughter, Barbara were with me and agreed we should gas up at Stuckey's, maybe purchase some candy, and then proceed onward to Fond du Lac, and my father's house.

That's what we did: I picked up a few things, totaling about $10. I put them on the counter for the salesperson to see, along with a $20 bill. She took the items and put them in a bag and the money for the register. I asked, "Where is my change?" adding "I gave you a $20 bill." She shook her head negatively and called the manager over. She told him that I gave her a $10 bill.

They gave up on further discussion as I argued that I knew I had given her a $20 because I had just come from my bank and all I had in my purse were twenties. She reluctantly handed me a $10 bill as change. The three of us beat a hasty path to our car and headed towards Dad's house. I suddenly remembered, "Oh, she was right! Before we left Chicago, I gassed up the car so I did have a ten among the $20's when we stopped at Stuckey's!

HANNIBAL, MISSOURI

It was quite a different trip than the three of us (Bill, Barbara and I) had imagined. It started out plain and simple, but, oh, the twists and turns.

It started when I read a real estate ad in the paper, "Southern mansion, with flying staircase, $18,000. On the Mississippi River". I wrote to the owner and received the okay to come at any time. I called a Hannibal motel and got adjoining rooms. I had called the river boat for three dinner reservations on a Saturday night when they serve prime rib, drinks, and have a Dixieland band.

I called the riverboat from the motel, and didn't quite understand the set-up for that Saturday night. We drove down to the pier where we saw a couple in casual clothes and young people arrive in formal wear. I registered at the desk, giving her my name, which has only six letters, but she confirmed with a name that had about 12 letters in it. We walked the plank to the boat and then past the display of food--no prime rib, no drinks and church music piped in, instead of the live Dixieland band.

We sat at a table where a young married couple joined us. When they asked where we were from: Bill said "Chicago", I said, "Milwaukee", and Barbara said, "Wisconsin"--all at once, mixed up like a tossed salad. We saw the "mansion" with the flying buttresses, which was truly flying, since it wasn't attached to anything and was about to fall down. The holes in the ceilings and floors were scary and seeing the slave's quarters in the basement made us all want to run out of there, pronto! We moved onto the truly gorgeous mansions around Hannibal that were filled with exquisite china and delftware. Bill kept annoying the man giving us the tour of his home by asking if something was for sale, and he kept replying, "NO, I said this was my private collection!"

We really enjoyed seeing Samuel Clemens (Mark Twain's) home and recreations of Tom Sawyer's shenanigans.

We crossed the Mississippi River at Quincy, Il. And had dinner at the Ramada Inn where we had a tasty seafood buffet, where we stuffed ourselves with crab legs.

LAKE PUCKAWAY

In 1983, we bought a vacation home on Lake Puckaway, a 5600-acre reservoir in central Wisconsin. It was a wonderful refuge on the '50' yard line of the sandy shore where we could see the whole lake from our glass-enclosed sun porch (which Bill dubbed 'the solarium'). We put up a 75' pier, and a lift for our bass boat. Our water supply came from an artesian well which supplied the house, and piped down to a live well where we could keep the day's catch in ever-moving fresh water. The underground pipe from the live well then took the water to the edge of the lake where, in winter, one would see deer come to drink because the rest of the lake was frozen solid. We could have made a dollar a day if we had charged five cents for every neighbor who came to get this crystal clear water to make their coffee every day!

My oldest sister, Tess, and her husband Francis, married at age 65 a few years before us, lived close enough to visit us whenever we were at this lovely location--an invigorating retreat for them and for the rest of our family. They loved having meals like prime rib roast that they could not make for themselves. The best dinners that all of us enjoyed were the freshwater perch that we filleted, then breaded lightly and deep fried.

There were many species of fish that we caught: bluegills, walleye, northern pike, and catfish--all good eating. There were also white bass, smallmouth and largemouth bass, sheephead, and carp. But our favorite to dine on was the perch. Never a fishy taste, just delicious. It was seldom that we came back empty-handed from fishing. It was amazing that there was an abundance of fish, considering that the lake was only six feet at its deepest spot in the middle. In fact, that's one of the main reasons that we bought on Lake Puckaway. I don't swim and neither does Barb, and the thought of being on a deep lake was terrifying to us. So we really were thrilled to find a place on a shallow lake.

On our best day, Bill and I caught 100 perch. That was during the noon hours when fishing should be at its worst. For us, the best part was the pristine setting, hosting only a few small resorts and residences, and one small town on the opposite shore. Even on holidays, there were only a few boats on the lake and, almost never, the sound of a jet ski or a boat pulling water skiers.

We finally succumbed to the natives' custom and bought and ice-fishing tent, a heater, an auger to dig the fishing hole, some poles with tip-ups--all the comforts of home. But, alas and alack, no fish were ever caught, our catch matching the temperature…ZERO.

Meanwhile, back at the ranch, while the men were having so much fun, swapping fish tales and trading snow crickets (don't ask if you don't know), my daughter, my son's girlfriend, and I went to work building a fire in the stately fireplace to cozy things up for the men's return-- for their cold hands, a warm hearth--and some vittles. We mistakenly presumed that the damper was open. A few minutes after we lit the kindling and logs, we could hardly see each other through the smoke.

Although the weather was frigid, we had toe open all the doors and windows and began flailing at the smoke with bath towels. When the men came in, they wondered why we were sweating, our eyes burning, and the house seemed cold. We managed to distract them with a much-welcomed meal that we had prepared.

In October 1985, I arranged for a hot air balloon ride for my son-in-law Chuck's birthday. A company in nearby Ripon had one vacancy available. I had no burning desire to ever go myself, but they offered me and option: if there was a cancellation, they would call me at the lake house. That was highly unlikely, I thought. So I told my husband and daughter Barb and her husband, that I would go up in the balloon for a ride if they did call. Barb was not thrilled, knowing my fear of heights. My daughter had my three-month-old son, Joshua, to take care of and my husband had no desire to go up either.

No one called in the next couple of hours, so I was sure there had not been a cancellation. Just as my husband, daughter, her husband, Chuck, and I were heading out to see the launching of the balloon, the telephone rang. I answered it. I said nothing, but my daughter could tell by my facial response that I was being invited to join the flight. I had no choice but to accept the opportunity. She was right. I was the victim of my own entrapment when I had offered to go, if someone chickened out. Now I was the chicken.

We got to the launch pad a the flames were being fanned into the balloon to inflate it. The passenger basket wasn't chest high as I had imagined. It was slightly under waist high. As Oliver Hardy might have quipped, "Another fine mess, I got me into". It turned out to be unlike anything I had expected. You don't feel any movement at all; you're traveling with the wind. The field of vision is unbelievable. I could see Bill's car following our route. I could see deer jumping fences--mostly their white tails straight up like antennas. We came close to duck hunters, but their shotgun pellets didn't reach the balloon height of ¼ mile like a rifle's bullet would.

After about two hours, we landed in a farmer's muddy field. As the balloon hit the ground, it toppled over enough for me to get even with a snooty woman (who emptied her entire inventory of stupid remarks on the trip) as I couldn't avoid falling on her. The balloon master had all of us meet in Ripon at his father's floral shop were we were treated to the customary champagne and some apples. He said he had given champagne also to the farmer where we landed, true to tradition--about the fifteenth bottle! He usually tried to land in that same field because he has a blanket permission to do so any time without calling ahead. It was an interesting, once-in-a-lifetime experience for us.

Since this was October, duck hunters set up their blinds on Lake Puckaway near the spot that we called "heron island"--an ancient-looking habitat of tall dead trees where the blue herons made their nests. When their fledglings leave home, just prior to Memorial Day, the Cormorants take over. My son, Alan, visited us one Memorial Day and tried fishing next to Heron Island. The fishing was productive, but the racket of dozens of baby heron chicks was unnerving, he said.

During the rest of the year, we would see Sandhill Cranes, Great Blue Herons, White Egrets, Terns, Cormorants, Nighthawks, and an occasional Bald Eagle. There were many pure white squirrels that hung around our property. I started at the shore and dropped peanuts in the shell all the way up to our cottage, spaced about a yard apart, to watch the squirrels follow the trail--usually with Blue jays dive-bombing them to snatch a peanut.

We had very friendly neighbors, most of whom were the first settlers there in the early fifties, living in trailers until their year-round homes were constructed. It is sad that I am the only survivor of that group.

We traded recipes and shared whatever we cooked. Old "Sam" Bradley next door had a black Labrador Retriever as we had. It was his seventh one, he said. When one died, he immediately got another. Sam was in his 80's and was very sociable. He gave me a recipe for refrigerator bread-and-butter pickles, which are ready to eat in an hour. Sam's son was a police officer in Milwaukee. When my husband retired, he gave his bullet-proof vest to Sam's son.

On the other side was "Mac", a retired plumber. He was an inveterate cook, made soup for the whole neighborhood every day, shared the rare morel mushrooms when he went hunting for them (he said only Bohemians know which are edible mushrooms, and we took his word on that), and gave us a copy of his newly-published cookbook which included anecdotes about his family in addition to the recipes. Its title was, "Everything But the Kitchen Sink, by the Bohemian Plumber."

His good friend, Darryl Christensen, a professional bass fisherman and local conservationist, hired out as fishing guide on Lake Puckaway as well as surrounding lakes. He also wrote for a magazine about various outdoor subjects, such as carp control, actions of the Sierra Club, introduction of muskies into Lake Puckaway, and the restocking of wild turkeys in the area.

Taking Montello for Granite

Our property was located midway between the towns of Montello and Princeton. Montello was known for its Christmas tree farms (one made it to the White House a few years ago) and for its granite. Streets in Chicago were made from that granite until it became too hard to cut. That town also is the site of the largest dogwood tree in the state of Wisconsin. Princeton is famed for its summer-long flea market that takes up one whole square block, and had many quaint Victorian homes that house antique collections. We still like to make an annual trek to that area even though we sold our property on Lake Puckaway after Bill passed away in 1988.

Time to Beat the Odds?

Bill was what you might call superstitious when it came to retirement, or perhaps a realist. He said that he wouldn't stay on the police force until retirement age. He had seen one too many men stay until the 'last dog was hung' and never got to see their first pension check. He suggested that we retire at age 58, which we did in May of 1985.

We both looked forward to our retirement years, dividing our time between the interesting side trips that we liked and spending time at our Lake Puckaway home. What an exhilarating feeling of freedom for the first time in our lives: no more strict work schedules, no more midnight shifts for Bill. The next six months held the enchantment of Shangri La.

Six short months later, in January of 1986, our lives were abruptly changed. Bill felt a bean-shaped lump under his chin, thinking it was a cold or flu symptom, was advised by his pharmacist to see a doctor, immediately. What was the urgency? Since we had no family doctor, we took my daughter's recommendation of hers. He spent little time in examining Bill; he made an appointment with a surgeon for him.

We drove to the hospital where I sat in the waiting room while Bill was in an uncomfortably long time in the surgeon's office. I grew more concerned with each passing moment until Bill emerged, looking ashen and worried. As we walked out to the parking lot, Bill took his pack of cigarettes from his shirt pocket and tossed it into a garbage receptacle, whispering to himself 'son-of-a-bitch'! When we got to our car, he said the surgeon decided 'on the spot' to remove a baseball-sized lump in his armpit with just a local anesthetic. He said he could hear tendons or ligaments snap as the doctor operated. It was completely unexpected, obviously a very serious situation.

Life was never the same after that. The "C" word, however, was never spoken by either of us. It denial was something he needed to lean on, I would not pull out the rug from under him. I let him volunteer any comments or information. I knew little about specific types of cancer until I looked in a medical book and deduced that he had it in his lymph glands--under his jaw and in his armpit. It appeared that it would continue its travels throughout his lymph gland system.

The doctor ordered a series of 25 chemotherapy treatments with an equal amount of lung x-rays. I didn't know what to expect for a future.

I couldn't call from home, so I called the primary physician from a supermarket pay phone. He said that Bill could be expected to live 8-18 months. I asked, "Does Bill know?" He said, "No, it would be inhumane to deny a man hope." Those words have roosted in my brain ever since.

It wasn't long after he began the regimen of radiation treatments that he lost his sense of taste. He said that everything tasted metallic. Much of our time thereafter was spent going to the hospital for his treatments, blood tests, and chest x-rays. We were not living 'the life of Riley" as others thought we were. Ironically, I could hear that catchphrase that William Bendix used to say in portraying Riley in that family sitcom, "What a revoltin' development this is!"

We tried to stay upbeat, but it became obvious that it would be wise to sell our house which was not illness-friendly--long stairs to go in and out, no bathroom on the first floor, no help for me to get Bill in and out of the car. I knew it would be traumatic for him to leave the house that we loved. He had put so much heart into it, but I sold him on the idea by saying that I wanted to be near my daughter and grandchildren who had moved the past June to the vibrant suburb of Schaumburg. The highly-rated Alexian Brothers Medical Center was also in that area to continue treatment, and as it was pointed out to us by the doctor, it had a hospice unit.

PULLING UP STAKES

We put our house up for sale, and I began packing our three-story home plus basement, and the big garage that Bill had built. In December, 1986, our suburban, 3-bedroom ranch house with 1/3 acre lot was ready to occupy. Bill's chemotherapy treatments in and out of the hospital continued through 1987. Christmas arrived, which was an awkward time for selecting gifts for him since we usually got Bill gifts that included tools. I told everyone to continue that practice. Not to do so would emphasize his terminal condition.

His brother, Don and his wife, Eve, were angels throughout the entire crisis with visits and helping to transport him back and forth to continue treatments at the Chicago hospital for a few months. I drove there every day, bringing him a strawberry shake from McDonald's--the only food that actually sustained him. He was ever hopeful about recovery.

As he passed the 18-month mark, I got apprehensive but couldn't share my concern. It was ironic, when he couldn't eat at all, he kept watching food shows on TV and even tried writing down recipes as if to believe he'd get nourishment by just watching food being prepared.

I prepared all his favorites: baked French onion soup which we shared with a visiting nurse. I'd steam crab legs and lobster tails, serve them with clarified butter, and he'd apologetically say, "Sorry, I just can't eat any more"--when, in fact, we both knew he hadn't touched any of it.

I ordered an adjustable hospital bed to be put in the living room where it was warmer than our master bedroom and would allow us to watch shows together. My son, Tom, programmed Bill's retirement Seiko watch to have numbers of family members and emergency services so it would be handy for Bill to use if I were out of the house getting groceries or medications.

In mid-September 1987, at his regular hospital exam, he was told that there was no more sign of cancer in his chest x-ray--that he was obviously in remission. We were so happy to be able to spend a week at Lake Puckaway and invited my daughter and family to join us the following day to give us time to stock up on provisions.

The morning after their arrival, Bill came out of his bedroom with a grotesquely swollen leg. I drove him to the nearest hospital in Berlin, Wisconsin, where we were surprised at the high level of their equipment and professional personnel. We expected the verdict of the CT scan to be a blocked vein, but the doctor gave us the crushing news that the cancer had returned--spread throughout his lymph node system, just as I earlier had feared.

Throughout his death sentence, Bill never mentioned the word, "Cancer." Though I know he was in much pain, I'm sure he wanted to appear to be brave in front of his family, especially me...who might be thinking he let me down.

We stayed a few days while Bill underwent some testing and while Barbara helped me close up the cottage. Her husband, Chuck, drove Bill carefully stretched out in their minivan back to Alexian Brothers Medical Center back home, and I drove Barbara and her young sons back to our homes in Schaumburg. Bill came home before Christmas, but I could tell our days together were numbered. It was so strange to not look forward to Christmas. My children and I hoped that Bill would last through the holidays. The hospice visiting nurse was pleasant, loving, and gentle with Bill in bathing him, talking to him while she applied soothing lotion on him--making him feel at ease and comfortable, and giving me strength to go on. When I had an earlier tour of the hospice unit, I understood that, when it was obvious the patient could no longer be cared for at home, they would admit him.

When I called the hospital on March 14 to advise them that his condition had worsened and needed to be admitted to the hospice unit. I was told a doctor would have to visit him at home and make that decision. I called our wonderful visiting nurse to intercede for me as I cried uncontrollably. I said that I physically could not help him. I knew he needed pain relief with a morphine drip because the commonly prescribed drugs were not helping him. She agreed that it was cruel to have patients wait until they were at death's door. I said, "That's not the way it was explained to me during the hospice tour." She explained that a new group had taken over the hospice unit in December and were running it differently than had been Alexian Brothers' practice.

When I knew in the last few days that Bill was at home, that the end was imminent, I wondered it I would know what to do if Bill passed away in my presence. I had never faced that dilemma before. I felt a terrible guilt in not wanting to be around because I wouldn't know what to do if he said, "Help me". I was sure it wouldn't be beautifully dramatic or peaceful for him to hear "I love you" as my last words and then blissfully drift off. I was scared, probably more scared than he was of dying.

Finally, a hospital doctor did come and made the decision. As the paramedics carried him into the ambulance, I saw that only a skeleton of a man remained. He had not let me see his arms for some time. Then I knew why. I stayed with him night and day from that moment on, in the hospice unit. My children visited him every day. Their friends called every day, hoping for good news--maybe a miracle.

Bill's stepsons and their families visited him in those last days, too. By Wednesday, Barbara's 30th birthday on March 16, Bill could no longer close his eyes. He couldn't speak. The Police Department chaplain, Rev. George Rice, the man who married us, stopped in and prayed with us. As the clock ticked toward the 17th, Barb said it was the last present Bill would ever give her, not to pass away on her birthday. On that Thursday, Saint Patrick's Day, a volunteer gentleman (who had lost his wife to cancer) said he would make Reuben sandwiches for my sons and me, and that it would be okay to have a beer with them. Food and drink can be good tranquilizers, we discovered. After my sons left, I went back to Bill's room and sat in a chair next to his bed. I don't know if he was aware of my being there, holding his cold hand, but it mattered to me to be there.

The next morning, March 18, I stepped out of the room to get a cup of coffee. The nurse came down to the coffee shop and gave me the news. She told me to wait a little while until she would get the room cleaned up. I felt guilty not being there for him in his final moments. The nurse encouraged me not to feel guilty, that people often prefer dying alone.

I couldn't believe that my "knight in shining armor" had fallen off his horse, never more to ride to be my protector, to save me from earthly harm. I never was afraid of anything when he was alive.

I went to his room and said goodbye to him. Then I went out to the parking lot and cried and cried. I couldn't stop crying for hours, as I got in my car and drove home--screaming to myself all the way home to unleash my emotions. I wept all day, every day, for weeks after his funeral.

I kept remembering the last sentence I heard from him, "I'd be happy to live like this if only I could stay with you."

YOU HADDA BE THERE!

I had just turned 70 when I got the acting bug again and decided to audition for community theater, specifically the part of an elderly lady, a character role, with the play set in a retirement home. Although my lifelong experience has been most frequently in musical comedy, I thought it might be interesting to give comedy/drama a try.

When I arrived at the theater, I chose to audition for an inebriated old lady. It was fun to get into the part in speaking and body language. I saw the director in the audience, and he seemed to be paying undivided attention. I did not get the role. I attended the opening performance when, afterward, I sought the director and, out of professional curiosity, I asked for his critique of my audition as to why I didn't get the part. He said he thought I was a genuine alcoholic, too risky to cast me in the part. I assured him I wasn't really drunk at the audition. I had never had that problem before, being too realistic!

In one of my secretarial positions, I was asked to bring some confidential files into the president's office where the vice president and executive director had joined him for an obvious top-level meeting. They asked me to close the door--which I did, *(thinking I was going to witness something really big going down)*. Then they added, "From the other side." Oops! I made a red-faced exit.

In the same office as above, where most of the employees occupied a large, open area office, but the male officers were located in offices on the perimeter. Their doors were always open so the rest of us could overhear their conversations, especially when they would cuss out someone. One day, a young Jewish executive loudly shouted, "JESUS CHRIST!" Without missing a beat, I commented, "NAME DROPPER!"

In my very first office job, I was an assistant to the straight-laced, elderly president of a company that used felt material in its manufacturing process. It was an open office where everyone was visible and within hearing distance of each other. One of the devious male executives enjoyed embarrassing me by asking, "Joan, do you want to join me in the factory and get *felt?*"

The same joker in that office used to stop by my desk for brief conversations which, one day, turned to music. He was surprised that I played trombone, one that had belonged to my father. I said my Dad would still borrow it occasionally to show his ability to play a simple tune by moving the slide with his foot. Just then, the president stopped by my desk also, and the joker seriously interjected, "Did you know that Joan's father plays with his feet?!" You hadda be there!

SPRING VALLEY CONCERT BAND

A Community Band with a Mission

The Band was incorporated November 4, 1994 under Illinois' Charitable Act and as a not-for-profit 501(c)(3) organization by the IRS--allowing tax-deductible donations from private and corporate sector.

It is a venue for volunteer adult musicians for healthful physical and mental exercise, self-improvement, wholesome recreation, and self-expression as they perform community service. In any one year they perform a combined total of 5,000 hours. Because of this selfless dedication, the band won Schaumburg village's 2004 "Volunteer of the Year" organization award.

Most of the annual performances benefit local charities and the 'forgotten' populations of Veteran's hospitals and nursing/rehab centers who otherwise would never see nor hear live music.

Concert repertoire includes a mix of genres on a single program, of interest for all ages that include classics and revered marches such as our national anthem, STAR SPANGLED BANNER and our national march, THE STARS AND STRIPES FOREVER.

In the Sousa tradition, we frequently feature professional-level vocalists to add further listening pleasure.

Just as education is not complete without music, a community is not complete without an adult concert band. In Schaumburg, that niche is filled by the SPRING VALLEY CONCERT BAND.

> *Music is the only language that cannot say anything bad or hurtful. It is not a journey of hate or prejudice. It is non-discriminate as to race, or age, or gender.*
>
> *--Anonymous*

CONCERT BAND ENTERTAINS ABROAD

(and quite a few gentlemen, too!)

In June 1995, Prince Philip Ernst of the Schaumburg-Lippe region of Germany came to visit Schaumburg, Illinois, as part of a Sister Cities exchange arrangement. Our community band, Spring Valley Concert Band, was invited by the local Sister Cities organization to play outdoors in Schaumburg's municipal plaza as part of the local reception. The band, which had only been in existence for six months, was honored by the opportunity and was well-received.

A couple of months later, I met with the local Sister Cities Commission's president, Barbara Laubenstein, wife of the Township's director, Vern Laubenstein, to suggest a musical ambassadors' exchange--our band to perform at music festivals in Germany in June 1996 for Schaumburg's annual Septemberfest celebration on Labor Day weekend.

Between the two sister cities organizations, the plans were finalized: rosters were made up on both sides of the Atlantic Ocean: listing the visitors' names, ages, instruments, relationships (husband/wife, brother/sister, etc.), special diets, religion preferences, and any other pertinent information that would be helpful to the host family.

In June 1996, 'D' day arrived, that's D for Departure. A group of forty which included musicians and special guests left O'Hare airport for Washington, D.C.-the first leg of our trip. There we picked up a trumpet player (a retired school counselor) from Mount Laurel, New Jersey, and a trombone player (a professor and band conductor from South Carolina) who responded to our invitation published in the Association of Concert Bands' newsletter.

Our next stop was Frankfort, Germany; from there a smaller aircraft to Hannover, Germany; then by bus to Rinteln, Germany where we were met by our hosts and hostesses. We were paired accordingly to our personal profile information that had been provided to them. I loved my host family--the parents, daughter Meike, and son Marco-- the latter having given up his room in a kind of an English basement arrangement, with a television, and a private bathroom with a shower. They were friendly and accommodating, and made their lovely home a comfortable place to be.

A few of our band members were initially hesitant to make the trip, not knowing what kind of environment to expect. Everyone was pleasantly surprised that our hosts and the living quarters exceeded any possible anticipation. Their houses were impeccably neat and charming. There wasn't even a gum wrapper on the sidewalks in town. We musicians began comparing notes and wondered if we could make it that much of a pleasant surprise when they visited us in September. We had a long way to go to match their hospitality.

During the day, when the residents were at the jobs, the board members of the German Sister Cities organization had tours arranged for us every day: to a very modern electric company; a tour of the countryside; a day to shop; a day to visit Old World places of interest such as Hameln, where costumed adults and children dressed as mice on an outdoor stage, reenacted the legend of the Pied Piper of Hameln; and a 100-foot-long buffet of meats, breads, salads, and scrumptious desserts at a brewery where, as you might expect, we could select a brew from an endless variety of fine beers. There's no way we could ever match that display of gourmet hospitality when their entourage would visit us in September.

Our band performed outdoors on a beautiful, sunshiny day in the market square at Rinteln, where we socialized over the creamiest ice cream we ever tasted. All of our hosts and hostesses admitted their 'addiction' to it, also. There were various shops around the square, and a rathskeller where we enjoyed liquid and solid sustenance. Atop the rathskeller was a huge ballroom that we used as a rehearsal facility prior to the outdoor concert. One of the evening concerts was held nearby in a concert hall, the Bruckentorsaal, where we performed separately and then with their youth orchestra, the Jugendblasorchester.

A few of our hosts lived in Rinteln; others lived in Mindan, Krainhagen, and other small towns. Krainhagen was the site of an all-day, all-night celebration of German-American Day. Under a huge tent, there was a hospitality area at the entrance with free beer for everyone. Inside, there was a stage, the length of the enclosure, set up for three bands; a jazz band, our concert band, and the youth orchestra. The whole place was decorated with banners and flowers everywhere. There were dozens of tables and chairs on one-half of the room; the rest of the room was left for dancing. At the far end, there was a homemade dessert and coffee section.

My hosts, Mr. and Mrs. Peter Pietsch, took a day off from work to take me to some interesting sights. Their daughter, Meike, took me to the university where she was studying to become an English teacher. In our country, we would see a huge parking lot for all the students' vehicles. There the parking lot was a sea of bicycles. Meike had hoped it might be the day when a random streaker named "Ernie" would ride nude across the campus as he was known to do at least once a week! His likeness appeared on a commercially-printed post card.

We had a lovely visit to the palace in Buckeburg, the residence of Prince Philip Ernst and his family. The female guides were dressed in authentic vintage attire.

At the end of our 10-day visit, we left by bus from Rinteln to go to Hannover where we caught our flight to Frankfort. From there, we had a non-stop flight back to Chicago. Our round-trip transportation cost $850. We had no further expense during our stay in Germany, except for a parting gift of flowers or candy for our hosts; and for any meal or libation we may have offered to pay; and for souvenirs.

MY FIRST, AND LAST, CRUISE

A Community Band at Sea

My son Tom, and his wife Pam, decided to take a Carnival Cruise in August, 1998 when I turned 73. We chose this particular cruise because it would afford us an opportunity to play with Colonel John Bourgeois--the legendary retired conductor of the "President's Own", the United States Marine Band, considered to be the best in the country.

We decided that we wanted to stay on the main deck because that's where the dining and rehearsal room were. As we walked to the rehearsal room, we passed the slot machines and a bar. While aboard ship, we spent about an hour each morning and afternoon rehearsing our band music.

The first day, I arrived a little early and saw a pleasant-looking older man placing music parts on the chairs that were set up for the band members. I thought he might be part of the agency who made the travel and concert plans. When rehearsal was finally called to order, that 'man' was none other than Col. Bourgeois himself!

I was one of three trombone players, and Tom was outstanding in the percussion section. It was an experience to remember. The maestro appeared to be humble and subdued as he directed with no baton, just slight movements of his hands and commanding facial expressions.

We played some of his classic arrangements and particularly liked "Americans We".

We played onshore at several Virgin Islands and aboard ship. Our free time was spent playing the slot machines, swimming in the main deck pool or just sunning ourselves. Our staterooms were comfortable, with showers and television, and huge picture windows looking out at the sea. We didn't get to make the first night stop at San Juan, Puerto Rico because we were delayed in rescuing 'boat people' fleeing from Haiti which I witnessed from my picture window.

Our dinners were delicious. We were told that the servers came from 19 different countries. They put on a show every night following dinner, going up and down the dining room aisles. The stateroom crew surprised everyone: every night when we were at dinner, they changed our bed linens and created a different animal or character out of our towels which we found sitting on our beds when we returned from dinner. They were really clever and efficient.

We had no complaints about anything. Ed Pio, of Salinas, California had made all necessary arrangements through his travel agency, Community Bands at Sea, with Carnival Cruise Lines for great price reductions for all musicians and their guests.

MY LEGACY: THE SPRING VALLEY CONCERT BAND

Having my fifteen minutes of fame wasn't what I was aspiring to when I picked up the gauntlet thrown me by my percussionist son, Tom, to pursue the idea of starting an adult concert band in this suburb of 77,000 residents called Schaumburg.

I had just celebrated my 69th birthday, settled down after my husband's passing, ready to enjoy retirement. But, I shall be ever grateful for my son's encouragement to ask the Mayor's help in locating a rehearsal space for a band--in case we got one started. With the help of a CPA I had known in the corporate world, one who was familiar with incorporating a 501(c)(3) organization, I approached the Mayor with our plans. Upon receiving approval from the Health and Human Services Commission, the Cultural Commission, and the Village Board of Trustees, we were given a 'home' in the performing arts center.

In the years since our incorporation of November 4, 1994, we have given the opportunity to hundreds of musicians to enjoy playing their instruments once more--some after a hiatus of 25 or 30 years, bringing immeasurable joy to themselves, their families and friends, and to the hundreds of institutionalized veterans and seniors who would otherwise not have an opportunity to hear live music that we bring to their doors:

Horn-of-Plenty concert to benefit the local food pantry;
Reception in the Village Plaza for a visiting German prince;
Jump-starting a national sales convention;
Annual pet memorial celebration;
Wedding prelude music for a band member;
Performances at music festivals in Germany, 1996 and 1999;
Benefit for Little Sisters of the Poor;
Raised funds/awareness for medical research;
Dedication of new Township center;
Library's summer concert series;
Dedication of new airport terminal;
National Anthem at local ballpark;
Traveling Viet Nam Memorial Wall;
Veterans Hospital concerts on Armed Forces Day;
Flag Day concert;
July 4 celebration;
9/11 Memorial concert;
Park District's 'Picnic at the Farm';
Cantigny War Memorial concert;
Schaumburg Park District's "Concert at the Cabin";
Memorial Day, St. Peter Lutheran Church;

Memorial Day, Streamwood's Veteran's Park;
Annual Holiday concerts.

Medical professionals could not have prescribed the benefits derived from this kind of therapeutic involvement for both the presenters and the receivers. It is a full-time activity that keeps us mentally, physically, and emotionally charged. It is a completely volunteer commitment with applause as remuneration.

The band received the "Volunteer Organization of the Year" award from the Village of Schaumburg in 2004 for its philanthropic outreach to audiences who otherwise would have not have opportunities to attend a live performance. On my 81st birthday in 2006, the Village President issued a Proclamation, declaring a week in my honor for having founded an adult volunteer concert band--the first such organization in this suburb.

PROCLAMATION

WHEREAS, Joan Kleppe is an amazing lady who defies the aging process by being forever young, and

WHEREAS, Joan Kleppe's youthful spunk caused her to meet with the Mayor to tell him what is missing in Schaumburg is its own community concert band and,

WHEREAS, Joan Kleppe is the founder and inspiration for the Spring Valley Concert Band, and

WHEREAS, thousands of music lovers, from seniors at Friendship Village to extended-care veterans at Hines VA Hospital to the stage of Schaumburg's Prairie Center for the Arts, have tapped their feet to the wonderful music that Joan Kleppe has brought to us, and

WHEREAS, Joan Kleppe closed her trombone case, put her golden instrument to sleep, and continued the full-time job of expanding the music library, fund-raising, publicity, and

WHEREAS, Joan Steiner-Wellander-Kleppe has lived the adage, "When God closes a door, He opens a window" and has been finding those open windows all her life, often helping open them with a crowbar, and

WHEREAS, Joan Kleppe's loving family, countless friends, thousands of fans and, certainly, the Mayor, want to honor this dynamite of a dame, this loving lady who has given so much joy and music pleasure,

NOW, THEREFORE, BE IT RESOLVED that by the power vested in me as President of the Village of Schaumburg, I hereby proclaim the week of August 20-26, 2006, as

JOAN KLEPPE WEEK

Here in the Village of Schaumburg, and urge all the citizens to join in celebration and thanksgiving for receiving the gift of this extraordinary lady.

IN WITNESS THEREOF, I have hereunto set my hand and caused the seal of the Village of Schaumburg to be affixed this 22nd day of August, 2006.

(Signed): Al Larson, Village President

REASONS TO FOUND A COMMUNITY BAND

The following excerpts were taken from articles saved over recent years to substantiate the purpose of founding the SPRING VALLEY CONCERT BAND.

1) Societies that flourish have music as a central thread in the fabric of community life.
2) The Community Band is a quintessential medium of "art for peoples' sake; to have a global effect on society, it must be widely heard. Throughout history, wind ensembles are the populist medium to bring artistic music to all strata of society."
3) Bands program music to create audience interests. Wind and percussion compositions, relatively short, that do not strain audience's attention span. Playing various genres on a single program help to increase the audience's enjoyment.

BIRTH OF A CONCERT BAND

My son and a friend approached me with, what I call, a brainstorm. Why me? Granted, concert band music is my favorite genre. As they presented their arguments, I 'tuned' into my own concerns, but did not want to dampen their sincere plans. However, their choice came with a price, to meet the necessary start-up expenses:

Free rehearsal space
Musicians
Membership dues structure
Conductor
Many (expensive) band arrangements
Folders for full band personnel
In-house music stands
Not-for-profit status
Constitution and by-laws
Registration with Secretary of State, Attorney General, IRS
Copier expenses, (paper and ink)
Letterheads
Envelopes, postage
P.O. Box
Publicity
CPA expense

Advertisers

Concert and rehearsal days/dates

I asked the mayor for suggestions. He took me across the plaza to the performing arts center, and asked me, "How's this?" I answered, "It'll do!" Cross item number one off the list.

REFLECTIONS

As far as I can remember, I was shy and sensitive, yet I wanted to be original and successful. In fact, in my lifetime, I never wanted to take on a project unless I was sure of its' success. That was unrealistic. But all that changed with my employment as a secretary in a Chicago Police district station. The commander empowered me with a dose of self-confidence: a trait that I had mistakenly identified as conceit. From that point, I asked myself, quite frequently, have I done all that I can do? My focus was changed to bring opportunities to others. That led to the founding of the boys' choir at age 50 and founding of an adult concert band at age nearly 70 and continued as executive director for that same band into my 80's. I'd like to think that my early years spent watching how my parents conducted their lives with dignity, honesty, and hard work helped shape me into the woman I became. They overcame so many obstacles that, when I was faced with so many seemingly insurmountable challenges, I felt that I could persevere, too. I felt their influence all through my life and always wanted to make them proud of me. That their guidance, whether it was through raising my children, or as a homeowner, or businessperson, was felt until this day. I think they would be proud of what I've accomplished, but more importantly, who I became because of the foundation they gave me, and my sisters back on the farm in Lomira, Wisconsin.

Printed in the United States
By Bookmasters